J. M. T. E.

JOURNAL OF MUSIC TEACHER EDUCATION

Yearbook

Volume 16

Fall 2006   Spring 2007

Published in partnership with
MENC: The National Association for Music Education
Frances S. Ponick, Director of Publications

Rowman & Littlefield Education
Lanham • New York • Toronto • Plymouth, UK

Published in partnership with
MENC: The National Association for Music Education

Published in the United States of America
by Rowman & Littlefield Education
A Division of Rowman & Littlefield Publishers, Inc.
A wholly owned subsidiary of
The Rowman & Littlefield Publishing Group, Inc.
4501 Forbes Boulevard, Suite 200, Lanham, Maryland 20706
www.rowmaneducation.com

Estover Road
Plymouth PL6 7PY
United Kingdom

Copyright © 2008 by MENC: The National Association for Music Education

All rights reserved. No part of this publication may be reproduced, stored in a retrieval system, or transmitted in any form or by any means, electronic, mechanical, photocopying, recording, or otherwise, without the prior permission of the publisher.

British Library Cataloguing in Publication Information Available

Library of Congress Control Number: 2007933605

ISBN 9781-57886-178-9

Fall 2006   Volume 16, Number 1

Society for Music Teacher Education Executive Committee

Chairperson
Don Ester
Ball State University

Eastern Representative
Susan Conkling
Eastman School of Music

Southwestern Representative
Robin Stein
Texas State University–San Marcos

North Central Representative
Janet R. Barrett
Northwestern University

Southern Representative
Janet Robbins
West Virginia University

Northwest Representative
Tina Bull
Oregon State University

Western Representative
Marg Schmidt
Arizona State University

Member-at-Large
Sara Bidner
Southeastern Louisiana University

Chair-Elect
Linda Thompson
Lee University

Journal of Music Teacher Education Editorial Committee
William E. Fredrickson, Editor
Florida State University

Gail Barnes
University of South Carolina

Debra Hedden
University of Kansas

Colleen Conway
University of Michigan–Ann Arbor

Mitchell Robinson
Michigan State University

Alan Gumm
Central Michigan University

Cecilia Wang
University of Kentucky

Alice Hammel
James Madison University

Molly Weaver
West Virginia University

MENC Staff

MENC Executive Director
John J. Mahlmann

Deputy Executive Director
Michael Blakeslee

Director of Publications
Frances Ponick

Managing Editor
Teresa K. Preston

The *Journal of Music Teacher Education* (ISSN 1057-0837) is published twice yearly by MENC: The National Association for Music Education, 1806 Robert Fulton Drive, Reston, VA 20191-4348.

Copyright © 2006 by MENC: The National Association for Music Education. You can read or download a single print of an MENC online journal exactly as if you had purchased a subscription to a journal in print form. You do not have any other rights or license to this material. This material cannot be reproduced, retransmitted, or reprinted without permission from MENC. This means multiple copies for handout or library reserve cannot be made. Placing on Web sites or school broadcast systems is prohibited, and printing in full or part in other documents is not permitted. To make use of an article or a journal in any of the aforementioned circumstances, please send a request to our editorial department (caroline@menc.org), fax a request to Caroline Arlington at 703-860-9443, or call for more information at 800-336-3768, x238.

Fall 2006   Volume 16, Number 1

CONTENTS

From the Chair
In Search of the Tipping Point
Don Ester
3

Commentary
History
William E. Fredrickson
5

The Relationship between Type of Teacher Talk and Student Attentiveness
By Jessica Napoles
7

Preservice Music Teachers' Perceptions of Vocal Hygiene: Findings from a National Survey
By Rhonda S. Hackworth
20

Enhancing Interaction between University and Public School Music Teachers: The Design and Impact of a Local Needs Assessment Project
By John W. Scheib and Frederick W. Burrack
32

The Effect of Personal and Situational Factors in the Attrition and Retention of Texas Music Educators
By Janice N. Killian and Vicki D. Baker
41

The Teaching of Secondary Instruments: A Survey of Instrumental Music Teacher Educators
By James R. Austin
55

A Four-Way Perspective on the Development and Importance of Music Learning Theory-Based PreK–16 Music Education Partnerships Involving Music for Special Learners
By Jennifer Scott Miceli, Elise Sobol, Maureen T. Makowski, and Izzet Mergen
65

Perspectives
An Approach for Mentoring the Vocal Graduate Teaching Assistant
By Martha Rowe
79

Book Review
The Power of Questions
By Suzanne Burton
82

Announcements
85

From the Chair
In Search of the Tipping Point
Don Ester
Chair, Society for Music Teacher Education

I am excited and humbled to assume the role of chair of the Society for Music Teacher Education (SMTE). David Teachout, my predecessor, has continued the quarter-century tradition of excellent leadership while guiding SMTE through an exceptionally active two years. The unqualified highlight of David's term was the 2005 Symposium on Music Teacher Education. His untiring effort and enthusiastic leadership of the SMTE Executive Committee and the Local Arrangements Team made possible an event that has added tremendous momentum to our profession's flywheel—a fitting metaphor that David drew on in his final "From the Chair" in the spring 2006 edition of this journal. Our continuing goal is to build on this momentum. Before sharing some thoughts about the future, however, I would like to reflect on the emerging impact of SMTE's first symposium.

As a follow-up to the 2005 Symposium, SMTE led a Teacher Preparation Special Focus Session during the 2006 MENC preconference activities in Salt Lake City, Utah. This session was very well attended and provided an opportunity for the continued work of the twelve Areas of Strategic Planning and Action (ASPA) originally established at the 2005 Symposium. It was exciting to see so many new members joining the founding ASPA members as each of the focus groups reviewed accomplishments and continued to develop action plans. The productivity of these groups over the first year since their inception is quite remarkable, with even more impressive results on the horizon. Extensive research summaries, calls for new research, policy action plans, and ambitious publication time lines are only a few of the highlights you will find by viewing the individual ASPA sections on the SMTE Web site (more on this later). If you are not already involved with one of these ASPAs, we invite you to identify the one that is of primary interest to you and contact the facilitator about sharing your expertise.

And now to the future. In *The Tipping Point: How Little Things Can Make a Big Difference* (New York: Little, Brown and Co., 2000), Malcolm Gladwell discusses the factors that lead to "social epidemics" or sudden changes in societal beliefs and behaviors. Is music teacher education nearing a tipping point? The serious music teacher shortage, the correlated myriad of alternative licensing practices, and a variety of other factors are certainly causing significant changes in the profession. Change is, of course, inevitable; the direction of change is not. SMTE has the opportunity, indeed the responsibility, to proactively address the critical issues of the present and work toward positive change. This is the collective purpose of the ASPAs—to engineer a constructive tipping point rather than reacting to a negative one. Gladwell's observations in *The Tipping Point* offer some interesting ideas about how this might be accomplished. He identifies three types of people who have significant influence on tipping points: *mavens*, the experts who pass on knowledge to others; *connectors*, who serve as the hubs of the human social network; and *salesmen*, who subtly but effectively persuade people to change. With respect to music teacher education, SMTE members are certainly mavens in the profession, and there are those among us who are connectors and salesmen, as well. Most important, Gladwell's Law of the Few suggests that desired social change is unlikely to occur if this relatively small group of influential people is uninvolved. I am absolutely convinced that the 2005 Symposium was a crucial event in our search for a desirable tipping point, precisely because it was a productive gathering of "the few" (fascinatingly close to Dunbar's number of 150, by the way, a number Gladwell identifies as ideal for groups seeking social change). We must continue to build on this excellent foundation, continuing the work of the ASPAs. And we will do exactly that as we build toward the 2007 Symposium on Music Teacher Education.

In an effort to facilitate the communication necessary to optimize our efforts, SMTE is launching a completely redesigned Web site at www.smte.us. Here you will find valuable tools to enable our cooperative efforts at moving the profession forward. Each ASPA has its own area featuring a discussion forum and other resources developed by the group members. The site is designed to be flexible and easily updated so we can more quickly respond to the needs of the ASPAs and individual members. Access to issues of this journal and the variety of resources on the MENC Web site are included, as well. I want to thank the National Executive Board (NEB) of MENC for its support of this project. I encourage you to take a few minutes to browse the new site and see what it has to offer. Take particular note of the details related to the 2007 Symposium on Music Teacher Education as we announce the call for proposals and registration information.

As we enter another two-year cycle of SMTE leadership, I thank the outgoing members of the SMTE Executive Board for their outstanding service: Jeffrey Bush (Western Division) and Sara Bidner (member-at-large and 2002–2004 chair). Continuing their terms as division representatives will be Susan Conkling (Eastern Division), Tina Bull (Northwest Division), Janet Robbins (Southern Division), and Robin Stein (Southwestern Division). We welcome Marg Schmidt as the newly appointed Western Division representative, Janet Barrett as the North Central Division representative (after serving as the MENC NEB liaison to SMTE), and Barbara Payne McLain as the new NEB liaison. David Teachout will continue to serve, now in the member-at-large role, and we are excited that Linda Thompson has accepted the chair-elect position. I know each of the board members joins me in soliciting your input and support as we all work together in search of the next tipping point in music teacher education.

Commentary
History

William E. Fredrickson
Editor, Journal of Music Teacher Education

I am reminded almost every day that knowing something about what has come before plays an important role in being able to effectively handle the challenges we face. I started a new position in a new school, and the learning curve we all experience when we start a new job is keeping me very busy. I enjoy learning new things and meeting new people. But I am finding that the hardest part about adjusting to my new surroundings is not having the comfort of knowing the history of the various situations I encounter.

In my previous job, where I happily spent fourteen years, many of the new challenges that came my way during the course of a day felt easier to meet, in part because I knew something about what had transpired in the past. Knowing the people involved, living through various situations, and having information about how things had been handled in the past were all helpful sources when I was making my decisions. While on the one hand it has been said that familiarity breeds contempt, I think it more often breeds a sense of comfort. Our history with our situation provides us with a level of protection from the unknown.

Coming into my new situation has reminded me of the power of ambiguity. Not knowing what to do, how people will react, or what others have done in similar situations raises both the level of attention (keeping me on my toes) and anxiety (worrying about the outcome). My previous experience in other, similar situations with the same kinds of events does not completely ameliorate the situation.

I mention this because it occurred to me that our newest music teachers, starting their first year in classrooms this fall, are experiencing many of the same feelings. Most are in schools that are the same in theory but different in fact from their own previous environments. Field experience, student teaching, and their own high school/middle school experiences provide some history. But there is nothing like the time they will spend in the next three to five years, if they make it past the first year, to help them feel in control of their environment. There are lots of experienced teachers who have changed jobs and find themselves in situations similar to mine. They have successful history to lean on, but it is not enough to make up for new surroundings, new rules, and new people. I've heard it said, and found it personally to be true, that the first year in a new teaching position is difficult no matter how long you've been teaching.

The best tool any of us has when we come into these new environments is our ability to logically analyze our situation, look for evidence that leads us to a reasonable answer to our question, and then move forward with our decisions with the knowledge that we've made our best effort. I worry about young teachers, and some of my colleagues, who believe that their "instinct" will carry them through—that they will somehow just "know" what to do because they want to do the right thing. Some of my students seem to think that they can act one way while in college and that once they graduate they will suddenly be different people—able to get up early in the morning, balance their personal budget, and get their tasks done in a timely manner. Yet doing that while they are studying to be teachers (or adults of any kind) seems to them like a separate issue. What I do is not as important as what I intend to do. Personally, my observations lead me to believe that what I do is who I am.

Whether we are talking about our personal history, or the history of the situation/institution in which we find ourselves, knowing what has come before gives us many clues to the answers we must find every day. For that reason, as well as many others, I was particularly happy that Jere Humphreys received MENC's Senior Researcher Award at the biennial conference in Salt Lake City this past April. Jere's talents as a researcher are extensive and not confined to historical inquiry. But he seems to me to have made historical inquiry his passion, and I think he sets a wonderful example for our profession as a teacher who uses our history as music educators as an integral component of his philosophy and the daily application of that philosophy.

The *Journal of Music Teacher Education*'s history now includes two wonderful editorial board colleagues who finished their service this past July. Kim Walls and Barbara Brinson made important contributions to *JMTE* and the music education profession. I want to thank them publicly for their work, and I look forward to working with Gail Barnes, Colleen Conway, and Debra Hedden as our newest editorial board members.

I've always felt that the great thing about teaching was that we always have a point at which we can at least attempt a new beginning. The new school year brings challenge and promise along with the opportunity to start again, get it right this time, continue to improve, and/or just continue doing what we love. It doesn't matter whether you are a new teacher this fall, or a consummate professional at the top of your game like Jere. Each new start holds promise. My history, your history, our history plays an integral role and we ignore it at our peril—and sometimes wish for more when we have too little.

The Relationship between Type of Teacher Talk and Student Attentiveness

By Jessica Napoles

Jessica Napoles is an assistant professor of music education at the University of Utah in Salt Lake City. She can be reached at JessicaNapoles@comcast.net.

Effective teaching has been described in terms of student attentiveness. If the student is attentive (following class rules the teacher sets forth), an important goal has been achieved, and the likelihood that learning will occur is increased. Murray (1975), Kuhn (1975), Yarbrough (1975), Yarbrough and Price (1981), and Price (1983) agree that attentiveness is an important component of the learning process.

Student attentiveness has been viewed in relation to effective use of class time and time spent in performance activities (Forsythe, 1975, 1977; Moore, 1976, 1987; Wagner & Strul, 1979; Yarbrough & Price, 1981). Discipline problems may be greatly reduced when the student is actively participating and time is structured to provide more periods of performance activities. Interestingly, Forsythe (1975) found that students in music classes are less off-task than in other classes. Since music is believed to provide its own reward (Gordon, 1979; Madsen & Geringer, 1976; Steele, 1971), students apparently prefer to spend time in performance than in nonperformance activities. For instance, Spradling (1985) suggested that nonperformance intervals function as "timeout from reinforcement." Murray (1975), Thurman (1977), and Witt (1986) asserted that stops themselves function as punishment in rehearsal situations. Because music is intrinsically rewarding, and because performance keeps students engaged, timeout from performance functions as punishment.

It is during this period of timeout from performance that much off-task behavior occurs. Numerous scholars have noted that students are most attentive during performance intervals. Madsen and Alley (1979), Madsen and Madsen (1972), and Madsen, Wolfe, and Madsen (1969) noted that students who are active participants in class are more on task. Madsen and Geringer (1983) and Moore (1987) added that most off-task behavior occurs during transition or "getting ready" time. Dunn (1997), Forsythe (1977), Kostka (1984), Price (1983), Witt (1986), and Yarbrough and Price (1981) calculated student off-task rates and found them to be lower during performance intervals. Clearly, timeout from performance in rehearsals negatively influences student attentiveness.

Because students are reinforced by music and are more attentive during periods of performance, the goal of effective teachers seems to be to keep students performing and reduce teacher verbalization. Price (1983); Thurman (1977); Witt (1986); and Yarbrough and Price (1981) found that directors spend large amounts of rehearsal time verbalizing about music. Grechesky (1985) found a strong relationship between a high quantity of talking and "less effective" directors. Perhaps experience level is a factor in how much teachers talk. In a comparison of student teachers, novice teachers, and experienced teachers, Goolsby (1996) observed that student teachers talked most and allowed students to play least, while experienced teachers talked the least during rehearsals.

Several studies have described the verbal behavior of music teachers in terms of the content of teacher verbalization and categories of teacher verbalization. Caldwell (1980) analyzed time use in a high school chorus and categorized verbal behavior as music instruction, 55%; illustration, 21%; and evaluation, 24%. Cavitt (2003) observed 10 band directors (five at the middle school level, five at the high school level) and found that rehearsal frames that addressed intonation/tone targets were most frequently observed, followed by rehearsal frames that addressed articulation, rhythm, multiple targets, dynamics, tempo, pitch accuracy, unidentified targets, and technical facility. Carpenter (1988) found a different order of importance using junior high and senior high school band directors: verbal instruction was devoted to rhythm, articulations/style, dynamics/expression, instrumental fundamentals, tempo, intonation, notes, balance/blend, and tone (in order of frequency). Similarly, Pontious (1982) analyzed the verbal behavior of outstanding band directors and noted that most verbal instruction was devoted to rhythm, followed by phrasing/dynamics, pitch, style, balance, and tone quality. Watkins (1986) studied types of verbal behavior used by 33 successful high school choir directors using the categories of modeling, metaphorical language, and musical/technical language. The top three verbal modes used during rehearsal verbalization were musical/technical language (40.3%), modeling and musical/technical language (15.4%), and modeling (12.4%).

Price (1992) and Yarbrough and Price (1989) used a sequential patterns model as a basis for observation of rehearsals. This model defines three steps of a teaching unit: (1) teacher presentation of information, (2) student response, and (3) teacher feedback. The first step of the sequence is further divided into musical/academic information and/or modeling (1a), directions (1d), and other (1o) including social tasks, off-task, and questions. The third step is further categorized as approval (3a) or disapproval (3d). Research has shown that sequential patterns of instruction can effectively be increased by self-analysis of videotape (Arnold, 1991). Band directors who used complete sequential patterns were effective in producing good performance while maintaining high student attentiveness and positive student attitudes (Price, 1983). Sequential patterns can be applied to other curricular areas, for Bowers (1997) demonstrated that elementary education majors could use sequential patterns to increase their teaching effectiveness.

Because a relationship has been suggested between performance activities and increased student attentiveness, and because teacher verbalization purportedly serves as "timeout from reinforcement," it may be useful to examine whether there is a difference between types of teacher verbalization and student attentiveness. Sequential patterns seem to provide useful categorization for teacher and student behaviors, and the model can serve as a guide for differentiating types of teacher talk. Will student attentiveness be affected differently when teachers are talking about the music as opposed to giving directions only? Will students be more attentive when teachers are providing reinforcement along with the academic task presentation? Does teacher verbalization differ between grade levels in frequency, duration, or content?

The purpose of this study was to investigate possible effects of different types of verbal behaviors of teachers in music rehearsal settings at the middle school, senior high, and university levels on student attentiveness. For this study, only the first and third steps of a sequential patterns model were observed, since these focus on teacher behaviors exclusively. An additional purpose of this study was to compare amount and type of teacher verbalization across grade levels and observe whether student attentiveness is affected differently, since research up to this point has not focused on differences among grade levels.

The research questions were as follows:

1. Does the amount of time teachers spend talking differ across levels (middle school, high school, and university)?
2. How does the amount of time teachers spend talking relate to student attentiveness?
3. Is student attentiveness in response to teacher talk different across levels?
4. How does the type of teacher talk relate to student attentiveness?
5. Is student attentiveness in response to different types of teacher talk different across levels?
6. How much time do teachers spend on each type of talk?
7. Does the amount of time teachers spend on specific types of talk differ by levels?

Method

Independent and Dependent Variables. The independent variables for this study included type of teacher talk, duration of teacher talk, and age level of musical ensemble (middle school, senior high school, and university). Teacher verbalization was measured using sequential patterns as discussed by Price and Yarbrough (1981). Each period between performance intervals was considered a single teacher verbalization unit (the period between the time the conductor cut the ensemble off and the subsequent cue to perform), even when more than one type of verbalization was employed. Thus, many of the units included combinations of two, three, or four types of teacher talk. Because total individual categories and subsequent combinations yielded at least 10 different types of teacher talk, the data were grouped into four categories: (a) 1a: those intervals of teacher talk that included academic information, (b) 31a: those intervals of teacher talk that included reinforcement and academic information, (c) no 1a: intervals that did not include academic information but instead focused on student questions, social tasks, reinforcement only, and other nonacademic matters; and (d) 1d: directions only. If, for example, type 1a (academic information) and type 3a (teacher approval) were both found in the same period, that unit would be labeled 31a.

In addition to the type of teacher talk, the duration of each period was recorded. The data were presented in terms of the percentage of the entire observed rehearsal (e.g., 9 seconds of teacher verbalization constituted 1% of the rehearsal, since the entire observed rehearsal was 15 minutes, or 900 seconds). In the same way, the number of students off-task was computed as a percentage of the entire class (7 students off-task constituted 25% of the class, assuming class size was 28).

The dependent variable was student attentiveness.

Participants. Thirty music rehearsals were observed across middle school, senior high school, and university levels. Six middle school teachers (2 choral, 1 band, and 3 orchestral), six senior high school teachers (4 choral and 2 band), and eight university teachers (3 choral and 5 band), a total of 20 teachers, were participants in this study. Among directors, 8 were female and 12 were male. Experience levels ranged from 2 years of experience to over 20 years of experience. All schools were from the same city in the state of Florida. The observations included both vocal and instrumental groups.

Observations. Rehearsals were observed in 15-minute segments, immediately following warm-ups, sight-reading, announcements, and opening routines. Transition times between activities were not included in the data. All observations took place in the natural setting with the usual teacher. The rehearsals were either videotaped or audiorecorded (when videotaping was deemed obtrusive). In either instance, the researcher sat in front of the class, off to the side, and took data by hand on number of students off-task (by visually scanning the room using 10-second observe/record intervals) and on types of teacher talk. No information was given to the class regarding who the observer was. Reliability of 100% was established for types of teacher talk through repeated viewings of videotapes or listening to audiorecordings. Students in rehearsals were observed only during those segments that included teacher verbalization. Attentiveness was not recorded during performance intervals. Attentiveness was defined according to the classroom rules that the teacher had previously set forth. In all instances, teachers defined attentiveness in terms of not speaking with other ensemble members and providing eye contact while the teacher was speaking.

Results

The purpose of this study was to investigate possible effects of different types of verbal behaviors of teachers in music rehearsal settings at the middle school, senior high, and university levels on student attentiveness. The following relationships were examined using a Pearson correlation: (a) duration of teacher talk and student off-task behavior at the middle school level, (b) duration of teacher talk and student off-task behavior at the high school level, (c) duration of teacher talk and student off-task behavior at the university level, and (d) duration of teacher talk and student off-task behavior for all levels. Note that each instance of teacher talk was considered one data point, so degrees of freedom were different in each analysis.

In addition to correlational data, a two-way analysis of variance (ANOVA) examined level of group and type of teacher talk as independent variables and student off-task behavior (expressed as a percentage of all students in the class) as the dependent variable. A second two-way analysis of variance examined the effects of level of group and type of talk on time spent in each type of talk. See the Complete Results at the end of this article.

As can be seen in Figure 1, irrespective of the type of talk, the overall amount of total teacher talk was highest at the middle school level, then at the high school level and then at the university level, although there are slight differences in the no 1a category (where university teachers spoke slightly longer than high school teachers) and in the 1d category (where high school teachers spoke slightly longer than middle school teachers). The same trend can be observed in Figure 2 for percentages of student off-task behavior ($M = 13.5\%$ for middle school, $M = 8.7\%$ for high school, and $M = 3.1\%$ for university). The mean time of teacher talk was 29.1 seconds at the middle school level, 13.7 seconds at the high school level, and 15.0 seconds at the university level.

Discussion

In answer to the research questions posed,

1. The amount of time teachers spent talking differed across levels. Middle school teachers spent the most time talking ($M = 29.1$ seconds per instance; high school teachers, $M = 13.7$ seconds; university teachers, $M = 15.0$ seconds).
2. The amount of time teachers spent talking related negatively to student attentiveness.
3. Student attentiveness in response to teacher talk was similar across levels. Students in each group were less attentive during longer periods of teacher talk.
4. Type of teacher talk was related to student attentiveness. Students were most off-task

during the no 1a condition ($M = 10.2\%$), when they were not receiving academic information. Students were least off-task during the 1d condition ($M = 4.4\%$), when they were receiving directions only.

5. Student attentiveness in response to different types of teacher talk was somewhat different across levels. Middle school students were most off-task during the no 1a condition ($M = 17.2\%$), while high school and university students were most off-task during the 31a condition (high school, $M = 10.4\%$; university, $M = 4.5\%$).

6. Teachers spent the most time in the 1a category ($M = 22.2$ seconds) and the least amount of time in the 1d category ($M = 7.0$ seconds).

7. The amount of time teachers spent on specific types of talk differed only somewhat by levels. Middle school teachers spent more than twice the time ($M = 37.1$ seconds) as any other level (high school, $M = 15.4$ seconds; university, $M = 16.5$ seconds) in the 1a category. Similarly, all groups spent the least amount of time in the 1d category, but middle school teachers spent more time ($M = 12$ seconds) in that category than high school teachers ($M = 5.8$ seconds) and university teachers ($M = 5.7$ seconds).

One of the most important findings was the significant positive correlation between time of teacher talk and off-task behavior across all levels. There seemed to be a negative relationship between the time a teacher talked and the attentiveness of the students. While inconsistent with previous research (Spradling, 1985), this is consistent with the other observed significant differences in that the longer episodes of teacher talk yielded a greater number of inattentive students. Teachers spent the least time in 1d across all levels, and this may help to explain why the student off-task behavior was so low during this type of teacher talk. Also consistent are the differences between levels within each type of teacher talk, mainly because the occurrence of off-task behavior of middle school students was so much higher than the other levels and because the time the middle school teachers spent in each type of talk was so much greater than at the other levels. Although significant, the overall correlation between duration of teacher talk and off-task percentages was still only $r = .26$, suggesting that there are still other factors that could have accounted for the increased off-task behavior.

It is interesting to observe that so much time was spent in the no 1a category, especially at the middle school level. Subsequently, much off-task behavior was observed during these periods of teacher talk. It is difficult to determine what accounted for this, but perhaps the fact that the teacher was engaged in off-task behavior or social tasks allowed the students to think it was permissible to be off-task as well.

In answer to the question of whether there was a relationship between the type of teacher talk and student attentiveness, one may be tempted to answer yes, given the list of statistically significant differences between each. However, practically speaking, student attentiveness did not appear to be affected by the type of teacher talk during the researcher's observations. More often, student attentiveness was affected by the rehearsal setting, the teachers' patterns of reinforcement, how much they enforced silence during periods of teacher verbalization, the overall discipline of the group, distractions throughout the rehearsal, and other intangibles. Some teachers did not apply any contingencies to student attentiveness, and other teachers were diligent about not allowing students to talk while the teacher was talking.

In answer to the question of whether teacher verbalization differed between grade levels in duration, the answer is yes. Middle school teachers in these observations talked much more than teachers at any other level. Even in the 1d category, where all teachers consistently talked the least, middle school teachers averaged 12 seconds per instruction, more than twice that of the high school teachers and university teachers. In terms of content, no practical differences were observed. As an average, middle school teachers spent the largest amount of their time in 1a ($M = 37.1$ seconds; see figure 3), high school teachers spent the largest amount of their time in 31a ($M = 19.4$ seconds), and university teachers spent the largest amount of their time in 1a ($M = 16.5$ seconds). All three categories included musical academic task preparation, so the majority of time was being spent in some form of musical instruction.

It is not advisable to generalize these results to other settings. The observations represented only the teachers of one school district in one county in the Southeast. Further research may perhaps focus on comparisons within levels using a variety of populations and at-risk students versus non-at-risk students. While much research has been done in the field of off-task behavior, the question of what contributes to students' off-task behavior can only partially be explained. Forsythe (1977) and Madsen and Geringer (1983) propose that the type of classroom activity affects student attentiveness, and Witt (1986) suggests that it is the teacher's use of class time. It seems to be attributable to both of these factors in addition to many intangibles.

This study has several important implications for music teacher preparation programs. The tendency of beginning music educators is always to talk too much, give too many instructions, and spend too little time in performance. Thus, music teacher preparation courses could include instruction in reducing teacher talk. Research consistently indicates that in order to maintain students' attentiveness, teachers should talk less and keep students actively engaged in performance. This study corroborates previous research. The finding that such little off-task behavior occurred during 1d indicates that sometimes it is best for teachers to give a starting point in as few words as possible and get the students performing again quickly. While observing students during rehearsals, it was often the case that students tuned out the teacher's verbalizations until the next starting place was given, so perhaps another important teaching technique would focus on how to maintain student attentiveness during periods of teacher instructions. Nevertheless, keeping instructions short takes practice and contributes to good pacing, which is certainly a desirable trait for all music educators.

References

Arnold, J. A. (1991). Using videotape self-analysis to improve teaching during rehearsals. *Update, 10*(1), 10–14.

Bowers, J. (1997). Sequential patterns and the music teaching effectiveness of elementary education majors. *Journal of Research in Music Education, 45*(3), 428–43.

Caldwell, W. M. (1980). A time analysis of selected musical elements and leadership behaviors of successful high school choral conductors. (Doctoral dissertation, Florida State University, 1980). *Dissertation Abstracts International, 41* (3A), 976.

Carpenter, R. A. (1988). A descriptive analysis of relationships between verbal behaviors of teacher-conductors and ratings of selected junior and senior high school band rehearsals. *Update 7*(1), 37–40.

Cavitt, M. E. (2003). A descriptive analysis of error correction in instrumental music rehearsals. *Journal of Research in Music Education, 51*(3), 218–30.

Dunn, D. E. (1997). Effect of rehearsal hierarchy and reinforcement on attention, achievement, and attitude of selected choirs. *Journal of Research in Music Education, 45*(4), 547–67.

Forsythe, J. L. (1975). The effect of teacher approval, disapproval, and errors on student attentiveness: music versus classroom teachers. In C. K. Madsen, R. D. Greer, & C. H. Madsen, Jr. (Eds.), *Research in music behavior* (pp. 49–55). New York: Teachers College Press.

Forsythe, J. L. (1977). Elementary student attending behavior as a function of classroom activities. *Journal of Research in Music Education, 25*(3), 228–39.

Goolsby, T. W. (1996). Time use in instrumental rehearsals: A comparison of experienced, novice, and student teachers. *Journal of Research in Music Education, 44*(4), 286–303.

Gordon, M. (1979). Instrumental music instruction as a contingency for increases in reading behavior. *Journal of Research in Music Education, 27*(2), 87–102.

Grechesky, R. N. (1985). *An analysis of non-verbal and verbal conducting behaviors and their relationships to expressive musical performance.* Unpublished doctoral dissertation, University of Wisconsin–Madison.

Kostka, M. J. (1984). An investigation of reinforcements, time use, and student attentiveness in piano lessons. *Journal of Research in Music Education, 32*(2), 113–22.

Kuhn, T. L. (1975). The effect of teacher approval and disapproval on attentiveness, musical achievement, and attitude of fifth grade students. In C. K. Madsen, R. D. Greer, & C. H. Madsen, Jr. (Eds.), *Research in music behavior* (pp. 40–48). New York: Teachers College Press.

Madsen, C. K., & Alley, J. (1979). The effect of reinforcement on attentiveness: A comparison of behaviorally trained music therapists and other professionals with implications for competency-based academic preparation. *Journal of Music Therapy, 16*(2), 70–82.

Madsen, C. K., & Geringer, J. M. (1976). Choice of televised music lessons versus free play in relationship to academic improvement. *Journal of Music Therapy, 13*(4), 154–62.

Madsen, C. K., & Geringer, J. M. (1983). Attending behavior as a function of in-class activity in university music classes. *Journal of Music Therapy, 20*(1), 30–38.

Madsen, C. K., & Madsen, C. H. Jr. (1972). Selection of music listening or candy as a function of contingent versus non-contingent reinforcement and scale singing. *Journal of Music Therapy, 9*(4), 190–98.

Madsen, C. K., Wolfe, D. E., & Madsen, C. H. Jr. (1969). The effect of reinforcement and directional scalar methodology on intonational improvement. *Council for Research in Music Education, 18*, 22–33.

Moore, R. S. (1976). Effect of differential teaching techniques on achievement, attitude, and teaching skills. *Journal of Research in Music Education, 24*(3), 129–41.

Moore, R. S. (1987). Effects of age, sex, and activity on children's attentiveness in elementary music classes. In C. K. Madsen & C. Prickett (Eds.), *Applications of research in music behavior* (pp. 26–31). Tuscaloosa: University of Alabama Press.

Murray, K. C. (1975). The effect of teacher approval/disapproval on musical performance, attentiveness, and attitude of high school choruses. In C. K. Madsen, R. D. Greer, & C. H. Madsen, Jr. (Eds.), *Research in music behavior* (pp. 165–80). New York: Teacher College Press.

Pontious, M. F. (1982). *A profile of rehearsal techniques and interaction of selected band conductors.* Unpublished doctoral dissertation, University of Illinois, Urbana-Champaign.

Price, H. E. (1983). The effect of conductor academic task presentation, conductor reinforcement, and ensemble practice on performers' musical achievement, attentiveness, and attitude. *Journal of Research in Music Education, 31*(4), 245–57.

Price, H. E. (1992). Sequential patterns of music instruction and learning to use them. *Journal of Research in Music Education, 40*(1), 14–29.

Spradling, R. L. (1985). The effect of timeout from performance on attentiveness and attitude of university band students. *Journal of Research in Music Education, 33*(2), 123–37.

Steele, A. L. (1971). Music therapy: An effective solution to problems in related disciplines. *Journal of Music Therapy, 8*(4), 131–39.

Thurman, V. L. (1977). A frequency and time description of selected rehearsal behaviors used by five choral directors. *Dissertation Abstracts International, 38*(6), 3135-A.

Wagner, M. J., & Strul, E. P. (1979). Comparisons of beginning versus experienced elementary music educators in the use of teaching time. *Journal of Research in Music Education, 27*(2), 113–25.

Watkins, R. E. (1986). A descriptive study of high school choral directors' use of modeling, metaphorical language, and musical/technical language related to student attentiveness. (Doctoral dissertation, University of Texas at Austin, 1986). *Dissertation Abstracts International*, 47(05A), 1644.

Witt, A. C. (1986). Use of class time and student attentiveness in secondary instrumental music rehearsals. *Journal of Research in Music Education, 34*(1), 34–42.

Yarbrough, C. (1975). Effect of magnitude of conductor behavior on students in selected mixed choruses. *Journal of Research in Music Education, 23*(2), 134–46.

Yarbrough, C., & Price, H. E. (1981). Prediction of performer attentiveness based on rehearsal activity and teacher behavior. *Journal of Research in Music Education, 29*(3), 209–17.

Yarbrough, C., & Price, H. E. (1989). Sequential patterns of instruction in music. *Journal of Research in Music Education, 37*(3), 179–87.

Complete Results

Correlation Analyses
Pearson correlation between duration of teacher talk and student off-task behavior

Middle school level:	$r = .18$	$df = 190$	$p < .01$
High school level:	$r = .45$	$df = 266$	$p < .0001$
University level:	$r = .41$	$df = 187$	$p < .0001$
All groups:	$r = .26$	$df = 647$	$p < .0001$

ANOVA Results

Independent variables: Level of group and type of talk
Dependent variable: Percentage of students off-task

Overall significant difference between types of talk
$F = 4.8; df = 3; p < .01$

Overall significant difference between levels
$F = 31.3; df = 2; p < .0001$

No interaction

Tukey HSD post-hoc analysis
Significant differences between

MS 1a and MS no1a	$p < .01$	MS and U 1a	$p < .01$
MS 31a and MS no 1a	$p < .01$	HS 1a and U 1a	$p < .01$
MS no 1a and MS 1d	$p < .01$	MS no1a and U no1a	$p < .01$
HS 1a and HS 1d	$p < .01$	HS no1a and U no1a	$p < .01$
HS no1a and HS 1d	$p < .01$	MS 1d and HS 1d	$p < .05$
HS 31a and HS 1d	$p < .01$	MS 1d and U 1d	$p < .01$
U 31a and U 1d	$p < .05$		
Total 1a and 1d	$p < .05$		
Total 31a and 1d	$p < .05$		
Total no 1a and 1d	$p < .01$		
MS total off-task and HS total off-task	$p < .05$		
HS total off-task and U total off-task	$p < .01$		
MS total off-task and U total off-task	$p < .01$		

ANOVA results

Independent variables: Level of group and type of talk

Dependent variable: Time spent in each type of talk

Overall significant difference between time spent in different types of talk

$F = 4.0; df = 3; p < .01$

Overall significant difference between levels in time spent in different types of talk

$F = 11.5; df = 2; p < .0001$

No interaction effect

Tukey HSD post-hoc analysis

Significant differences between

MS 1a and HS 1a	$p < .01$	MS 1a and MS 31a	$p < .05$
MS 1a and U 1a	$p < .01$	MS 1a and MS 1d	$p < .01$
MS no 1a and HS no1a	$p < .01$	MS no 1a and MS 1d	$p < .01$
MS no1 and U no1a	$p < .05$	MS 31a and MS 1d	$p < .01$
Total MS and HS	$p < .01$	HS 1a and HS 1d	$p < .05$
Total MS and U	$p < .01$	HS 31a and HS 1d	$p < .01$
		U 1a and U 1d	$p < .01$
		U no 1a and U 1d	$p < .05$
		U 31a and U 1d	$p < .01$
		Total 1a and 1d	$p < .01$
		Total 31a and 1d	$p < .01$
		Total no 1a and 1d	$p < .01$

Figure 1. Total Time Spent in Each Type of Talk

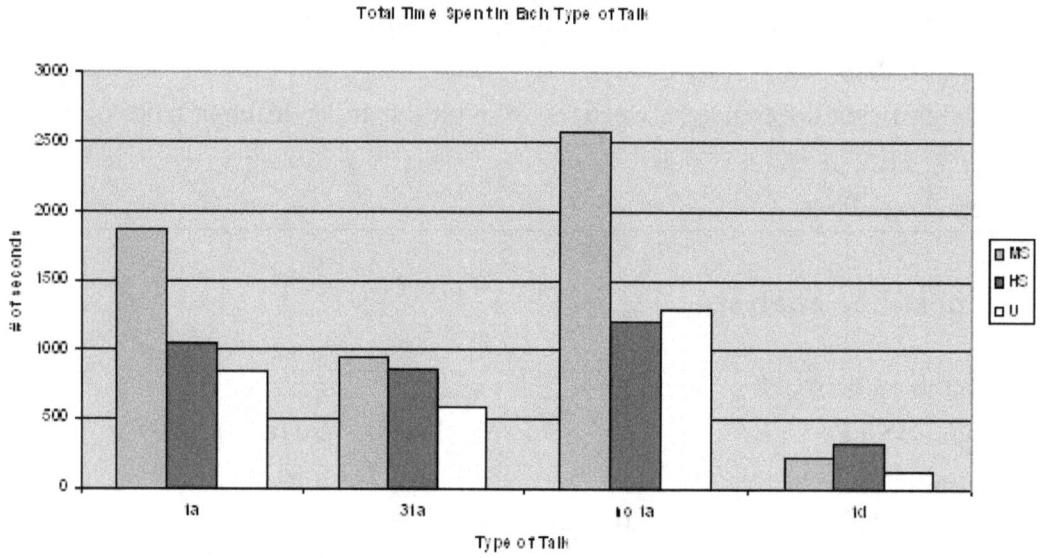

Figure 2. Mean Off-Task Behavior by Talk

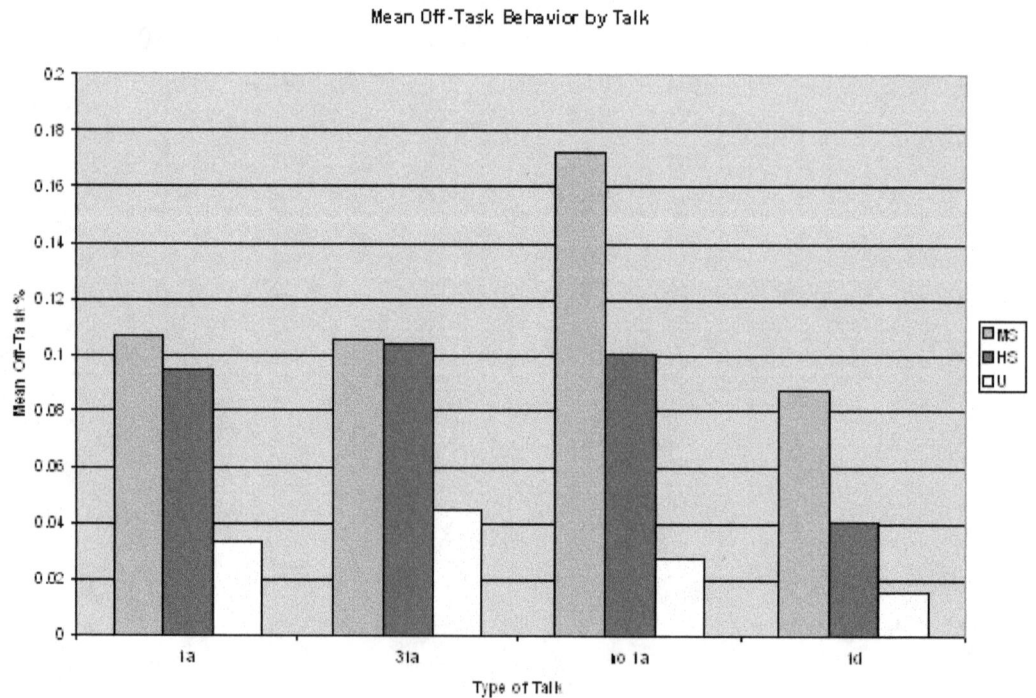

Figure 3. Mean Time Spent in Each Type of Talk

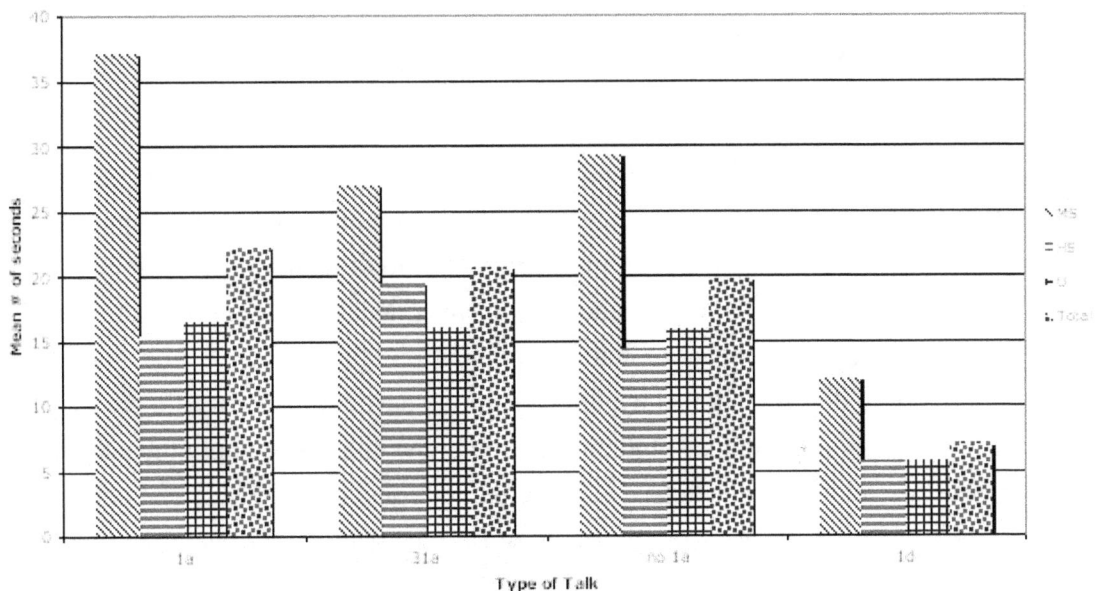

Preservice Music Teachers' Perceptions of Vocal Hygiene: Findings from a National Survey
By Rhonda S. Hackworth

Rhonda Hackworth is assistant professor of choral music education at the Mason Gross School of the Arts at Rutgers, The State University of New Jersey in New Brunswick. She can be reached at rshackwo@rci.rutgers.edu.

The voice is an important teaching tool in the music classroom. Music teachers use their voices in a variety of ways for long periods of time. Therefore, voice disorders can be a common problem. A teacher may take his or her vocal health for granted, giving no thought to prevention, until a problem surfaces (Martin & Darnley, 2004). If prevention is to work, ideas about maintaining a healthy voice may need to take root during the years of teacher preparation.

Before attempting to develop a vocal hygiene education curriculum for music education majors, it might be prudent to first find out what students already know or believe about the subject. This study sought to answer the following questions: (1) What perceptions do preservice teachers have about how they will use their voices in the classroom? (2) Do preservice teachers believe the teaching profession is at high risk for voice disorders, and do they believe voice problems might affect their career? (3) Are preservice teachers familiar with the term vocal hygiene, and what beliefs do they have about caring for the voice? (4) What teaching activities do preservice teachers believe are most harmful to the voice? (5) Do instrumental majors differ from vocal majors in their opinions on vocal hygiene?

Review of Literature

Research has recognized teaching as an occupation at high risk for voice disorders (Herrington-Hall, Lee, Stemple, Niemi, & McHone, 1988; Mattiske, Oates, & Greenwood, 1998; Morton & Watson, 1998; Rantala, Haataja, & Vilkman, 1997; Roy, Merrill, Thibeault, Gray, & Smith, 2004; Roy, Merrill, Thibeault, Parsa et al., 2004; Russell, Oates, & Greenwood, 1998; Smith, Lemke, Taylor, Kirchner, & Hoffman, 1998; Verdolini & Ramig, 2001; Vilkman, 2000), and the problem is increasing over time (Simberg, Sala, Vehmas, & Laine, 2005). Smith et al. found a significant difference between the number of voice problems reported by teachers and the number reported by people in other professions (32% versus 1%, $p < .05$). Teachers were more likely to have current and past voice problems, more likely to miss work due to those problems, and more likely to seek a physician's care for their voices than people in other occupations (Roy, Merrill, Thibeault, Parsa et al., 2004; Smith, Gray, Dove, Kirchner, & Heras, 1997). Sapir, Keidar, and Mathers-Schmidt (1993) observed ($N = 237$) a large number of reported voice-related problems, including missed work and interference with teaching responsibilities. Teachers were also more likely than people in other professions to consider a career change as a result of voice disorders (Roy, Merrill, Thibeault, Gray et al., 2004).

The voice is an important teaching tool for all teachers, but it is especially important for music teachers. Nolteriek (1985) found that music educators teach significantly more often ($p < .001$) in a large-group setting than a small-group setting, and their verbal response rate is significantly higher (p

< .001) to students in a large-group versus small-group setting. Thibeault, Merrill, Roy, Gray, and Smith (2004) found music teachers at higher risk for voice disorders when compared to other types of teachers. According to Bernstorf and Burk (1996), illness or allergies can contribute to vocal problems, but music teachers usually encounter problems simply because the nature of their job may cause overuse or misuse of the vocal mechanism. Almost one-half of the instrumental teachers and the majority of vocal teachers in Hendry's (2001) study reported speaking and singing problems. In Askren's (2000) survey, 21% of music teachers ($N = 63$) reported experiencing vocal attrition once or more per month, and 44% had sought medical treatment for vocal problems.

There is evidence supporting certain treatments for teachers with voice disorders. Roy et al. (2001) tested two methods of treatment (vocal hygiene vs. vocal function exercises) for 6 weeks with 58 voice-disordered teachers. Their findings showed a significant reduction in symptoms from the vocal function exercises group only, suggesting vocal hygiene alone may not be sufficient to treat some teachers who have already developed disorders. On the other hand, any type of treatment may be better than none. Roy et al. (2002) found minimal differences between vocal hygiene and voice amplification treatment methods, but both groups improved significantly more than the control group. The researchers concluded, "The significant deterioration of the nontreatment control group ... over the course of the 6-week trial also indicates that, in the absence of voice treatment, many voice-disordered teachers will experience worsening of their level of voice handicap" (p. 634).

Vocal hygiene has been encouraged as a method of preventing voice disorders in future professional voice users (Morton & Watson, 1998; Timmermans, De Bodt, Wuyts, & Van de Heyning, 2004). Simberg et al. (2005) stated, "Voice training programs should be routinely available to all teachers, not only occasionally. It would be of great importance to make voice-training programs a part of the normal schedule both for teachers and for those who are training to be teachers" (p. 101). Chan (1994) determined that education had a positive effect on the vocal habits of kindergarten teachers. Duffy & Hazlett (2004) determined positive results for education students participating in direct or indirect vocal training when compared to control subjects. Broaddus-Lawrence, Treole, McCabe, Allen, and Toppin (2000) discovered no significant difference in vocal hygiene habits of subjects before and after vocal hygiene education, although their subjects reported a positive perceived value of the knowledge gained. A vocal hygiene program created specifically for kindergarten students ($N = 66$) significantly increased knowledge that could possibly prevent bad vocal habits from becoming habitual (Scrimgeour & Meyer, 2002).

According to Richardson (1996), life experiences strongly influence beliefs about teaching and learning, and the three most prominent sources of teacher beliefs are "personal experience, experience with schooling and instruction, and experience with formal knowledge" (pp. 105–106). The most important role models for music education students in Conway's (2002) study were applied teachers and ensemble conductors; therefore, preservice teachers' beliefs may be influenced by these instructors. Some of what students already believe about teaching is often maintained throughout their undergraduate education and carried with them into their teaching career. Although methods courses provide many opportunities for preservice teachers to define anew their concepts of teaching (Gohlke, 1994), students may complete an education degree and continue to "think as they were taught" (Austin & Reinhardt, 1999, Discussion section, ¶ 5). According to Bridges (1993), much of what graduates wish they had been told about teaching was actually relayed to them at some point in their education and forgotten, possibly because "their need to know was not sufficiently strong at that point in their journey" (p. 71).

Preservice music teachers gave responses similar to those of experienced music teachers when asked to rate the level of importance of teaching skills and behaviors (Teachout, 1997), showing that their perceptive abilities are honed even as students. When asked about voice problems, practicing teachers perceived their voices to be significantly worse than prospective teachers (Yiu, 2002). Both preservice and practicing teachers stated a belief that having information on vocal hygiene strategies would be helpful (Yiu).

Method

Subjects were 140 music education undergraduates from five large universities with similar sized music education programs in distinctly different regions of the United States. Students responded to a written survey (see the complete survey at the end of the article), giving opinions about their personal voice use and its impact on their future teaching careers, rating the impact of behaviors/conditions on the voice, rating the impact of teaching activities on the voice, and providing demographic information (including year in school, major and secondary instruments, voice lesson experience, and future teaching plans). Only undergraduate students with no prior contractual teaching experience were asked to complete the survey. Prior to the survey's distribution, it was piloted with students in a graduate music education course.

Respondents were asked to speculate how many hours they would spend once their teaching careers began (a) giving verbal instruction, (b) planning, (c) singing, (d) playing an instrument, and (e) rehearsing after/before school hours, using a 4-point scale (1 = less than two hours, 2= two to three hours, 3 = four to five hours, 4 = more than five hours). They were also asked if they believed a voice disorder might affect their teaching career and/or make them consider changing careers.

Preservice teachers indicated whether they were familiar with the term *vocal hygiene* and then rated behaviors/conditions (such as talking in noisy environments, adequate sleep, drinking water, smoking, stress, etc.) on a 6-point scale (1 = very healthy, 6 = very unhealthy). Ratings were analyzed for overall means, and a series of independent *t*-tests was performed to compare ratings of vocal versus instrumental majors.

Following the ratings of behaviors/conditions, preservice teachers indicated whether they believed the teaching profession to be an occupation at low, medium, or high risk for voice disorders. Percentages for the entire population, vocal versus instrumental majors, and individual classes were analyzed. Subjects also rated teaching activities for perceived vocal stress on a 7-point scale (1 = least vocal stress, 7 = most vocal stress). The ratings of vocal versus instrumental majors were analyzed using a series of independent *t*-tests.

In the final section of the survey, respondents provided information about their year in school, gender, primary and secondary instruments, voice lesson experience, and what type/level of music they would like to teach after graduation. These responses made possible the group assignment for testing other areas of the survey.

Thirty-six respondents indicated voice as a primary or secondary instrument, and 112 indicated an instrument other than voice as primary. For a more balanced comparison of ratings between vocal and instrumental majors on survey questions 5 and 7 (see the complete survey), a smaller group of instrumental students ($n = 36$) was randomly selected and compared to the group of vocal students ($n = 36$). Selected instrumental students indicated something other than voice as primary and secondary instruments and had never taken voice lessons. Independent t-tests were performed to compare the ratings of vocal versus instrumental majors on survey questions 5 and 7.

Results

Thirty-seven percent of preservice teachers believe they will use their voices between 2 and 3 hours daily for vocal instruction. Twenty-six percent believe that number will be between 4 and 5 hours, and 22% believe they will verbally instruct more than 5 hours per day. A majority of respondents (56%) believe they will spend two to three hours rehearsing before or after school hours; however, 55% believe they will spend less than 2 hours per day singing. See Table 1 for a complete summary.

Almost one-half (48%) of preservice teachers believe the teaching profession is at high risk for voice disorders. Six percent believe it is at low risk, and 46% believe it is a medium risk occupation. A majority (60%) of the preservice teachers surveyed believe developing a vocal problem will have an effect on their career. Only 9% believe a vocal problem would not affect their career, and 31% answered "maybe." Of the 106 preservice teachers answering the next question ("would you consider changing your career in order to preserve your voice?"), 68% answered "no," 7% answered "yes," and 25% answered "maybe."

The term *vocal hygiene*, or care of the voice, was familiar to 53% of respondents and unfamiliar to 47%. When asked to rate a variety of behaviors/conditions affecting the voice on a 6-point scale (see question 5 on the survey), preservice teachers rated drinking water, warming up the voice, and exercising as the healthiest behaviors/conditions. Smoking, exposure to secondhand smoke, and acid reflux disease were rated the unhealthiest behaviors/conditions. See Table 2 for a complete summary. When ratings from a smaller group of instrumental ($n = 36$) and vocal ($n = 36$) majors were compared using a series of independent t-tests, no significant differences were found in any of these behavioral categories.

Preservice teachers were asked to rate several teaching activities for vocal stress on a 7-point scale. The activities rated highest for vocal stress included (a) speaking over noisy classroom conditions (e.g., air conditioning, fans, hallway noise) ($M = 5.68, SD = 1.25$); (b) verbally instructing students while they play instruments ($M = 5.52, SD = 1.32$); (c) lunchroom duty ($M = 5.28, SD = 1.48$); (d) bus duty ($M = 5.16, SD = 1.50$); and (e) classroom management ($M = 4.93, SD = 1.57$). Teaching activities rated lowest for vocal stress included (a) demonstration singing (alone) ($M = 2.60, SD = 1.35$); (b) verbally instructing students during structured listening activities ($M = 3.04, SD = 1.29$); (c) opening remarks/giving instructions ($M = 3.22, SD = 1.40$); (d) demonstration singing with recordings ($M = 3.74, SD = 1.41$); and (e) demonstration singing with students also singing ($M = 3.85, SD = 1.45$).

When the ratings of a smaller group of instrumental ($n = 36$) and vocal ($n = 36$) majors were compared using a series independent t-tests, significant differences were found in two categories. Instrumental majors ($M = 2.78$, $SD = 1.31$) rated "demonstration singing (alone)" as having significantly more vocal stress than did vocal majors ($M = 1.81$, $SD = 1.04$), $t(70) = 1.67$, $p < .001$. The category of "demonstration singing with students also singing" was also rated significantly higher for vocal stress by instrumental majors ($M = 3.97$, $SD = 1.59$) than by vocal majors ($M = 3.33$, $SD = 1.60$) $t(70) = 1.67$, $p < .05$. A summary of results is shown in Table 3.

Discussion

There is no clear majority opinion about how many hours preservice teachers believe they will use their voices each day giving vocal instruction. The variety of respondents (different classes, different instrument majors, and different levels of exposure to teaching) may account for the range of responses in this category. It is interesting to note that a majority of preservice teachers (56%) believe they will spend two to three hours rehearsing after school, while 55% believe they will sing less than two hours in the entire day. Most of the respondents (81%) indicated their primary instrument to be something other than voice; therefore, these preservice teachers may not believe they will spend a considerable amount of the teaching day engaged in singing activities.

Sixty percent of preservice teachers believe a voice disorder *would* affect their career, and another 31% believe a disorder *might* affect their career. These responses indicate a strong awareness of the risk teachers face, possibly because these preservice teachers know a teacher with vocal problems or have had exposure to earlier cited research on the subject. A large number of preservice teachers also believe the teaching profession is at either high risk (48%) or medium risk (46%) for voice disorders.

Preservice teachers who believe a voice disorder would affect their career are not willing to give up the career in order to preserve their voices. A large majority (68%) indicated they would not consider changing their career, even if a voice disorder developed. However, it should be noted that the combined percentage of those who *would* consider (7%) or *might* consider (25%) a change adds up to 32% (even though the discussion of music teacher retention is beyond the scope of the survey employed for this study and encompasses many more variables than vocal health alone).

Familiarity with the term *vocal hygiene*, or care of the voice, was split. A slight majority of preservice teachers (53%) were familiar with the term, and 47% were not. This does not necessarily indicate that 47% lack knowledge about vocal care; it may simply mean the terminology is unknown. In fact, preservice teachers seemed to have strong opinions about healthy or unhealthy personal behaviors/conditions related to vocal care. Those behaviors emerging as "healthiest" (drinking water, warming up the voice, and getting adequate sleep) have health benefits in addition to vocal care, and many people may find it logical to incorporate them into an overall healthy lifestyle. Consequently, behaviors/conditions rated "unhealthiest" (smoking, secondhand smoke, and acid reflux disease) may be perceived as unhealthy for a variety of reasons. The general nature of these behaviors/conditions could also be a factor in similar ratings of instrumental and vocal majors.

Speaking over noisy classroom conditions was rated by preservice teachers as the teaching activity with the most vocal stress. There are many sources of classroom noise, and this survey question specifically asked about environmental noise (e.g., air conditioning, fans, hallway noise) to make a distinction between environmental sounds and other music classroom sounds. The teaching activity rated second-highest for vocal stress was verbally instructing students while they play instruments. No specific number of students and/or type of instrument was indicated in the rating choice. This choice may indicate preservice teachers' perception that talking over any number of students playing instruments produces vocal stress. Teaching activities rated for the least amount of vocal stress were demonstration singing (alone) and verbally instructing students during structured listening activities. Again, no amount of time or frequency of occurrence for these activities was indicated in the rating choice.

The significant differences found between the ratings of instrumental and vocal majors are interesting. Instrumental majors rated both demonstration singing categories (demonstration singing alone and demonstration singing with students also singing) significantly higher for vocal stress than did vocal majors. It is possible that vocal majors see these activities as something for which they are well trained and not a large threat to their vocal health. Instrumental majors, on the other hand, may view singing as a stressful activity in general and transfer that stress to the voice. Instrumental majors may believe they will sing only occasionally and experience more vocal stress as a result.

Future research in this area should ask more specific questions about how preservice music teachers believe they will use their voices. More pertinent questions regarding vocal stress in teaching activities could facilitate a more complete analysis of perceptions. Additionally, it would be interesting to compare the responses from freshman, sophomores, juniors, and seniors to see if any changes in perception occur during the completion of a degree. Finally, it would be interesting to compare the opinions and perceptions of preservice teachers to those of experienced teachers. Despite these remaining questions, this study provides preliminary information of the awareness preservice teachers already possess about the risks of developing voice disorders as a result of career choice. Talking to music education students about vocal stress, its prevention, and its treatment prior to teaching will likely benefit the students and possibly benefit the overall future of the profession.

References

Askren, K. A. W. (2000). *Vocal attrition and the vocal educator.* Unpublished master's thesis: University of Missouri–Kansas City.

Austin, J. R. & Reinhardt, D. (1999). Philosophy and advocacy: An examination of preservice music teachers' beliefs [Electronic version]. *Journal of Research in Music Education, 47*(1), 18–30.

Bernstorf, E. D., & Burk, K. W. (1996). Vocal integrity of elementary vocal music teachers: Personal and environmental factors. *Journal of Research in Music Education, 44*(4), 369–83.

Bridges, M. S. (1993). What our graduates wish we had told them. *Quarterly Journal of Music Teaching and Learning, 4*(1), 68–72.

Broaddus-Lawrence, P. L., Treole, K., McCabe, R. B., Allen, R. L., & Toppin, L. (2000). The effects of preventive vocal hygiene education on the vocal hygiene habits and perceptual vocal characteristics of training singers. *Journal of Voice, 14*(1), 58–71.

Chan, R. (1994). Does the voice improve with vocal hygiene education? A study of some instrumental voice measures in a group of kindergarten teachers. *Journal of Voice, 8*(3), 279–91.

Conway, C. (2002). Perceptions of beginning teachers, their mentors, and administrators regarding preservice music teacher preparation [Electronic version]. *Journal of Research in Music*

Education, 50(1), 20–36.

Duffy, O. M., & Hazlett, D. E. (2004). The impact of preventive voice care programs for training teachers: A longitudinal study. *Journal of Voice, 18*(1), 63–70.

Gohlke, L. J. (1994). The music methods class: Acquisition of pedagogical content knowledge by preservice music teachers. *Dissertation Abstracts International, 55(09A)*, 2757. (UMI No. 9504621)

Hendry, K. L. (2001). Burnout and self-reported vocal health among music teachers and other educators. *Dissertation Abstracts International, 62* (05), 1767A. (UMI No. 3014770)

Herrington-Hall, B. L., Lee, L., Stemple, J. C., Niemi, K. R., & McHone, M. (1988). Description of laryngeal pathology by age, sex, and occupation in a treatment-seeking sample. *Journal of Speech and Hearing Disorders, 53,* 57–54.

Martin, S., & Darnley, L. (2004). *The teaching voice* (2nd ed.). London: Whurr.

Mattiske, J. A., Oates, J. M., & Greenwood, K. M. (1998). Vocal problems among teachers: A review of prevalence, causes, prevention, and treatment. *Journal of Voice, 12*(4), 489–99.

Morton, V., & Watson, D. R. (1998). The teaching voice: Problems and perceptions. *Logopedics, Phoniatrics, Vocology, 23*(3), 133–39.

Nolteriek, M. A. (1985). A description of teacher and student behavior within single and multiple group teaching structures in elementary and general music education classrooms. *Dissertation Abstracts International, 45* (08), 2435A. (UMI No. 8424727)

Rantala, L., Haataja, K., & Vilkman, E. (1997). Measuring voice under teachers' working circumstances: F_0 and perturbation features in maximally sustained phonation. *Folia Phoniatrica and Logopedics, 49,* 281–91.

Richardson, V. (1996). The role of attitudes and beliefs in learning to teach. In J. Sikula (Ed.), *Handbook of research on teacher education* (2nd ed., pp. 3–13). New York: Simon & Schuster Macmillan.

Roy, N., Gray, S. D., Simon, M., Dove, H., Corbin-Lewis, K., & Stemple, J. C. (2001). An evaluation of the effects of two treatment approaches for teachers with voice disorders: A prospective randomized clinical trial. *Journal of Speech, Language, and Hearing Research, 44*(2), 286–96

Roy, N., Merrill, R. M., Thibeault, S., Gray, S. D., & Smith, E. M. (2004). Voice disorders in teachers and the general population: Effects on work performance, attendance, and future career choices. *Journal of Speech, Language, and Hearing Research, 47*(3), 542–51.

Roy, N., Merrill, R. M., Thibeault, S., Parsa, R. A., Gray, S. D., & Smith E. M. (2004). Prevalence of voice disorders in teachers and the general population. *Journal of Speech, Language, and Hearing Research, 47*(2), 281–93.

Roy, N., Weinrich, B., Gray, S. D., Tanner, K., Toledo, S. W., Dove, H. et al. (2002). Voice amplification versus vocal hygiene instruction for teachers with voice disorders: A treatment outcomes study. *Journal of Speech, Language, and Hearing Research, 45*(4), 625–38.

Russell, A., Oates, J., & Greenwood, K. M. (1998). Prevalence of voice problems in teachers. *Journal of Voice, 12*(4), 467–79.

Sapir, S., Keidar, A., & Mathers-Schmidt, B. (1993). Vocal attrition in teachers: Survey finding. *European Journal of Disorders of Communication, 28,* 177–85.

Scrimgeour, K., & Meyer, S. E. (2002). Effectiveness of a hearing conservation and vocal hygiene program for kindergarten children. *Special Services in the School, 18*(1–2), 133–50.

Simberg, S., Sala, E., Vehmas, K., Laine, A. (2005). Changes in the prevalence of vocal symptoms among teachers during a twelve year period. *Journal of Voice, 19*(1), 95–102.

Smith, E., Gray, S. D., Dove, H., Kirchner, L., & Heras, H. (1997). Frequency and effects of teachers' voice problems. *Journal of Voice, 11*(1), 81–87.

Smith, E., Lemke, J., Taylor, M., Kirchner, H. L., & Hoffman, H. (1998). Frequency of voice problems among teachers and other occupations. *Journal of Voice, 12*(4), 480–88.

Teachout, D. J. (1997). Preservice and experienced teachers' opinions of skills and behaviors important to successful music teaching [Electronic version]. *Journal of Research in Music Education, 45*(1), 41–50.

Thibeault, S. L., Merrill, R. M., Roy, N., Gray, S. D., & Smith, E. M. (2004). Occupational risk factors associated with voice disorders among teachers. *Ann Epidemiol, 14*(10), 786–92.

Timmermans, B., De Bodt, M., Wuyts, F., & Van de Heyning, P. H. (2004). Training outcome in future professional voice users after 18 months of voice training. *Folia Phoniatrica et Logopaedica, 56*(2), 120–29.

Verdolini, K., Ramig, L. O. (2001). Review: Occupational risks for voice problems. *Logopedics, Phoniatrics, Vocology, 26*(1), 37–46.

Vilkman, E. (2000). Voice problems at work: A challenge for occupational safety and health arrangement. *Folia Phoniatrica and Logopedics, 52*(1–3), 120–25.

Yiu, E. (2002). Impact and prevention of voice problems in the teaching profession: Embracing the consumers' view. *Journal of Voice 16*(2), 215–28.

Survey of Future Music Educators

1. When you begin your career as a music teacher, how many hours per day do you believe you will spend performing the following activities: *(circle one)*

   a. giving verbal instruction   less than 2   2–3   4–5   more than 5
   b. planning   less than 2   2–3   4–5   more than 5
   c. singing   less than 2   2–3   4–5   more than 5
   d. playing an instrument   less than 2   2–3   4–5   more than 5
   e. rehearsing after/before school hours   less than 2   2–3   4–5   more than 5

2. If you develop vocal problems while teaching, do you believe it might affect your career?

   Yes   No   Maybe

3. If you answered "yes" to question #2, would you consider changing your career in order to preserve your voice?

   Yes   No   Maybe

4. Are you familiar with the term *vocal hygiene*?

   Yes   No

5. Rate each of the following from 1 to 6 (1=very healthy, 6=very **un**healthy) in order to give your opinion about its impact on the health of your voice.

	Very healthy				Very unhealthy	
Talking in noisy environments	1	2	3	4	5	6
Drinking water	1	2	3	4	5	6
Wearing proper clothing	1	2	3	4	5	6
Clearing your throat	1	2	3	4	5	6
Warming up your voice	1	2	3	4	5	6
Exercising	1	2	3	4	5	6
Using alcohol	1	2	3	4	5	6
Experiencing stress	1	2	3	4	5	6
Using caffeine	1	2	3	4	5	6
Eating a balanced diet	1	2	3	4	5	6
Smoking	1	2	3	4	5	6
Coughing	1	2	3	4	5	6
Adequate sleep	1	2	3	4	5	6
Acid Reflux disease	1	2	3	4	5	6
Secondhand smoke	1	2	3	4	5	6

6. Place an X by the statement with which you agree most. (*Choose only one*):

   _____ I consider the teaching profession to be an occupation at **low** risk for voice disorders.
   _____ I consider the teaching profession to be an occupation at **medium** risk for voice disorders.

_____ I consider the teaching profession to be an occupation at **high** risk for voice disorders.

7. Rate the following teaching activities for the amount of vocal stress you believe they render:

Least Vocal Stress					Most Vocal Stress	
1	2	3	4	5	6	7

_____ Opening remarks/giving instructions
_____ Verbally instructing students while they are playing instruments
_____ Verbally instructing students while they are singing
_____ Verbally instructing students during structured listening activities
_____ Demonstration singing (alone)
_____ Demonstration singing with students also singing
_____ Demonstration singing with recordings
_____ Classroom management/discipline
_____ Speaking over noisy classroom conditions (a/c, fans, computers, hallway noise, etc.)
_____ Hall supervision
_____ Bus supervision
_____ Lunchroom duty
_____ Other _____
_____ Other _____

8. Circle your year in school: freshman   sophomore   junior   senior

9. Gender: female   male

10. Primary instrument: _____

   years of lessons: _____

11. Secondary instrument: _____

   years of lessons: _____

12. If voice is not your primary or secondary instrument, have you taken voice lessons?
       Yes   No
    If yes, how many years? _____

13. What would you like to teach after graduation? (*check all that apply*)
_____ elementary   _____ middle/junior high   _____ high school   _____ college
_____ general music   _____ band   _____ choir   _____ orchestra
_____ keyboard   _____ musical theater   _____ guitar

Table 1. Preservice Teachers' (N = 140) Perceptions of Amount of Voice Use in Teaching

Task	Hours			
	Less than 2	2–3	4–5	More than 5
	% of responses			
Giving verbal instruction	16 %	37 %	26 %	22 %
Planning	19 %	**51 %**	21 %	9 %
Singing	**55 %**	25 %	14 %	6 %
Playing instruments	36 %	35 %	20 %	9 %
Rehearsing before/after school	21 %	**56 %**	15 %	8 %

Table 2. Healthiest and Unhealthiest Vocal Hygiene Behaviors/Conditions Rated by Preservice Teachers (N = 140)

Healthiest Behaviors/Conditions	% of Respondent Ratings					
	1	2	3	4	5	6
Drinking water	86 %	13 %	1 %	—	—	—
Warming up the voice	73 %	20 %	5%	1%	—	1%
Getting adequate sleep	66%	23%	6%	2%	1%	2%
Eating a balanced diet	57%	29%	13%	1%	—	—
Unhealthiest Behaviors/Conditions						
Smoking	1%	1%	—	—	7%	91%
Secondhand smoke	—	2%	1%	11%	25%	61%
Acid reflux disease	2%	—	1%	13%	32%	52%
Experiencing stress	—	1%	3%	23%	43%	30%

Note. Ratings made on a six-point scale (1 = very healthy, 6 = very **un**healthy)

Table 3. Instrumental vs. Vocal Majors' Ratings of Vocal Stress in Selected Teaching Activities

Teaching Activity	Group	Mean	Standard Deviation
Speaking over noisy conditions (fans, hallway noise, etc.)	Instrumental ($n = 36$)	5.94	.92
	Vocal ($n = 36$)	6.08	1.13
Verbally instructing students while they play instruments	Instrumental	5.25	1.52
	Vocal	5.86	1.22
Lunchroom duty	Instrumental	5.19	1.41
	Vocal	5.54	1.54
Bus duty	Instrumental	5.19	1.56
	Vocal	5.39	1.40
Classroom management	Instrumental	5.07	1.63
	Vocal	5.19	1.49
Verbally instructing students while they sing	Instrumental	4.81	1.33
	Vocal	5.25	1.20
Hall duty	Instrumental	4.56	1.44
	Vocal	5.14	1.59
Demonstration singing with students also singing	Instrumental	3.97*	1.59
	Vocal	3.33	1.60
Demonstration singing with recordings	Instrumental	3.58	1.42
	Vocal	3.39	1.52
Opening remarks/giving instructions	Instrumental	3.39	1.42
	Vocal	3.47	1.44
Verbally instructing students during structured listening activities	Instrumental	3.00	1.20
	Vocal	3.03	1.03
Demonstration singing (alone)	Instrumental	2.78**	1.31
	Vocal	1.81	1.04

Note. Ratings made on a seven-point scale (1 = least vocal stress, 7 = most vocal stress).
*$p < .001$.
**$p < .05$.

Enhancing Interaction between University and Public School Music Teachers: The Design and Impact of a Local Needs Assessment Project
By John W. Scheib and Frederick W. Burrack

John W. Scheib is an assistant professor of music education at Ball State University in Muncie, Indiana. He can be reached at jwscheib@bsu.edu. Frederick W. Burrack is an assistant professor of music at Kansas State University in Manhattan. He can be reached at fburrack@ksu.edu.

University faculty have the awesome responsibility of overseeing the placement and supervision of music education student teachers. Familiarity with public school music programs and their instructors is an essential component of this responsibility. As new faculty members at a large midwestern university music education program, it was necessary for us to become familiar with the nature of music instruction in local school systems. In doing so, we confirmed a need for enhanced communication between the schools and the university. Initiating dialogues with school music teachers was important in better guiding the placement of music student teachers in the field and also for becoming familiar with the particular needs of these local school music programs. What developed from this need for enhanced communication was an assessment study to initiate conversations with practicing music teachers and to observe them in their teaching environments.

Project Design

As found by Grice (1986), needs assessments can elicit valuable insights about the educational goals of instrumental music programs, lead to staff development strategies to assist educational needs, and assist in focusing teacher education around the needs of the practitioner. The primary goals of this project were to determine the values, attitudes, performance levels, instructional needs, and conditions of instrumental music educators in the elementary through high schools located within a 65-mile radius of the university. Additional goals were to lay groundwork for future relationships and create an informational database to assist in future communication with practicing teachers.

Undertaking an investigation that examined perceived needs of practicing teachers rather than observing measurable behaviors exhibited during teaching necessitated a design that provided an environment of trust and cooperation. All unfamiliar elementary, middle, and high school instrumental music instructors within a 65-mile radius of the university were contacted (66 teachers from 55 different schools) through a standard mailing that introduced the instrumental music teacher-education faculty and stated a desire to become acquainted with all the area school instrumental music teachers. This letter was designed with the intent of being nonthreatening out of consideration for those who may perceive university faculty as judgmental toward their program.

The letters were followed by telephone calls with a purpose of coordinating a meeting at each prospective school. Each meeting (60 teachers from 52 different schools) included informal introductions, tour of the music facilities, and a 30 to 45 minute interview with the teacher. In order to further promote a nonthreatening atmosphere for these initial meetings, interviews were not recorded. Interviews focused on the curricular offerings of the instrumental music program, educational emphases, and school culture. Information leading to an understanding of the instructors' background, perceived struggles, and needs as practicing school music teachers was also pursued (see figure 1 for interview questions). To conclude, investigators asked each individual to offer advice to preservice music teachers preparing to enter the field. Follow-up visits with many of the directors (over 50%) offered further observations of instruction as well as opportunities for the investigators to serve as guest ensemble clinicians.

Detailed field notes were taken and transcribed immediately following each meeting. The case studies were synthesized through cross-analysis by identifying recurring themes and patterns among the instrumental programs while exposing uniqueness. The aggregation of data did not aim to exclude independent needs but treated each item as an important data source. All data collection took place during the 2003–2004 academic year.

Findings

Similar to a needs study of Barnett and Greenough (1999), four broad areas of concern emerged from the interviews. In understanding school music program culture, it was first necessary to provide context for the discussion. Since this project was primarily a study of directors' perceptions, understanding their work environment was important to establishing this context. Second, a look at the needs and struggles of the directors, collectively, was warranted to help identify and further support what was important to them (e.g., education-related philosophy). From this, the investigators discovered each program's unique (and possibly restricting) characteristics in relation to its director's philosophical understandings and gained an overall understanding of school music teaching within the context of the local school music program culture. Third, examining the directors' declared advice for music teachers soon to be entering the profession for the first time "triangulated" the data (e.g., what they gave for advice is likely to be directly influenced by the program's culture, their philosophy, and ideas of struggles and needs). All three lenses enhanced the understanding of what it was, for these directors, to be a school music teacher.

Program Emphases. While each school music program certainly had its own unique and specific culture, data generated through this project presented four general areas of commonality. It appeared that competition through performance was an important component of local school music program culture. Linked to this theme, a focus on student performance achievement helped support this ideology. However, somewhat in contrast to the performance foci, several programs also reported a more comprehensive approach to school music instruction. Finally, most of the school music directors reported that music teaching and learning was a social event and their programs reflected this characteristic.

Success in competition. Many directors reported a strong interest in achieving success, as a program, through several competition-related activities and arenas. From marching-related endeavors (e.g., state-sponsored marching band contests, winter drum line, winter guard) to the concert wind-band setting, success in the form of rankings and ratings at large-group contests was high on the priority list for many directors. As a result, directors focused on a smaller scope of repertoire over the course of an academic year.

Student achievement. Programs appeared to be geared toward student achievement above all else. Ratings, rankings, awards, accolades, trophies, and trinkets were all important representations of student achievement. Large ensembles consisting of as many students as possible seemed to be the desire of many directors—little attention or focus was placed on chamber music opportunities for students. Directors emphasized the need for high student enrollment in their band programs; recruiting and retaining students were important discussion points in the conversations. Accolades for student productivity in the form of achievement through various contests and competitions were motivational tools to keep students involved in the band programs.

Comprehensive musicianship. While many programs seemed quite traditional in their offerings and curricula, several others demonstrated an emphasis toward comprehensive musical experiences for students. Many programs offered jazz education before or after school. Some programs included not only a big band setting but also several smaller jazz combo opportunities for students to learn improvisation in a more intimate setting. Several of the programs that offered these types of experiences were also more likely to offer a wider variety of other musical experiences, such as chamber ensemble work, composition or music theory instruction, music technology education, and cross-disciplinary collaborations (e.g., vocal music, theater/drama).

Social learning. Overall, most directors held social learning and quality of work environment in high regard. Directors reported the desire to create environments where students worked comfortably with each other, enjoyed the experiences of making music in an ensemble, and cooperatively interacted toward a unified goal or objective. Various ensemble performance tours often provided this necessary social environment. For example, through the competitive marching band circuit, students executed duties beyond performing within an ensemble setting. These opportunities were intended to provide the students with understandings of the social-environment-enhancing concepts of work ethic, personal responsibility, cooperation, collaboration, and collective ownership of the process and product. For many directors, having students engaged in developing these life skills was a central component and emphasis of their music program.

Needs and Struggles. Beyond describing individual and collective school music program characteristics, this project also had the specific intent of identifying the needs of the directors. A better idea of the culture that surrounds and supports each program was achieved through understanding the needs, struggles, and emphases of each director. These needs and struggles often walked hand in hand; understanding one led to understanding the other. These directors were quite forthcoming with information, and the resulting analysis of the data from the interviews yielded three thematic streams that represented the relationships of their self-reported struggles as school music teachers: (1) student-related struggles, (2) schedule-related struggles, and (3) support-related struggles.

Student-related. Supporting findings from Heston, Dedrick, Raschke, and Whitehead (1996), when discussing student-related struggles the most mentioned issue dealt with the perceived poor (or lacking) student work ethic. Many directors stated that the majority of their students were not highly committed to the band program. Directors struggled with finding ways to motivate their students to not only practice, but also be involved with the program beyond the minimum expectations. This lack of effort by the students in turn created inhibited performance skills, which had a negative impact on the performance level of the ensembles. Ultimately, the lowered ability/skill level of the ensemble was the most pressing issue for many of these directors as the success level of the program was at stake.

Schedule-related. Directors also mentioned several issues relating to the often complicated and time-restrictive schedules in which they operated their music programs. As the research literature also claims (e.g., Hamann & Daugherty, 1984; Heston et al., 1996; Scheib, 2003, 2004), the most often cited complaint dealt with not having enough time to fulfill all the duties, or expectations, of their job as band directors—both in administrative tasks and instructional responsibilities. Part of the problem, for several of these directors, was due to having to operate their programs within various schoolwide schedules that did not allow them adequate time for instruction on a day-to-day basis. In a few examples, directors were responsible for teaching courses outside of instrumental music. In addition to being responsible for the band program, a few directors were also assigned to teaching one or two periods of a nonmusic subject (e.g., English, math, science). For these directors, being a "part-time music teacher" was a constant struggle.

Support-related. The third area most reported as a struggle involved a lack of support upon which to operate music programs—issues also well documented in the existing research literature (e.g., Gordon, 2000; Krueger, 2000; Madsen & Hancock, 2002; Nimmo, 1986; Scheib, 2004, 2006). Among the issues, directors mentioned that a lack of financial, administrative, and parental support were all problems they encountered on a daily basis. This perceived lack of support presented itself with issues relating to inadequate staffing for their programs, inadequate facilities in which to operate their programs, and an overall schoolwide educational emphasis away from the arts. As a result, directors felt they continually needed to be proactive in music and arts advocacy in their school and community, an expectation that can be all too consuming in their occupation as a school music teacher. The needed time to adequately fulfill the multiple roles expected of them (e.g., teacher, administrator, advocate) was at a premium and resulted in little time left for a satisfactory personal life (e.g., role as spouse, parent, individual). Additionally, adequate time for lesson planning and student assessment was difficult to maintain due to the consuming nature of the administrator and advocate roles for these directors. These *role conflicts* (Kahn, Wolfe, Quinn, & Snoek, 1964; Scheib, 2003) appeared to be a significant part of the day-to-day struggle for these directors.

State and federally mandated standardized testing added a third layer to their struggles where music courses, because of their marginalized status as a "special" or "nonacademic" subject, were not required nor emphasized within these initiatives. While most directors were relieved that music was not a part of this annual districtwide standardized testing, being absent from the cohort of subjects further perpetuated the notion that music was excluded from the list of "official" or "important" learning. Also, music students who performed poorly on standardized tests were removed from music rehearsals in order to receive remediation in the core academic areas in which they were determined to be deficient—a further blow to the academic or official status of music as an important subject to be studied.

Advice for New Teachers. In addition to providing information on their programs and professional needs, directors interviewed for this study were quick to give advice to preservice teachers soon to be entering the profession. Among all things, many directors mentioned the ability to multitask as a critical skill needed for any music teacher. According to Zehava (2001), multitasking, or multiskilling, positively contributes to surviving the expectations of teaching and deters the onset of burnout. The need for teachers to be organized, have well-thought-out plans, and thoroughly understand the content they teach are all additional bits of counsel communicated by these directors that should help the newly inducted novice teacher successfully navigate a busy professional life.

Directors were also thoughtful in encouraging new teachers to be patient with students, though firm and assertive, when dealing with both instructional and behavioral problems in class. However, they strongly advised against singling out students in front of their peers (e.g., in rehearsal). In agreement with Hewitt (1999), they believed that confrontation occurs in classrooms where the teacher is not properly trained to manage severe behavioral problems.

Communication was a central theme of several of the directors' prescriptions for success on the job. New teachers should be diligent but professional in their communication with colleagues, administration, and parents, in particular. One way toward this goal was to identify oneself as being an educator first and foremost—a *music* educator second. The need for networking with other *educators* was also among the most referenced tips.

Many of the directors suggested the need for pursuing graduate work as soon as possible. The benefits of this, reportedly, were twofold: it helped further the teachers' professional development, and it provided them with financial compensation in the form of an increase in salary.

Finally, directors supported the need for new music teachers to take great care of their personal and professional lives. "Enjoy your triumphs, no matter how small," was mentioned specifically by one director weighing the need for professional self-acknowledgment of success during those difficult (and sometimes victory-barren) first few years of teaching. The need for committing oneself to activities outside of school was also mentioned as critical to maintaining balance in one's life, especially considering the demanding professional schedule of the school music teacher that all too often tips the scale away from having a life removed from the job's responsibilities.

Impact on Music Teacher Education Program

The findings from this study helped us to understand local instrumental school music culture. However, as Graue and Walsh (1998) remind us, valid research should have ends that benefit the profession. Likewise, answering Kimpton's (2005) call to arms and supporting Robbins and Stein's (2005) suggestions in the Spring 2005 *JMTE* special issue on the future of music teacher education, the findings from this project needed to have "legs." As for the results of this study and their impact on preparing school music teachers at our institution, the ramifications were far-reaching.

Methods courses. Information collected from the area directors regarding their specific program designs, local school and community culture, and professional needs and struggles greatly enhanced instruction in methods courses through both curricula and course design. A critical part of methods course instruction deals with attempting to best prepare students to enter the complex world of teaching. To do so, preservice teachers need to understand the context in which they will be expected to teach (e.g., the school setting). In agreement with Paul (1998), field experiences are crucial for students to understand this context. Having this information helped us identify programs that would be best suited for methods course-related field experiences. Understandings gained from this study also transferred to the methods classroom and often provided the needed frame for discussions and dialogue concerning broader pedagogical issues.

Administration course. As a result of the communication with area music teachers, collaborations were developed to enhance a course for all music education majors titled Administration of School Music Programs. This course covers many essential administrative skills and necessary understandings relevant to teaching music in the schools. Prior to this study, most if not all topics were handled conceptually through readings and discussion. This study exposed strengths of area teachers, providing opportunities to allow them to share their expertise with the music education students. Selected teachers discussed working with parents, fund-raising, organizing trips and traveling with students, solving scheduling conflicts, planning within a block schedule, and dealing with classroom management situations.

Collaborative projects were developed that allowed students to experience authentic administrative duties of music teachers while assisting area teachers in fulfilling their responsibilities. One project taught students the budget process involved in equipment purchasing. This budget project focused on schools of area teachers who had described equipment needs. The teacher provided a detailed equipment inventory, with the replacement and repair needs, student participation list, and program goals. The music education students assessed the equipment purchase and repair needs for the next five years. At the completion of the project, the teacher was presented with a formal purchase proposal with researched bids, thorough rationale, and appropriate letters to administration.

Another project involved music education students researching, proposing, and developing travel itineraries for area schools intent on future music trips. Service projects also included organizing and filing printed music, inventorying instruments, and assisting with scheduling for local schools. As research confirms (e.g., Paul et al., 2001), instructional activities that replicate the authentic teaching experience in schools give students the opportunity to experience the role of a practitioner that allows them to become familiar with the context they will experience as teachers.

Instrumental techniques courses. Instrumental techniques courses also benefited from the information gained from this project. Local contact offered opportunities for music education students learning a new instrument to experience teaching *actual* beginners on this unfamiliar instrument. This authentic teaching experience has been valuable and enlightening for the novice teachers. To provide context in understanding the process of starting beginners on instruments, area teachers volunteered to be interviewed by music education students concerning the organization of their starter program.

Field experience and student teaching. As stated earlier, the process of assigning field experience sites for students was greatly informed through the findings of this project—not only in identifying sites, but also in being able to expand placement opportunities. Contacts made to area teachers exposed talented teachers not previously involved with the university. These contacts expanded observation opportunities for music education students to experience outstanding music teaching in inner-city situations. The exposure through school visits and having these teachers as guest speakers has benefited our students by encouraging us to consider such sites for student-teaching experiences. A database of important information on each music program with detailed findings from this project specific to each school was created and used. Efforts to track directors and programs as they evolve over time continue to be an important component of maintaining this database. Future field-experience and student-teaching sites can be determined more effectively and efficiently by correlating student data with site characteristics.

Project Conclusions

Enhanced communication of the university faculty with teachers in the field and understanding of the educational needs of practicing teachers allowed for collaborations, outreach opportunities, and expanded research possibilities. Similar to an educational needs assessment by Barbe (1984), course offerings to the music education students were enhanced and understandings of area music programs contributed to matching appropriate placements for student teachers.

Increased exposure of the music education faculty to practicing teachers made a positive impact upon the relationship of the university with practicing music teachers. It is advantageous for university faculty to develop professional relationships with area schools and their instructors. Familiarity provides a foundation for future associations between the music education department and surrounding schools. This relationship of trust between school music teachers and university faculty supports opportunities for professional development for practitioners, pre-service teachers, and university music education faculty alike—a partnership that truly yields benefits for all. Understanding the local context in which music education exists is a critical first step toward developing these opportunities.

References

Barbe, R. (1984). *A statewide teacher education needs assessment.* (ERIC Document Reproduction Services No. ED246042) Paper presented at the annual meeting of the American Educational Research Association, New Orleans.

Barnett, L., & Greenough, R. (1999). *The evolving context for teaching and learning in the Northwest: The 1999 regional education needs assessment.* (ERIC Document Reproduction Services No. ED447158) Office of Educational Research and Improvement, Washington, DC.

Gordon, D. (2000). Sources of stress for the public school music teacher: Four case studies. *Contributions to Music Education, 27*(1), 27–40.

Graue, M. E., & Walsh, D. J. (1998). *Studying children in context: Theories, methods, and ethics.* Thousand Oaks, CA: Sage Publications.

Grice, M. (1986). *Discipline-based art education: Needs assessment analysis.* (ERIC Document Reproduction Services No. ED287753) Getty Center for Education in the Arts, Los Angeles.

Hamann, D. L., & Daugherty, E. D. (1984). Teacher burnout: The cost of caring. *Update, 2*(3), 7–10.

Heston, M. L., Dedrick, C., Raschke, D., & Whitehead, J. (1996). Job satisfaction and stress among band directors. *Journal of Research in Music Education, 44*(4), 319–27.

Hewitt, M. B. (1999). The control game: Exploring oppositional behavior. *Reclaiming Children and Youth, 8,* 30–33.

Kahn, R. L., Wolfe, D. M., Quinn, R. P., & Snoek, J. D. (1964). *Organizational stress: Studies in role conflict and ambiguity.* New York: Wiley.

Kimpton, J. (2005). What to do about music teacher education: Our profession at a crossroads. *Journal of Music Teacher Education, 14*(2), 8–21.

Krueger, P. J. (2000). Beginning music teachers: Will they leave the profession? *Update: Applications of Research in Music Education 19*(1), 22–26.

Madsen, C.K., & Hancock, C.B. (2002). Support for music education: A case study of issues concerning teacher retention and attrition. *Journal of Research in Music Education 50*(1), 6–19.

Nimmo, D. J. (1986). *Factors of attrition among high school band directors.* Unpublished doctoral dissertation, Arizona State University, Phoenix.

Paul, S. (1998). The effects of peer teaching experiences on the professional teacher role development of undergraduate instrumental music education majors. *Bulletin of the Council for Research in Music Education, 137*, 73–92.

Paul, S., Teachout, D., Sullivan, J., Kelly, S., Bauer, W., & Raiber, M. (2001). Authentic-context learning activities in instrumental music teacher education. *Journal of Research in Music Education, 49*(2), 136–45.

Robbins, J., & Stein, R. (2005). What partnerships must we create, build, or reenergize in K–12 higher and professional education for music teacher education in the future? *Journal of Music Teacher Education, 14*(2), 22–29.

Scheib, J.W. (2003). Role stress in the professional life of the school music teacher: A collective case study. *Journal of Research in Music Education, 51*(2), 124–36.

Scheib, J.W. (2004). Why band directors leave: From the mouths of maestros. *Music Educators Journal, 91*(1), 53–57.

Scheib, J.W. (2006). Tension in the life of the school music teacher: A conflict of ideologies. *Update: Applications of Research in Music Education, 24*(2), 5–13.

Zehava, R. (2001). Teachers' multiple roles and skill flexibility: Effects on work attitudes. *Educational Administration Quarterly, 37*(5), 684–708.

Figure 1: Interview questions

1. [Background] Tell us a little bit about your background, where you grew up, what school(s) you attended, activities you were involved with (e.g., bands, corps, youth orchestras, jazz, musicals)? How did you come to be here?

2. [Demographics] How many students in the total school population? How many students involved with the band program? What other music (non-band-related) offerings are available to students? What type of schedule does the school operate (e.g., 7 periods, block)?

3. [Curriculum] What are the different ensembles/courses/topics you offer students through your band program? When do they meet? What is the emphasis of the program (e.g., marching, concert, jazz, chamber, solo/ensemble)? What would a graduating band student say about what they got out of being involved in your program?

4. [Beliefs/Needs] What are the struggles you face as a school band director/schoolteacher? What are the joys? What advice would you give to a new school music teacher just entering their first job? What do you believe to be the most important understandings/abilities a music teacher should possess?

The Effect of Personal and Situational Factors in the Attrition and Retention of Texas Music Educators

By Janice N. Killian and Vicki D. Baker

Janice N. Killian is professor of music education at Texas Tech University in Lubbock. She can be reached at janice.killian@ttu.edu. Vicki D. Baker is assistant professor of music education at the University of Texas–Arlington. She can be reached at vbaker@uta.edu.

One of the most critical challenges facing the field of education today is the retention of qualified teachers. The teacher shortage, coupled with the high rate of attrition, is an epidemic that plagues all areas of education in the United States (Conway, Krueger, Robinson, Haack, & Smith, 2002). According to the United States Department of Education, as many as 2.7 million new teachers will be needed in public schools by 2009 (Henke, Choy, Geis, & Broughman, 1996). The critical shortage of teachers in American schools over the past two decades has led to a substantial body of literature focused on teacher attrition (Ingersoll, 2001a).

Historically, the entire teaching profession has experienced high rates of turnover and substantial attrition (Heyns, 1988). Schlechty and Vance (1983) determined that 40–50 % of beginning teachers leave the profession during their first 7 years of teaching. Ingersoll (2001b) uses the metaphor of pouring water into a bucket with a hole to describe the problem of hiring a sufficient number of teachers for America's classrooms.

What impact does the high rate of teacher attrition have on schools? Ingersoll (2001a) characterizes teacher turnover as being a "revolving door" whereby teachers enter the profession and shortly thereafter leave in large numbers. This increases demand for new teachers and creates staffing problems that can cause disruption in program planning and continuity, impede student learning, and lead to higher recruiting and hiring expenditures by school districts (Shen, 1997).

In order to develop an intervention to retain qualified teachers, it is necessary to first examine the causes of attrition. Ingersoll (2001a) indicates that two of the primary reasons teachers leave the profession are inadequate support from school administration and problems dealing with student discipline. A positive correlation between teacher retention and administrative support was further verified by a study conducted by the National Center of Educational Statistics in which inadequate administrative support was the most common reason cited for leaving the teaching profession (Natale, 1993). Research into administrative assistance offered to beginning teachers in Oregon determined that school administrators reported that they offered more assistance than the beginning teachers reported they received, and the teachers described the support as being "ceremonial and ritualistic" (Myton, 1984, as cited in DeLorenzo, 1992, p. 11). In terms of retaining beginning teachers, administrators can have an impact on attrition by "shaping the tone and quality of a new teacher's first teaching experience" (Chapman, 1984, p. 655).

Student discipline is an additional reason teachers leave the profession. Research confirms that beginning teachers in elementary through secondary schools, both in the United States and abroad, consistently name classroom discipline as their greatest challenge (Madsen & Madsen, 1998; Veenman, 1984).

The field of music education is unique, however, and requires a more discipline-based investigation. Madsen and Hancock (2002) point out that "although these [general education] findings suggest relationships transferable to an investigation of music educators, the reinforcing nature of music, idiosyncratic teacher prerequisites, and unique demands placed on the in-service music teacher (e.g., performances) obfuscate generalization" (p. 8). Thus, the examination of discipline-based research relative to music education is necessary.

The teaching shortage is felt acutely in the field of music education, with the demand for music teachers rising, while the number of students training to become music teachers is declining (Asmus, 1999). A recent research report published by the Music Educators National Conference (MENC) (Hill, 2003) states that each year in the United States approximately 11,000 new music teachers are needed to replace those who leave; however, only about 5,500 new music educators join the profession each year. Further, music teacher attrition can create serious problems for music education in schools because continuity of teaching personnel is key to developing high-quality music programs (Krueger, 2000). To compound the problem, at current staffing levels, between 9 and 27 million students in the United States do not receive an adequate music education, as defined by MENC, the primary professional organization in the field. As a profession, music educators recognized these challenges, as evidenced by recent publications. (The entire spring 2005 issue of the *Journal of Music Teacher Education* was devoted to the topic.) More data, however, would appear necessary to determine ways to address the issue in a systematic way.

Administrative support is an issue that concerns music educators as well. Madsen and Hancock (2002) found that beginning music teachers expressed a number of concerns regarding administrative support. These issues included "differing understandings of the importance of music education, a perception of music as an extracurricular activity, challenges to the content of instruction, apathy for music education, music valued solely for utilitarian purposes, and music classes used as a respite for 'academic' teachers" (p. 15).

In one of the relatively few studies conducted regarding music teacher attrition, DeLorenzo (1992) found that beginning music teachers wanted administrators who were accessible, encouraging, and supportive. As one respondent remarked, you should "have an open invitation to sit down and discuss problems without feeling you are taking valuable time from them or that you are chasing them down for answers" (p. 21). Baker (2005) found, in comparing early career music educators' perception of administrative support with that of their administrators, that few educators felt they had specific types of administrative support, while their administrators believed they were highly supportive.

In an effort to examine the possible causes of music educator attrition, the present investigation was designed to explore factors that might provide additional insight into the differences between music educators who decide to remain in the profession and those who decide to leave the profession.

Method

Subjects consisted of self-identified new members of Texas Music Education Association (TMEA). In 1999, in an ongoing effort to identify, welcome, and mentor new music educators, TMEA requested that new teachers or new-to-Texas teachers indicate this fact on their membership registrations. Secondary music educators are required to join TMEA if they wish to enter students in all-region and all-state events; however, membership is completely voluntary for elementary teachers (see TMEA Constitution at tmea.org). Therefore, the resulting data might be assumed to include more secondary and fewer elementary teachers than in the general population. The resulting 5 years of data were thus limited to self-identified and self-defined first-year teachers or first-year-in-Texas teachers who were currently or had been teaching at some time during the past 5 years.

E-mails were sent to the music educators inviting them to respond to a survey on the retention and attrition of music educators. Discarding 63 who indicated no e-mail, 15 duplicate addresses and 240 undeliverable e-mail addresses, the remaining pool consisted of 597 music educators who entered the profession or moved to Texas from March 1999 to March 2003. The surveys were solicited completely by e-mail and, following procedures established by Johnson and Stewart (2004), volunteer subjects logged onto an Internet address to complete the online survey. It was hoped that using an online format would include a wider potential sampling, ensure ease of response, be less expensive that the traditional mail-out survey, and perhaps draw a higher response rate. A reminder to participate in the survey was sent to each potential respondent three times during March through May 2003. Surveys were completed by 223 subjects for a 37.35% return rate, which the researchers deemed sufficient for further analysis.

Survey questions were based on previous research from both music (Madsen & Hancock, 2002) and nonmusic sources (Chapman, 1984; Ingersoll, 2001a). The researchers developed the survey; four experienced music educators examined it for validity, made suggested changes, piloted both the questions and the e-mail process using subjects not represented in the final survey, made more revisions, and arrived at the final version of the survey.[1]

Survey questions included Personal Characteristics (gender, age, race, marital status, spouse employment as a teacher, and number of children); Educational Experience (degree, certification, year of certification, quality of collegiate preparation [Madsen & Hancock, 2002], quality of precollege preparation [Chapman, 1984; Madsen & Hancock, 2002]), and grade point average); and Teaching Venue (currently teaching, levels taught, areas taught, number of years taught, number of positions held [Madsen & Hancock, 2002], school size, school location [Ingersoll, 2001a], position, and number of campuses served). Respondents were asked if they planned to continue teaching, and, if not, to indicate their reasons for leaving. This question was considered the most important of the survey in our attempt to gain insight into why teachers consider leaving the music education profession.

Additional areas of interest included Mentoring and Professional Memberships. Based on previous literature supporting the value of mentoring in music classrooms (Conway et al., 2002; Haack & Smith, 2000; Krueger, 1999) and of professional organizations in the retention of teachers (DeLorenzo, 1992), respondents were asked whether they were mentored as first-year teachers and, if not, how mentoring would have assisted them, the number of professional music organization memberships held, and how many conferences they attended annually.

---

[1] The experimenters wish to thank the Texas Tech Teaching, Learning, and Technology Center for its able assistance in putting the survey online.

Results

Results, based on 223 returned surveys, consisted of frequency of responses to each question on the survey. The chi-square statistic was used throughout to analyze possible statistical differences in the frequency data; where appropriate, results are presented in terms of percentages for ease of comparison.

Overall, demographic data indicated that the survey sample (Table 1) consisted of significantly more females (x^2 [1,222] = 6.48 $p < .01$) and indicated significant differences in age (x^2 [3,222] = 124.14, $p < .0001$), race (x^2 [3,222] = 432.09, $p < .0001$), marital status (x^2 [2,220] = 99.51 $p < .0001$), number of spouses employed as teachers (x^2 [1,195] = 46.04 $p < .0001$), and number of children (x^2 [3,222] = 178.24 $p < .0001$).

The Educational Experience of the survey sample (Table 1) consisted of the majority (67%) holding bachelor's degrees and 91% holding music certification. Significantly more indicated a positive evaluation of both their college preparation (x^2 [4,220] = 125.27 $p < .0001$), and their precollege preparation (x^2 [4,220] = 164.16 $p < .0001$).

Teaching Venue data (Table 2) indicated that 98% of the respondents were currently teaching, and among those 97% were teaching in public schools. There were significant differences by school location (x^2 [2,222] = 54.49 $p < .0001$) and grade levels taught (x^2 [4,247] = 186.64 $p < .0001$). Note that respondents could check more than one grade level. As expected, due to the TMEA membership requirement for secondary teachers, many more secondary than elementary teachers were represented.

A significant difference appeared among the area (band, orchestra, choir, elementary) currently teaching (x^2 [6,337] = 143.18 $p < .0001$). Again, note that teachers could check multiple areas. Thus 218 teachers currently teaching taught in 338 areas. Likewise significant differences were noted among number of certified teachers assigned to music (x^2 [2,222] = 4.99 $p < .05$). This question was asked to determine whether teaching in isolation (only certified music teacher on campus) might be a differentiating factor in the stay/leave decision. Details appear in Table 2.

Significant differences (Table 2) occurred in position held (head director, assistant, neither) (x^2 [2,222] = 11.69 $p < .003$), number of campuses taught (x^2 [3,222] = 203.21 $p < .0001$), years taught (x^2 [4,222] = 69.26 $p < .0001$), and number of positions held (x^2 [4,222] = 109.8 $p < .0001$).

Perhaps the most important question queried future teaching plans. Eighty percent of the respondents ($n = 179$) indicated that they planned to stay in the profession, while 20% indicated that they planned to leave ($n = 39$) or had left ($n = 5$). In an effort to examine any differences between those electing to stay or leave the profession, chi-square analyses were performed for each of the above categories by the stay/leave decision.

Significantly more Females (x^2[1,222]=5.17, $p < .023$) indicated that they would leave the profession. Females equaled 75% of total leavers vs 59% of total respondents (Table 1). No other differences between Stayers and Leavers were significant. Thus there were no significant differences between Leavers and Stayers (Table 1) regarding teacher age, teacher race, marital status, whether spouse teaches, number of children, degree held, certification, quality of college or precollege preparation, college grade point average, private or public school, school location (urban, suburban, rural), size of school, grade level taught, area taught (band, orchestra, choir, elementary), number of certified teachers in the music area, position held, number of campuses served, number of years taught, number of different positions held, professional organization memberships, number of conferences attended per year, or presence of a mentor. The stereotype of a teacher who works alone, does not have any support, does not attend conferences, fails to be mentored, and finally drops out of teaching was not supported by these data.

Analysis of those intending to leave. Those indicating plans to leave the music teaching profession ($n = 44$) were asked to respond to reasons for leaving. Based on previous research indicating factors affecting the decision to stay or leave, the survey included a checklist of possible reasons for leaving. Categories in the frequency order in which they were checked appear in Table 3. Note that the 201 comments were made by 44 persons (average number of comments = 4.02).

Checklist responses (Table 3) were counted and categorized into dissatisfaction with administration ($n = 101$), dissatisfaction with students ($n = 46$), career enhancement opportunities ($n = 28$), personal reasons ($n = 20$) and school staffing issues ($n = 6$). Statistical analyses ($x^2 [3,200] = 146.87\ p < .0001$) indicated significantly more comments regarding students and administration than any other category. Twelve subjects responded to the free-response section inviting other reasons for leaving. Their comments (Table 3), subjected to an item analysis and categorized by two independent researchers, echoed the checklist categorizations for the most part. Two new categories appeared that included workload issues (too busy with feeder schools, too many demands for one person, etc.) and scheduling challenges (problems with block scheduling, assigned to teach nonmusic classes, etc.).

The Leaving teachers were asked if they would consider returning to teaching. The vast majority (39 of the 44 Leavers) said that they would and listed the circumstances under which they would return in a free-response format (Table 3). Again, independent analyses determined that the majority of the 33 responses were consistent with the concerns teachers had listed above.

Mentoring and professional membership. All 223 respondents were asked whether they had received formal or informal mentoring during the first years of their teaching experience. A significant number replied affirmatively ($n=148$, $x^2 [1,222] = 24.0\ p < .0001$). There was no significant difference between the Stayers and Leavers regarding whether they had received mentoring ($x^2 [1,221] = 0.17\ p > .68$).

Frequency of Yearly Attendance at Music Conferences revealed significant differences ($x^2 [5,222] = 201.71\ p < .0001$), with the frequency of attendance from highest to lowest being two per year = 107, one per year = 57, three per year = 27, five or more per year = 14, four per year = 9, and zero conferences = 9. Remarkable was the very large number of teachers who attended conferences.

There were, however, no significant differences between Stayers and Leavers in regard to conference membership or attendance ($x^2 [4,222] = 3.71\ p > .45$).

Results may be summarized as follows:
1. Significantly more persons (80%) intended to stay in the profession than intended to leave.
2. Significantly more women than men intended to leave the profession.
3. There were no significant differences between Leavers and Stayers regarding

demographic information, quality of college or pre-college preparation, teaching experience, teaching venue, number of years taught, number of positions held, membership in professional organizations or the presence of a mentor.
4. Reasons for leaving the profession included significantly more comments about lack of administrative support and dissatisfaction with student behavior than any other category.
5. Respondents indicated that 66% had been formally or informally mentored during their first years of teaching.
6. Ninety-six percent of respondents attended at least one conference annually.

Discussion

Teacher attrition does pose a problem to music education. This study indicates that 19.73% of the respondents, approximately one in five, intended to leave the teaching profession. This percentage is consistent with earlier research in the field of general education (Conway et al., 2002; Ingersoll, 2001a), as well as music education (DeLorenzo, 1992; Fallin & Royse, 1994; Madsen & Hancock, 2002). When this attrition rate is considered in combination with the increasing demand for new music educators and the decline in students training to become music teachers (Asmus, 1999; Hill, 2003), major deficits result.

In terms of gender, this study reveals that a significantly larger number of women than men intended to leave the profession. This finding is consistent with previous studies conducted surveying the general teaching population (Adams, 1996; Heyns, 1988; Ingersoll, 2001a; Murnane, Singer, & Willett, 1988), as well as the field of music education (Madsen & Hancock, 2002). Perhaps childbearing issues that are unique to young female teachers can explain the difference in genders. Gender differences may also indicate expanding opportunities for women in careers other than teaching.

In an effort to determine any causal factors, the survey contained detailed questions concerning demographic information, quality of college or precollege preparation, teaching experience, teaching venue, number of years taught, number of positions held, membership in professional organizations and the presence of a mentor. Although these data indicated intriguing trends worthy of future study (e.g., the tendency for a greater percentage of teachers with lower grade point averages to stay in the profession), there were no significant differences between the teachers staying and those leaving the profession. It might seem surprising, given the large number of factors listed, that no significant differences were found. Perhaps this suggests that causes of teacher attrition are idiosyncratic, cannot be generalized in accordance with personal or situational influences, or cannot be determined by means of a survey.

When Leavers were asked to give reasons for leaving the teaching profession, a significant number of replies included lack of administrative support and problems with student discipline. These findings are in keeping with previous studies (Baker, 2005; Chapman, 1984; Chapman & Green, 1986; DeLorenzo, 1992; Ingersoll, 2001a; Krueger, 2000; Madsen & Hancock, 2002; Madsen & Madsen, 1998). These data suggest that perhaps an improvement in situational conditions, namely increased support from school administration and the reduction of student discipline problems, would diminish the rate of attrition. As one respondent stated, "The lack of enforced policies and weak administration are my main stress. I have had to learn to fully discipline [students] myself because the administration is not harsh for most offenses that occur. Students get away with being rude, telling off teachers, and doing as they please because of weak administration." This statement also exemplifies the connection between administration support and student discipline.

A majority of respondents (66%) indicated that they had received mentoring during their first year of teaching. However, in this study, having a mentor did not have a significant affect on teacher retention. Although mentoring has received much support (Conway et al., 2002; Haack & Smith, 2000; Krueger, 1999), there is a lack of research linking mentoring with a reduction in teacher attrition. The respondents were not asked to rate the quality of their mentoring experience; further research might do so. A number of respondents, both those who had and had not received mentoring, suggested ways to improve the mentoring process. One respondent suggested that a mentor could be useful to "teach me about the other parts of teaching besides music, like paper work, deadlines for auditions, contests, etc., as well as inner-school policies and politics." Perhaps mentoring would play a more significant role in attrition if greater attention were given to the specific needs of the beginning teacher. Certainly systematic data-based studies regarding the specifics of mentoring would be in order.

This study seems to substantiate the fact that teacher attrition among music educators in the state of Texas is a critical problem. Data suggest that the attrition rate could be diminished by increased support from school administrators and by reducing the student discipline problems. While this study suggested that mentoring does not appear to be related to teacher attrition, perhaps further investigation might reveal the type of support provided by mentors that is most beneficial to new teachers, thus encouraging them to remain in teaching.

Of special interest is a comparison of the reasons for leaving the profession with what would have to change if the leaving teachers were to return (Table 3). For example, poor salary is not a top priority (ranked number 7 out of 24 topics), but it ties with changing schools or positions as the top problem to be solved if teachers were to return. It is gratifying to note that the vast majority of Leavers (89%) indicated that they would return to the profession. Perhaps further studies should explore whether teachers do indeed return after child-care issues have been solved or when offered a new position at a different school in (presumably) a better teaching situation. It should be remembered that this survey asked teachers' opinions but had no way of verifying the willingness of teachers to act on those opinions. Thus, further research tracking music educators throughout their careers (changes in positions, grade levels taught, returning after children are older, returning part-time, etc.) would provide valuable information in determining attrition causality.

Because this study is limited to members of a single state professional organization and does not represent an equal sample of elementary and secondary music educators, the results are indicative of a specific geographic region and are not necessarily representative of the national population of music educators. Additionally the response rate (37.4%) was relatively low, but consistent with other response rates on Internet surveys (Johnson & Stewart, 2004). Thus, the findings of this study should be generalized with caution. Also note that Leavers in this study indicated an intent to leave the profession; no attempt was made to verify whether or not they left. The results of this study are consistent with research conducted on the general teaching population in the U.S.; thus, music education associations of other states might want to investigate similar issues. Additionally, despite the potential lack of generalizeability, the data provide interesting and perhaps insightful information regarding 233 music educators, and, of those, why some would elect to leave the profession and what would cause them to return. Teacher educators might be cognizant of these results and discuss them with future music educators. Research might address whether knowledge of potential challenges as identified in this study would affect the retention of future music educators. Additional research might address in-depth analyses of teachers who elect to stay in the profession for 20-plus years. Those results could be shared with new educators and compared with the responses among Leavers as addressed by the present study. Clearly, further research is indicated to address this crucial problem.

References

Adams, G. J. (1996). Using a Cox regression model to examine voluntary teacher turnover. *The Journal of Experimental Education, 64*, 267–85.

Asmus, E. (1999). The increasing demand for music teachers. *Journal of Music Teacher Education, 8*(2), 5–6.

Baker, V. (2005). *Relationship between job satisfaction and the perception of administrative support among early career secondary choral music educators.* Unpublished doctoral dissertation, Texas Tech University, Lubbock.

Chapman, D. W. (1984). Teacher retention: The test of a model. *American Educational Research Journal, 21*, 645–58.

Chapman, D. W., & Green, J. S. (1986). Teacher retention: A further examination. *Journal of Educational Research, 79*(5), 273–79.

Conway, C., Krueger, P., Robinson, M., Haack, P. & Smith, M. V. (2002). Beginning music teacher induction and mentor policies: A cross-state perspective. *Arts Education Policy Review, 104*(2), 9–17.

DeLorenzo, L. C. (1992). The perceived problems of beginning music teachers. *Bulletin of the Council for Research in Music Education, 113*, 9–25.

Fallin, J., & Royse, D. (1994). Common problems of the new music teacher. *Journal of Music Teacher Education, 4*(1), 13–18.

Haack, P., & Smith, M. V. (2000). Mentoring new music teachers. *Music Educators Journal, 87*(3), 23–27.

Henke, R. R., Choy, S. P., Geis, S., & Broughman, S. (1996). *Schools and staffing in the United States: A statistical profile, 1993–94.* Washington, DC: U.S. Department of Education, National Center for Education Statistics. (NCES 96–124)

Heyns, B. (1988). Educational defectors: A first look at teacher attrition in the NLS-72. *Educational Researcher, 17*, 24–32.

Hill, W. L., Jr. (2003). The teacher shortage and policy. *Music Educators Journal, 89*(4), 6–7.

Ingersoll, R. M. (2001a). Teacher turnover and teacher shortages: An organizational analysis. *American Educational Research Journal, 38*(3), 499–534.

Ingersoll, R. M. (2001b). *Teacher turnover, teacher shortages and the organization of schools.* Seattle, WA: Center for the Study of Teaching and Policy, University of Washington.

Johnson, C. M., & Stewart, E. E. (2004). Effect of sex identification on instrument assignment by band directors. *Journal of Research in Music Education, 52*, 130–40.

Krueger, P. J. (1999). New music teachers speak out on mentoring. *Journal of Music Teacher Education, 8*(2), 1999.

Krueger, P. J. (2000). Beginning music teachers: Will they leave the profession? *Update, 19*(1), 22–26.

Madsen, C. K., & Hancock, C. B. (2002). Support for music education: A case study of issues concerning teacher retention and attrition. *Journal of Research in Music Education, 50*(1), 6–19.

Madsen, C. K. & Madsen, C. H. (1998). *Teaching/Discipline: A positive approach for educational development* (4th ed.). Raleigh, NC: Contemporary Publishing Company.

Murnane, R. J., Singer, J. D., & Willett, J. B. (1988). The career paths of teachers: Implications for teacher supply and methodological lessons for research. *Educational Researcher, 20*, 22–30.

Myton, D. V. (1984). *Study on needs of beginning teachers*. Salem, OR: Teachers Standards and Practices Commission. (ERIC document Reproduction Service No. ED275626)

Natale, J. (1993). Why teachers leave. *Executive Educator, 15*(7), 14–18.

Schlechty, P. C., & Vance, V. S. (1983). Recruitment, selection and retention: The shape of the teaching force. *Elementary School Journal, 83*(4), 469–87.

Shen, J. (1997). Teacher retention and attrition in public schools: Evidence from SASS91. *Journal of Educational Research, 91*, 81–88.

Veenman, S. (1984). Perceived problems of beginning teachers. *Review of Educational Research, 54*(2), 143–78.

Table 1. Respondents' Demographic Characteristics

	Stayers $n = 179$	Leavers $n = 44$	% Leavers	Total Respondents $N = 223$	% of Total Respondents
Gender					
Female	**98**	**33**	25%	**131**	59%
Male	**81**	**11**	12%	**92**	41%
Age					
20s	101	26	20%	**127**	57%
30s	30	8	21%	**38**	17%
40s	30	6	17%	**36**	16%
50s	18	4	18%	**22**	10%
Race					
Caucasian	151	38	20%	**189**	85%
Hispanic	20	3	13%	**23**	10%
Other	3	3	50%	**6**	3%
African-American	4	0	0%	**4**	2%
(unanswered = 1)					
Marital Status					
Married	105	23	18%	**128**	58%
Single	65	18	22%	**83**	38%
Divorced	6	3	33%	**9**	4%
(unanswered = 3)					
Spouse a Teacher?					
No	115	30	21%	**145**	74%
Yes	43	7	14%	**50**	26%
(unanswered = 28)					
Number of Children					
Zero	95	24	20%	**119**	64%
One	21	6	22%	**27**	12%
Two	23	6	21%	**29**	13%
Three or more	21	1	5%	**22**	11%
(unanswered = 26)					

continued on next page

Table 1 (cont.)

	Stayers $n = 179$	Leavers $n = 44$	% Leavers	Total Respondents $N = 223$	% of Total Respondents
Degree(s) Held					
Bachelor	120	30	20%	**150**	67%
Masters	56	14	20%	**70**	31%
Doctorate	3	0	0%	**3**	1%
Music Certification					
Yes	163	39	19%	**202**	91%
No	15	4	21%	**19**	9%
(unanswered = 1)					
College Preparation					
Excellent	57	9	14%	**66**	33%
Good	64	15	19%	**79**	40%
Average	29	12	29%	**41**	20%
Fair	10	2	17%	**12**	6%
Poor	0	1	100%	**1**	1%
(unanswered = 24)					
Precollege Preparation					
Excellent	71	16	18%	**87**	39%
Good	74	20	21%	**94**	42%
Average	23	4	15%	**27**	12%
Fair	10	2	17%	**12**	5%
Poor	1	2	67%	**3**	1%
College GPA					
3.5–4:0	90	25	22%	**115**	52%
3.0–3.5	64	16	20%	**80**	36%
2.5–3.0	24	3	11%	**27**	12%
2.0–2.5	1	0	0%	**1**	1%

Note. Boldface type indicates significant differences among groups.

Table 2. Respondents' Teaching Situations

	Stayers n = 179	Leavers n = 44	% Leavers	Total Respondents N = 223	% of Total Respondents
Currently Teaching					
Yes	179	39	18%	**218**	98%
No	0	5	100%	**5**	2%
School Type					
Public	175	42	19%	**217**	97%
Private	4	2	33%	**6**	3%
School Location					
Suburban	98	27	22%	**125**	56%
Urban	45	14	24%	**59**	26%
Rural	36	3	8%	**39**	17%
Level(s) Taught					
(multiple answers possible)					
Elementary	4	1	20%	**5**	2%
Middle School	89	19	18%	**108**	48%
Junior High	26	8	24%	**34**	15%
High School	78	15	16%	**93**	42%
College	8	0	0%	**8**	4%
Area(s) Taught					
(multiple answers possible)					
Band	87	13	13%	**100**	45%
Choir	55	17	24%	**72**	32%
Elementary	53	10	16%	**63**	28%
General Music	42	14	25%	**56**	25%
Orchestra	17	6	26%	**23**	10%
Other Music Classes	18	2	10%	**20**	9%
Nonmusic Classes	4	0	0%	**4**	2%
Current Campus Characteristics					
Certified Music Teachers					
One	64	15	19%	**79**	35%
Two	47	12	20%	**59**	26%
Three or more	68	17	20%	**85**	38%
Position					
Head Director	77	20	21%	**97**	43%
Assistant/Associate	57	13	19%	**70**	32%
Not Applicable	45	11	20%	**56**	25%

Continued on next page

Table 2. (cont.)

	Stayers $n = 179$	Leavers $n = 44$	% Leavers	Total Respondents $N = 223$	% of Total Respondents
Current Campus Characteristics (cont.)					
Campuses per Week					
One	113	33	23%	**146**	65%
Two	38	5	12%	**43**	19%
Three	19	1	5%	**20**	9%
Four or more	9	5	36%	**14**	6%
Years Taught					
One	28	8	22%	36	16%
Two	52	12	19%	64	29%
Three	24	7	23%	31	14%
Four	9	2	18%	11	5%
Five or more	66	15	19%	81	36%
Number of Positions Held					
One	79	24	23%	**103**	46%
Two	45	5	10%	**50**	22%
Three	24	7	23%	**31**	14%
Four	14	3	18%	**17**	8%
Five or more	17	5	23%	**22**	10%
School Sizes Currently Taught					
Elementary ≤ 399	29	3	9%	32	27%
Elementary 400–599	33	7	16%	45	38%
Elementary ≥ 600	33	12	30%	40	34%
Middle School ≤ 249	18	2	10%	20	17%
Middle School 250–649	38	11	22%	49	42%
Middle School ≥ 650	41	6	13%	47	41%
Junior High ≤ 249	6	2	25%	8	47%
Junior High 250–649	5	0	0%	5	29%
Junior High ≥ 650	3	1	25%	4	24%
High School ≤ 179	11	2	15%	13	14%
High School 180–344	5	1	17%	6	7%
High School 345–899	14	2	13%	16	17%
High School 900–1909	16	1	6%	17	18%
High School ≥ 1910	32	8	20%	40	43%

Note: Boldface type indicates significant differences among groups.

Table 3. Reasons for Leaving or Intending to Leave the Profession (*n* = 44)

	Checklist Responses (44 subjects checked 201 topics)	% of Subjects Checking Each Item	Free Response (12 subjects made 20 comments)	Would Return to Teaching if Specified Problems Were Solved (33 subjects made 40 comments) Would return = 39 Would not return = 5
Dissatisfaction with Administration				
Inadequate Administrative Support	17	39%	2	1
Lack of Influence over School Policies	16	36%		
Lack of Parental/Community Support	13	30%		
Poor Pay	12	27%	2	5
Lack of Adequate Preparation Time	11	25%	2	
Poor Opportunities for Advancement	10	23%		
Lack of Adequate Budget	9	20%		1
Isolation	9	20%		
Multicampus Duties	4	9%		
Workload issues			4	2
Scheduling Issues			2	1
Change in Schools or Positions				5
Dissatisfaction with Students				
Lack of Student Motivation	18	41%		
Lack of Student Discipline	17	39%	1	3
Classes Too Large	7	16%		
Unsafe Environment	4	9%		1
Resign to Change/Enhance Career				
Pursue Other Music Career	14	32%		
Attend Graduate School in Music	7	16%	1	3
Pursue Career Outside of Music	6	14%	3	4
Retirement	1	2%	1	1
Resign for Personal Reasons				
Pregnancy/Child Care	7	16%		4
Other Family Problems	6	14%		
Moving	5	11%		
Health	2	5%	1	1
Job Stress				2
Resign for School Staffing Issues				
Reduction in Staff	3	7%		
Elimination of Programs	2	5%		
School Closing	1	2%		
Unique Individual Comments			1	6

The Teaching of Secondary Instruments
A Survey of Instrumental Music Teacher Educators
By James R. Austin

James R. Austin is an associate professor and chair of music education at the University of Colorado at Boulder. He can be reached at James.Austin@colorado.edu

Music teachers manifest their musicianship in a variety of ways. Individuals who teach instrumental music in K–12 schools must be not only fine performers and teachers of their principal instrument, but also competent in the playing and teaching of secondary instruments. Secondary instrument or instrument technique classes have long been considered an important component of preservice music teacher education. The National Association of Schools of Music (NASM) lists "knowledge of and performance ability on wind, string, and percussion instruments sufficient to teach beginning students effectively in groups" as an essential competency for music education majors with an instrumental music teaching specialization (NASM, 2003). In many undergraduate programs, secondary instrument classes constitute a substantial portion of the credits required in music education (capstone methods courses and field experience representing other major components of music education course work).

Research on secondary instrument issues is limited. Five researchers (Conway, 2002; Cooper, 1994; Hillbrick, 1999; Jennings, 1998; Teachout, 1997) have studied teacher beliefs and opinions in relation to secondary instrument classes. Jennings (1988) surveyed 299 high school band directors and 21 college band directors to determine which preservice training courses contribute to the development of competencies viewed as most needed by school band directors. Secondary instrument courses were ranked 7th in terms of their effectiveness in basic competency development (behind student teaching, band ensembles, methods courses, conducting classes, applied lessons, and jazz ensemble). In a similar investigation, Cooper (1994) sought to identify the most important topics of study in the instrumental music education core curriculum. Nearly 75% of 275 respondents (high school band directors and college-level instructors) indicated that secondary instrument courses are important and should focus on a combination of performance and teaching skills. A majority of the high school band directors rated their experience in these courses as no better than adequate and expressed concern about course instructors lacking recent successful public school teaching experience.

Teachout (1997) surveyed 35 preservice and 35 experienced music teachers to determine which skills or competencies were considered most important to successful music teaching in the first three years of one's career. Experienced and preservice teachers believed that "being knowledgeable and proficient with secondary instruments" was an important competency for early career teachers. Out of the 40 skill categories rated, however, secondary instrument knowledge/proficiency was ranked 32nd in importance by preservice teachers and 37th by experienced teachers. In a study by Hillbrick (1999), over 2,000 junior high instrumental music teachers were asked to identify which instruments were taught most effectively within their undergraduate percussion techniques classes. Teachers felt most prepared to teach snare drum, and reasonably prepared to teach timpani, keyboard percussion, and auxiliary percussion. Most teachers felt inadequately prepared to teach drum set and also believed that more class time should have been devoted to percussion instrument maintenance and repair. Overall, music teachers rated the percussion techniques classes as being of average quality.

Conway (2002) interviewed 14 first-year music teachers, a majority of whom taught instrumental music at the middle and/or high school level, to assess most valuable and least valuable aspects of degree program work. Participants identified secondary instrument courses as being among the least valuable. For instrumental music teachers, major concerns centered on the lack of consistency across courses, the configuration of courses (class format being seen as preferable to individual instrument format), the need for more course content that focuses on how to teach and repair the instruments, and the qualifications of people assigned to teach such classes (i.e., faculty and teaching assistants from performance areas who may have limited training or experience in teaching instruments to beginners).

Two researchers have compared different approaches to configuring and delivering instruction within secondary instrument classes. Martin (1982) explored the relative benefits of teaching woodwind techniques classes using a mixed (heterogeneous) instrument format versus a like (homogeneous) instrument format. Data analyses revealed that students taught in mixed instrument woodwind techniques classes were better prepared to diagnose performance problems (whether presented in audio or visual formats) and prescribe solutions when teaching flute, clarinet, or saxophone. Lethco (1999) compared three approaches (emphasizing self-evaluation, observation of experienced teachers, or development of performance skills) to teaching an undergraduate brass techniques course. She found that brass techniques students' behaviors (time allocation) when teaching two lessons to band beginners did vary on the basis of instructional approach. Students in the self-evaluation group had the beginner class engaged in performance for a significantly greater amount of time than students in the other two groups. Student ability to perform on secondary brass instruments and attitude toward class instruction, however, were not affected by method of instruction.

In a group of related studies, Ambrose (1989), Sebald (1982), and Mueller (1997) focus on the effectiveness of using programmed materials or instructional technology in secondary instrument classes. Ambrose (1989) found that the use of a "specially-developed programmed text" to address matters of instrument assembly, breathing technique, embouchure formation, instrument/hand/finger position, and posture resulted in superior levels of performance on clarinet by woodwind techniques students (as compared to a group of students who used a traditional approach). Sebald (1991) designed an "automated slide-cassette and workbook learning package" for use in a woodwind techniques course. Comparison of pretest and posttest data revealed that the materials were effective in increasing student knowledge of supplementary information related to woodwind teaching and that students responded positively to their use in class. Mueller (1997) created a hypermedia CD-ROM program that presented a 13-step method for teaching upper string vibrato in group lessons. Students enrolled in a string techniques class responded favorably to the program, but the effects of the program on student ability to perform with and teach vibrato were inconclusive.

Study Need and Purpose

Research reveals that novice and experienced music educators generally view secondary instrument classes as an important component of preservice music teacher education, but they also rate their training in these classes as moderately effective at best and express concerns about course format, content, and instructors. There is some evidence that course format and technology use may affect student learning in secondary instrument classes. I found no research in which instrumental music education faculty were surveyed to determine how secondary instrument classes are configured, how instruction is delivered, or how teaching responsibilities are assigned. The purpose of this study was to explore how secondary instrument classes function within music schools throughout the United States. Voice and piano classes were not a part of this investigation, and no effort was made to assess the quality of instruction associated with particular models or approaches.

Method

In consultation with two other researchers, a 12-item questionnaire was developed and e-mailed to a sample of 40 music education faculty who had expressed interest in attending a colloquium for instrumental music teacher educators. Questionnaire items, which were derived from the related literature, addressed degree requirements, course configurations, instructor background, instructional time and academic credit, instructional coverage and emphasis, and supplemental expectations (see the complete questionnaire at the end of this article). Responses were received from 25 faculty (63% response rate), representing varied institutions (public and private schools, research and comprehensive universities as well as conservatories) and all U.S. census regions. Because of the small sample size, data analysis was restricted to basic descriptive statistics.

Results

Degree requirements and course configurations. Degree requirements related to secondary instrument classes tend to vary on the basis of student degree track and, to a lesser extent, principal instrument. At 70% of the institutions, for example, students pursuing choral-general tracks complete a two- or three-credit survey class on secondary instruments or choose two to four classes from among secondary instrument offerings. At the remaining institutions, all music education majors (regardless of degree track or emphasis) are required to complete the same number of classes/credits in instrument techniques. Differentiated requirements for string music education majors, as compared to wind, brass, and percussion majors, are evident at only three institutions. In those instances, string music education majors spend less time on woodwinds and brass techniques and more time on string techniques.

Three main models or configurations exist for secondary instrument classes: (a) classes built around each instrument family (woodwinds, brass, strings, percussion); (b) classes in which certain instrument families are split (e.g., upper and lower strings); and (c) classes devoted to each instrument (percussion being the exception). Overall, 24% of schools organize their secondary instrument classes according to instrument families, 56% use some form of a split-family arrangement, and 20% offer classes that focus primarily on individual instruments (see Figure 1).

Classes organized by family, rather than by individual instrument, more often are taught using a mixed-instrument format (42% of institutions) than a like-instrument format (26% of institutions). This may be due to a belief that the mixed-instrument format more closely resembles the types of teaching situations students will encounter out in the field, or because like-instrument formats require institutions to maintain a larger inventory of instruments. In 32% of the institutions that use an instrument-family configuration, there is a mixture of formats (e.g., woodwinds and percussion taught in a like-instrument format, brass and strings taught in a mixed-instrument format).

Instructor background. As was noted earlier, many students express concerns about the qualifications of individuals assigned to teach secondary instrument classes. Notions about who is and is not qualified to teach these classes may center on the instructor's performance expertise, teaching expertise (particularly as it pertains to class teaching in K–12 contexts), or a combination of the two. The results of this survey indicate that secondary instrument classes are most commonly taught by music education faculty (70% of institutions) and/or performance faculty (65% of institutions), but situations in which classes are taught by teaching assistants in performance (48% of institutions) or music education (35% of institutions), as well as adjunct faculty such as beginning band instructors (52% of institutions), are not uncommon. Almost every institution uses two or more different types of instructors, and over one-half of the institutions use a combination of faculty, teaching assistants, and/or adjunct faculty instructors. Distinct differences in course configuration, course content, and teaching methods are likely to emerge, and questions about the degree to which particular instructors are qualified likely will persist, when instructors bring such varied experience levels and types of expertise to secondary instrument class settings within a given institution.

Instructional time and academic credit. The vast majority (87%) of institutions allot 100 minutes or more of instruction a week to each secondary instrument class. The most typical schedule is two 50-minute periods per week for the entire semester, leading to one credit. At institutions where instruction is focused on individual instruments, classes usually are organized as 5- to 8-week modules and credit is accumulated across the modules. For example, students might spend 8 weeks studying clarinet and 8 weeks studying flute, and receive one-half credit for each class. Only a handful of schools award two credits for each instrument techniques class, and in those instances the classes typically meet for 100 to 180 minutes per week. At several institutions, students earn less credit for percussion techniques, even though the percussion techniques class may meet for the same number of minutes per week as woodwinds, brass, or string techniques classes. The total number of credits awarded by institutions for all required secondary instrument classes ranges from 4 to 14 semester credits, with 8 semester credits being the average.

Instructional coverage and emphasis. Depending on the institution, students enrolled in secondary instrument classes learn to play/teach two to five woodwind instruments (mean = 4.3), two to five brass instruments (mean = 3.9), and one to four string instruments (mean = 3.1). In one institution, guitar is part of the strings class, while at two institutions guitar is taught as a separate class. Students typically cover fewer instruments when classes are configured according to instrument families (or split families) than when they are configured according to individual instruments. In almost every school, students learn to play/teach snare drum (100% of institutions), timpani (96% of institutions), keyboard percussion (91% of schools), and auxiliary percussion (91% of schools). Drum set and ethnic percussion, by comparison, are addressed in approximately one-half of the schools. The breadth of instruments and techniques covered in percussion class seems daunting, particularly when considering the number of classes students take and/or the number of credits they receive for comparable coverage in winds and strings. Only one institution offers two separate classes in percussion techniques.

Faculty were asked to rank instructional goals for secondary instrument classes in terms of the amount of emphasis given to developing performance proficiency on instruments, increasing pedagogical knowledge, and refining diagnostic and prescriptive skills. Overall, pedagogical knowledge (mean rank = 1.7) was ranked higher than diagnostic/prescriptive skills (mean rank = 2.1) and performance proficiency (mean rank = 2.2). Several individuals, however, had difficulty responding to this item and gave the first two objectives (pedagogical knowledge and diagnostic/prescriptive skills) or all three objectives the same ranking. One individual commented that "this varies so dramatically from class to class, depending on who teaches, there is no way to say." At two institutions, students enroll in separate wind and string pedagogy classes to supplement the performance proficiency developed in instrumental technique classes.

Just over 30% of the institutions reported using any type of instructional technology in conjunction with secondary instrument classes. The diagnostic slide series developed by James Froseth, Smart Music (intelligent accompaniment software), and Finale (used by students to create arrangements customized for secondary instrument classes) are the types of technology applications most commonly in use.

Supplemental expectations. A final questionnaire item asked faculty whether music education students are expected to demonstrate secondary instrument expertise through any outside-of-class activities. In roughly 50% of the schools, students are encouraged or required to play secondary instruments in laboratory or nonauditioned ensembles. Recitals and exit interviews or exams that address secondary instrument teaching are evident in fewer than 10% of schools. No other supplemental expectations were identified by respondents.

Faculty comments and concerns. Faculty were encouraged to provide additional comments and ideas concerning their secondary instrument classes. Several individuals emphasized that they were making special efforts to further refine students' secondary instrument teaching skills. Strategies that were identified include peer teaching, field experiences (that might entail teaching elementary beginners or observing an experienced instructor), and lab ensembles in which students conduct or teach their peers who are playing minor instruments. As was noted earlier, some schools separate secondary instrument techniques classes (which emphasize performance proficiency) from pedagogy classes (which emphasize teaching strategies and resources). In one school, students attend a senior practicum (2 hours each week) during which they play secondary instruments and discuss teaching-related issues.

Several individuals articulated a concern about curricular coherence and the need for music education faculty to maintain some degree of supervisory control over class content and instructional process, most notably when secondary instrument classes are taught by performance faculty or teaching assistants. One person noted that he is attempting to implement a common syllabus for all secondary instrument classes so that some of the variability in course content and learning outcomes can be miminized.

Finally, some individuals express worry about the impact of degree program credit hour reductions on the minor instrument component of music education majors' training. As pressures increase on music education curricula to address a greater number of professional teacher standards using fewer credit hours, faculty fear they may have to consider less specialized class configurations that allow for fewer minutes of instructional time or exposure to fewer instruments.

Conclusions

The purpose of this exploratory study was to obtain preliminary data regarding how secondary instrument classes are structured and how instruction within such classes is delivered. Data for this investigation were gathered from a small and select sample of instrumental music education professors. Accordingly, inferences to the larger population of music schools and music education programs nationwide must be made with extreme caution. Clearly, additional research that involves nationwide random samples of music schools and/or case studies of model schools would further illuminate policy and practices related to the role of secondary instrument classes in undergraduate music education curricula.

An overarching theme that emerged from this study is that there is no common practice with respect to how secondary instrument classes are configured. Instrument groupings, schedules, credit allocations, instructor backgrounds, class content, and instructional priorities vary widely from school to school and even class to class within schools. It is unclear whether these inter- and intrainstitutional differences are manifestations of music school history, local politics, or logistical realities. It also is unclear whether students benefit from certain class configurations more than from others. Does it make pedagogical sense, for example, to teach some secondary instruments in a mixed-instrument family format, others in a like-instrument split-family format, and still others in individual classes? Is breadth of study or depth of study more important? Should students concentrate on learning to play the various instruments, learning to teach the various instruments, or both? Does it matter whether the person teaching a secondary instrument is an accomplished performer and pedagogue or an experienced K–12 music educator?

Greater coherence and/or uniform expectations across secondary instrument classes may be viewed as desirable and appropriate by some music education faculty, but an infringement on academic freedom by others. Given the importance of secondary instrument training in the preparation of K–12 music teachers, however, it behooves music education faculty to carefully consider the philosophical, curricular, and pedagogical bases for configuring secondary instrument classes. Only by gaining more collective professional wisdom about what works in the secondary instrument realm can some of the critical questions posed above be answered.

References

Ambrose, S. C. (1989). The development and trial of programmed materials for teaching selected clarinet performance skills in college woodwind techniques courses. (Doctoral dissertation, University of Cincinnati, 1989). *Dissertation Abstracts International, 50* (05), 1242.

Conway, C. (2002). Perceptions of beginning teachers, their mentors, and administrators regarding preservice music teacher preparation. *Journal of Research in Music Education, 50* (01), 20–36.

Cooper, L. G. (1994). A study of the core curriculum for the preparation of instrumental music educators. (Doctoral dissertation, University of Kentucky, 1994). *Dissertation Abstracts International, 55* (01), 37.

Froseth, J., & Hopkins, M. (2006). Visual Diagnostic Skills Program [Computer software]. Chicago: GIA Publications.

Hillbrick, J. R. (1999). A profile of the perception of instrumental ensemble directors in the states of Illinois, Missouri, and Wisconsin regarding the percussion techniques class. (Doctoral dissertation, University of Oklahoma, 1999). *Dissertation Abstracts International, 60* (06), 1954.

Jennings, D. L. (1989). The effectiveness of instrumental music teacher preservice training experiences as perceived by college and high school band directors. (Doctoral dissertation, Indiana University, 1988). *Dissertation Abstracts International, 50* (04), 825.

Lethco, L. M. (1999). Preparing undergraduate music majors to teach beginning instrumentalists: The effects of self-evaluation, teacher observation, and performance-oriented instructional approaches on teacher behaviors and pupil responses. (Doctoral dissertation, Louisiana State University, 1999). *Dissertation Abstracts International, 60* (04), 1058.

MakeMusic. (2005). SmartMusic and Finale [Computer software]. Eden Prairie, MN: MakeMusic, Inc.

Martin, D. K. (1982). Heterogeneous and homogeneous methods of instruction of college woodwind minor instrument techniques classes and their effect on the learning of diagnostic skills. (Doctoral dissertation, The Ohio State University, 1982). *Dissertation Abstracts International, 43* (05), 1463.

Mueller, R. A. (1997). The development and pilot testing of a hypermedia program to supplement undergraduate string techniques class instruction in upper string vibrato. (Doctoral dissertation, University of Illinois, 1997). *Dissertation Abstracts International, 57* (12), 5093.

National Association of Schools of Music (2003). *NASM Handbook: 2003–04*. Reston, VA: National Association of Schools of Music.

Sebald, D. C. (1982). The development and formative evaluation of multi-media learning packages in supplementary woodwind techniques for use in teacher training. (Doctoral dissertation, Michigan State University, 1981). *Dissertation Abstracts International, 42* (08), 3492.

Teachout, D. J. (1997). Preservice and experienced teachers' opinions of skills and behaviors important to successful music teaching. *Journal of Research in Music Education, 45*(1), 41–50.

Figure 1. Summary of Secondary Instrument Class Configurations

Family	Split Family								Instrument	
$N = 6$	$N = 5$[a]	$N = 2$	$N = 1$	$N = 1$	$N = 1$	$N = 2$[b]	$N = 2$	$N = 3$	$N = 2$
WW Class	WW Class	Flute Clarinet Sax Oboe Bassoon	Flute Clarinet Sax Oboe Bassoon	Flute Clarinet Sax Oboe Bassoon	Clarinet Flute Sax Oboe Bassoon	Clarinet Flute Sax Oboe Bassoon	Flute Clarinet Sax Oboe Bassoon	Flute Clarinet Sax Oboe Bassoon	Flute Clarinet Sax Oboe Bassoon
Brass Class	Brass Class	Trumpet Horn T-bone Euph Tuba	Trumpet Horn T-bone Euph Tuba	Trumpet Horn T-bone Euph Tuba	Trumpet Horn T-bone Euph Tuba	Trumpet Horn T-bone Euph Tuba	Trumpet Horn T-bone Euph Tuba	Trumpet Horn T-bone Euph Tuba	Trumpet Horn T-bone Euph Tuba
Strings Class	Violin Viola Cello Bass	Strings Class	Violin Viola Cello Bass	Violin Viola Cello Bass	Strings Class	Violin Viola Cello Bass	Strings Class	Strings Class	Violin Viola Cello Bass
Perc Class	Perc Class	Perc Class	Perc Class	SD/BD Cym Aux Timpani Keyboard	Perc Class	Perc Class	Perc Class	Perc Class	Perc Class

[a] The woodwind class is split at one institution, the brass class is split at one institution, the string class is split at two institutions (depicted), and both the woodwind and strings classes are split at one institution.
[b] Horn is taught with trumpet in one institution (depicted) and with low brass in another institution.

Secondary Instrument Classes Questionnaire

1. Please describe how minor instrument classes are configured at your institution. (For example, separate classes for each instrument family? Separate classes for single and double reeds, upper and lower brass, and upper and lower strings? Separate classes for each wind or string instrument?)

2. If you do not offer separate classes for each instrument, which of the following formats is used in conjunction with your minor instrument classes? (please mark one)

   _____ Like Instrument Format (e.g., all students playing flute at the same time)

   _____ Mixed Instrument Format (e.g., students divided among flute, clarinet, and saxophone)

3. How many semester or quarter credits do students receive for each of your minor instrument classes? (please list the appropriate number of credits or range of credits)

   _____ semester credits   _____ quarter credits

4. How is instructional time typically allocated for your minor instrument classes? (please list the appropriate numbers or ranges in each blank)

   _____ class sessions per week   _____ minutes per class session

   _____ total number of weeks

5. Who teaches minor instrument classes at your school? (please mark any that apply)

   _____ Performance Faculty   _____ Music Education Faculty

   _____ Adjunct Faculty   _____ Performance TAs

   _____ Music Education TAs   _____ Other (please describe):

6. How many instruments within each family do students learn to play/teach? (please list the appropriate number for each instrument family)

   _____ Woodwinds   _____ Brass   _____ Strings

7. Which areas of percussion do students learn to play/teach? (please mark any that apply)

   _____ Snare Drum/Bass Drum/Cymbals   _____ Keyboard Percussion

   _____ Timpani   _____ Drum Set

   _____ Auxiliary Percussion   _____ Ethnic Percussion

8. Rank each of the following instructional goals, in terms of the amount of emphasis typically given in your minor instrument classes, by placing the appropriate number in each blank (1 = highest priority, 2 = middle priority, 3 = lowest priority):

_____ developing performance proficiency on minor instruments

_____ increasing pedagogical knowledge related to minor instruments

_____ refining diagnostic and prescriptive skills related to teaching minor instruments

9. Are all music education students required to complete the same number of minor instrument classes? (please mark one)

_____ No (explain how requirements differ below)   _____ Yes

10. Beyond the specific requirements associated with minor instrument classes, through which of the following activities are your students expected to demonstrate minor instrument expertise? (please mark any that apply, or leave blank if none apply)

_____ exit interviews

_____ minor instrument recitals

_____ playing minor instruments in laboratory or non-auditioned ensembles

11. Do you use technological tools or applications in minor instrument classes? (please mark one)

_____ No   _____ Yes (please describe below)

12. Please list any other comments or ideas you may wish to share concerning minor instrument classes!

Thank you for participating in this survey!

A Four-Way Perspective on the Development and Importance of Music Learning Theory-Based PreK–16 Music Education Partnerships Involving Music for Special Learners

By Jennifer Scott Miceli, Elise Sobol, Maureen T. Makowski, and Izzet Mergen

Jennifer Scott Miceli is director of music education at Long Island University–C. W. Post in Brookville, New York. She can be reached at jennmiceli@optonline.net. Elise Sobol is adjunct professor of music education at Long Island University–C. W. Post. She can be reached at essobol@aol.com. Maureen T. Makowski is an elementary general music teacher at South Huntington Union Free School District in South Huntington, New York. She can be reached at maurmusic8@yahoo.com. Izzet Mergen is director of music education at Northport/East-Northport Union Free School District in Northport, New York. He can be reached at imergen@northport.k12.ny.us.

Kyle lives in a group home for people with developmental disabilities. He spends some days at a rehabilitation program and other days at a state-supported job where he performs light custodial work. Kyle enjoys a healthy social life that includes parties, parades, movies, exercise, and dinners shared with friends and family. He is physically active, highly personable, and able to manage personal tasks such as bathing, dressing, tying his shoes, and general personal hygiene. Kyle is able to write his name. He understands basic money skills and especially enjoys walking to a favorite coffee shop, where he prefers his coffee black.

When Kyle was born in 1950, the doctors told his mother that he would never learn. A woman of great personal strength and determination, she ignored the doctors and forged ahead with the business of learning how Kyle learned. What she realized was that Kyle was able to learn to perform life's tasks through music. With the help of Burl Ives' recordings, Kyle learned to crawl and to feed himself. Soon he learned to brush his teeth, button his shirts, and tie his shoes. During Kyle's childhood and teen years, he learned to dance to and sing along with the music of Johnny Cash and Neil Diamond. As a middle-aged adult, Kyle lights up when he hears the music that he associates with his childhood and teen years. Through music, Kyle learned who he was: a lifelong learner with a need for self-expression through song and dance. Kyle is my (Jennifer Miceli's) brother.

Children with special needs learn music through doing life's tasks and learn life's tasks through doing music. As we prepare preservice music teachers to teach in public school inclusion classrooms, it is important to provide preservice teaching opportunities that promote pedagogically sound music teaching and learning practices that have life relevance for special populations. According to David Circle, president of MENC: The National Association for Music Education,

> There is interdependency in this musical life cycle as students progress from Pre-K through college to become music educators. If there is a weak link at any stage of this cycle, the entire system suffers. It is incumbent upon every music educator to be cognizant of this interdependency and to be dedicated to working collaboratively with other music educators for the improvement of the quality of instruction regardless of the music specialty or instructional level. (2005, p. 3)

The purpose of this article is to present a four-way perspective on the development and importance of standards-based music teacher preparation collaborative models (PreK–16 music education partnerships) that adapt Edwin E. Gordon's music learning theory for children with special needs. Two college professors, a former college student/new teacher, and a public school music administrator, respectively, reflect on best practices and favorable outcomes related to (a) method into practice including sequential planning, adapting, presenting, and assessing; and (b) standards, trends, and policies that affect music teacher preparation.

Perspective I: Jennifer Scott Miceli, College Professor

Method into Practice. According to Robbins and Stein (2005), "Universities need to establish networks that provide professional development opportunities for both novice and expert teachers in the form of apprentice programs, professional development workshops, site-based methods classes, and collaborative research" (p. 24). The Rompertunes Early Childhood Music Teaching and Learning Program is a PreK–16 music education partnership that requires graduate and undergraduate music education students to participate in a semester-long music teaching and learning experience with three- and four-year-old children, including children with special needs. Edwin E. Gordon's music learning theory is the predominant methodology in the Rompertunes PreK–16 music education partnership. During class time in Elementary General Music Methods, college students focus on Gordon's Skill Learning Sequence and Content Learning Sequence (Gordon, 1997) along with current research findings having to do with similarities between language acquisition and music learning (Valerio, Reynolds, Bolton, & Taggart, 1998, pp 6–7). Students learn to recognize the stages of preparatory audiation, or "preliminary music thought processes," and gain an understanding of the role of play in a child's music learning (Valerio et al., 1998, pp. 8–11.)

Music learning theory is adapted for practice in the Rompertunes PreK–16 music education partnership. College students are assigned specific songs or chants with accompanying musical games that involve musical instruments, physical movement, and props such as play balls, scarves, children's books, and stuffed animals. When best teaching practices are modeled for the college students during PreK–16 music education partnership experiences, they have the opportunity to imitate, augment, and develop minilessons that are appropriate for three- and four-year-old children, including children with special needs. Minilessons are then evaluated through reflective practice exercises during which college students assess, discuss, and write about (a) personal teaching triumphs and challenges and (b) the teaching strengths of their peers.

Standards and Assessment in Music Teacher Preparation. As music education methods classes and aligned PreK–16 music education partnerships are developed, teacher educators need to consider state and national arts standards together with teacher training standards, such as the standards that were developed by the Interstate New Teacher Assessment Support Consortium (INTASC), a national standard-setting initiative to ensure a quality teacher workforce. Pertaining to standards and preservice teacher education, Madsen (2000) offers the following insight: "Every prospective teacher will be expected to demonstrate not only the skills and knowledge called for in the standards, including skills and knowledge in improvisation and composition, but also the ability to teach those skills and that knowledge" (p. 98).

As a direct result of participation in the Rompertunes PreK music education partnership, preservice teachers learn to improvise in various tonalities and meters. Preservice teachers learn to sing in tonalities and chant in meters that are the same as the Rompertunes song and chant literature so that they may achieve musical transitions between lesson activities. Lesson flow, particularly as it relates to transitions between classroom activities, is enhanced when children are directed to the next activity through music. For example, if the children move to a rhythmic chant in 5/8 meter, the preservice teachers direct the children to the next activity through class instructions and coordinated movement activities that are improvised in 5/8 meter. Preservice teachers achieve classroom management naturally when children are engaged in musical behavior throughout the duration of the lesson.

Students who gain familiarity with the National Standards, the New York Arts Standards, and the INTASC Standards during music education methods classes and during PreK–16 music education partnership programs such as Rompertunes are better prepared to teach to those standards upon entering the workforce. The INTASC Standards also inform portfolio assessment and teaching performance assessment during student teaching.

Figure 1 is a three-part assessment tool that is designed to measure the success of a peer-teaching segment. Part I of the assessment tool acknowledges five of the ten INTASC Standards. Hogan (2004) contains a complete version of the INTASC Standards (pp. 6–13). The five standards that are indicated on Part I of the teaching performance assessment tool pertain to presenting "Sidewalk Talk," an eight-measure, duple meter, rhythmic chant with words, at the acculturation stage of preparatory audiation (Valerio et al., 1998, p. 116). The INTASC Standards direct instructor comments.

Part II of the assessment tool is a rubric that converts subjective teacher comments into letter grades. Part III is an additive rating scale that allows for objective measurement of preservice teacher performance. Students are awarded one point for each observable criterion, for a total of eleven possible points. Raw scores may be converted to letter grades through the use of a bell-shaped curve, in which case the instructor should find the statistical average grade and assign it a C. The highest and lowest grades receive A and F respectively, and the other grades are assigned a letter grade based on their deviation from the statistical average.

Preservice teachers benefit from viewing videotaped examples of peer-teaching episodes or PreK–16 music education partnership teaching episodes during which they assess their own teaching performance using the same or different assessment tools as those used by their instructors. Follow-up reflective narratives allow for emergent insights and free dialoguing that may or may not be attended to on instructor-designed assessment tools.

Perspective II: Elise Sobol, College Professor

Method into Practice. Successful music teacher preparation programs provide preservice teachers with essential practical experience for adapting instructional methods to the diverse populations present in our 21st-century schools. It is important for teachers to understand that *fair* in special education means giving each student what he or she needs to succeed. When music education methods curricula ensure that preservice teachers write and implement classroom orientation and classroom management plans for children with special needs, they are more likely to transfer this practice from preservice to professional teaching and learning situations. Current research about the effects of preservice teaching opportunities on college students' comfort levels in working with special learners indicates field experience has a significantly positive effect in regard to college students' comfort in inclusive music education settings (VanWeelden &Whipple, 2005).

In addition to learning adaptive instructional techniques for challenged youngsters, whether they be talented and gifted or socially, emotionally, developmentally, physically or learning disabled, PreK–16 music education partnerships provide consistent relevance to current issues, mandates, and policies found in every school community. A study by Hammel (2001) revealed the importance of preservice teaching opportunities that include work with special learners. The study involved 653 Virginia elementary music teachers who were surveyed in order to identify what course work and experiences they received that focused on special learners during their preservice education. Many teachers stressed the importance of field experiences that include special learners during preservice education. One teacher indicated that preservice teachers needed more hands-on experiences and/or observation of how mainstreaming really functions on a day-to-day basis.

PreK–16 music education partnerships encourage joyful music-making experiences in child-centered teaching and learning situations and develop flexibility and confidence in preservice teachers. According to Madsen (2000), "The development of musical and personal flexibility is an important goal of preservice music teacher education. Accordingly, every prospective teacher will be expected to be able to...develop skill in teaching students with diverse learning styles"(p. 98).

Policies, Standards, and Assessment in Music Teacher Preparation. When first-year teachers get their class assignments, they should feel prepared as a result of the instruction they received in their college methods classes and coordinated PreK–16 music education partnership programs. Methods classes such as those that include music foundations for teaching special learners are designed to inform preservice teachers about the way in which the new No Child Left Behind laws may affect their public or private school inclusion programs. New teachers need to be familiar with standard vocabulary and processes used in special education and aware of updates including the Individuals with Disabilities Education Improvement Act of 2004. Preservice music teachers should be prepared to create lesson plans for their performance medium and small-group instruction as well as vocal and instrumental ensembles that include instructional adaptations for students with (a) learning disabilities, (b) speech and language impairments, (c) visual and/or hearing impairments, (d) mobility issues due to physical impairments and/or health issues, and (e) behavioral challenges. Figure 2 is a lesson plan outline that may serve as a guide for preservice music teachers who are learning to create meaningful lesson plans that meet state and national standards for children with special needs.

Music education methods classes that are designed to prepare preservice music teachers to work with children with special needs should make it clear that children with special needs must have lessons that speak of consistent life relevance. Lessons should be designed to assist special learners with learning life skills while attending to state and national standards for excellence in the arts. Preservice teachers should understand that content is *not* compromised when teaching music to special learners; instead, assessment tools are modified to accommodate individual differences. As such, the preservice teacher should design appropriate lesson plans with accompanying assessment tools that demonstrate the progress of each student.

The PreK–16 music education partnership experience enables the preservice music teacher to feel comfortable teaching young children with special needs as well as older children with, for instance, developmental disabilities. As an example, let's say that a newly hired teacher has been assigned to teach middle school inclusion students who have moderate to severe cognitive abilities. It is not uncommon for the school administrator to require a lesson abstract with an accompanying assessment tool, such as a rubric. Appropriate preservice music teacher education programs include the process for writing developmentally appropriate lesson plan abstracts and accompanying assessment tools. Figure 3 is a lesson plan abstract with accompanying rubric that measures student progress in chime ensemble. The lesson abstract and accompanying assessment tool are designed for middle school inclusion students who have moderate to severe cognitive abilities.

This lesson abstract and accompanying assessment tool address national, state, and district curriculum standards such as music reading; performing on instruments, alone and with others, a varied repertoire of music; language literacy; and social development. Also considered are cognitive and conceptual understanding, eye-hand coordination for reading, listening skills, and focused attention. Cross-curricular concepts are reinforced because children learn to associate chime length (size) with pitch (sound) and to follow teacher direction.

PreK–16 music education partnerships that link effective music education methods classes with outside learning institutions offer practical experiences to preservice music teachers. As a result, preservice music teachers develop into competent and confident first-year music teachers in public and private schools. Educational partnerships provide preservice teachers with the tools for successful teaching and learning at all levels of ability so that even the most impaired child can be a full participant in challenging music learning activities.

Perspective III: Maureen T. Makowski, New Teacher

Method into Practice. The theoretical and pedagogical knowledge that preservice teachers acquire during their undergraduate music-teacher-training programs should prepare them to create lesson plans that demonstrate an understanding of (a) sequential music skill learning, (b) sequential music content learning, (c) adaptations for special learners, and (d) strategies for classroom management. Music education methods classes together with PreK–16 teaching and learning experiences that include children with special needs provide preservice teachers with the confidence they need to establish successful music programs that attend to individual learning differences. The Rainbowtunes Early Childhood Music Teaching and Learning Program for Children with Special Needs, an offshoot of the Rompertunes PreK–16 music education partnership, encourages preservice music teachers to take ownership of sequential lesson planning, lesson presentation, classroom management, and student assessment that is appropriate for children with special needs.

The musical development of the children with special needs who participate in the Rainbowtunes PreK–16 music education partnership is exciting. Each year when the program begins, most children are at the beginning stages of preparatory audiation (Valerio et al., 1998). Many children within the autism spectrum do not make eye contact and require more music acculturation. Other children hum or sway to the music but are still limited in their participation. As the weeks progress, the children acculturate by watching and listening to the preservice teacher as he or she sings tonal patterns and chants rhythm patterns. Eventually the children reach a level of imitation during which time they begin to imitate tonal and rhythm patterns, sing songs, and participate in movement activities that accompany rhythmic chants. By the end of the school year, all children, including those with low cognitive abilities, will have acculturated to music. Some children will have reached a level of imitation by the end of the first year, and a few children transcend the imitation level of preparatory audiation and begin to assimilate musical experiences allowing them to improvise musical patterns in a meaningful fashion.

The Rainbowtunes class is set up with the teacher sitting on the floor in front of the children. The children are seated in chairs set up in a horseshoe fashion (Sobol, 2001, p. 5). This facilitates easy access between teacher and child. It also allows the children to see one another and to work cooperatively. Finally, it allows the teacher to place children with physical handicaps near the end of the horseshoe, allowing for more space and comfort. The children learn that it is important to share through the use of props such as instruments and scarves.

The Rainbowtunes PreK–16 music education partnership includes adaptations for special learners. For example, adaptations for children with hearing impairments include visual cues such as posters, sign language, props, and movements. For children with visual impairments, auditory cues are given along with tactile props such as scarves, instruments, balls, and parachutes. Special adaptations are made depending on the severity of a child's disability. Children with autism may need to experience music in a multisensory way that includes one-to-one attention. In order to feel the beat, children benefit from rocking or bouncing. In order to "see" high and low, we use scarves that float high as we sing high notes and low as we sing low notes. In order to facilitate preparatory audiation and to experience breath support, we use a parachute and take a deep breath while slowly raising it up and then exhale while lowering it to the ground.

Children with autism and other challenges do best with repetition. Consequently, all songs and chants are repeated several times throughout the course of a 20-minute learning session. When singing tonal patterns and chanting rhythm patterns, a preservice teacher sits directly in front of a child in order to promote visual focus. Once eye contact is secured, the preservice teacher invites the child to imitate a pattern by singing, "your turn" followed by a preparatory breath. The eye contact aids in audiation, and the verbal cue "your turn" followed by a prep breath stimulates in the child the desire to imitate. Reaching the imitation stage of preparatory audiation is a process that can take several weeks or months. Once preschool-age children move into the imitation stage of preparatory audiation, they become comfortable with their singing voices and feel free to use them.

Elementary-school-age children who are not given the opportunity to move through the stages of preparatory audiation during preschool may feel uncomfortable when singing alone in front of others because they may be unfamiliar with their own singing voices. Preschool-age children who experience music in a group setting, on the other hand, may be more familiar with their singing voices and with their peers' singing voices; consequently, they may participate in elementary general music activities to a greater degree than those children who have not participated in preschool music programs.

The children who are involved in the Rainbowtunes PreK–16 music education partnership demonstrate accelerated social and academic progress. Socially, they become more comfortable working as a team and staying on task. According to O'Loughlin (2000), "Autistic children appear to prefer an auditory stimulus of music over verbal. Music appears to enable the autistic child to attend to activity and reduce what appears to be boredom for the child" (p. 947).

The classroom teachers who are directly involved with exceptional children are enthusiastic about the Rainbowtunes PreK–16 music education partnership because they find that the children are better able to focus after a Rainbowtunes session. According to the classroom teachers, the children who participate in Rainbowtunes are better equipped to make connections between music lessons and classroom lessons. The classroom teachers stay in the room during the Rainbowtunes sessions and learn all songs, chants, and movement activities so that they are prepared to reinforce the songs, chants, and movement activities during regular class time. The classroom teachers report that they are incorporating musical activities into general learning activities more often as a result of having observed the positive effects that Rainbowtunes has had on the children. The classroom teachers have also expressed that some children have demonstrated a higher level of self-confidence as a result of their participation in Rainbowtunes because they are proud of their accomplishments in music.

Effect on Music Teacher Preparation. Preservice teachers who participate in PreK–16 music education partnerships that include children with special needs are given an opportunity for growth as teachers, as professionals, and as musicians. As teachers, they gain confidence working with and making adaptations for special populations. According to VanWeelden and Whipple (2005),

> during the field experience, [preservice] teachers had to plan and prepare the activities in order to adapt to the students' needs as well as modify rate of instruction and material covered during the actual lesson presentation. Thus, when the act of teaching was coupled with the myriad of challenges displayed by the needs of the special learners, the comfort of working with this population may have seemed difficult for beginners. Students within this study, however, ended with high levels of comfort in their abilities to work with students with special needs in different music education settings following their field experience. (p. 67)

Preservice teachers who participate in PreK–16 music education partnerships also have an opportunity to grow as professionals. The program allows them to work with other teachers, administrators, and therapists. Important interpersonal skills can be learned as each professional shares her views on best practices related to special populations. As musicians, the PreK–16 music education partnerships that are founded on the tenets of Edwin E. Gordon's music learning theory increase preservice teachers' comfort level and competence with diverse and challenging tonalities and meters. They become more flexible and fluent with musical expression through tonal and rhythmic improvisation.

Perspective IV: Izzet Mergen, Public School Music Administrator

Method into Practice. PreK–16 music education partnerships such as those that are centered in Edwin E. Gordon's music learning theory support the unique mode of knowing and thinking in music that is known as audiation (Gordon, 1997). Gardner (1993) acknowledges that music is one of seven intelligences. According to respected educational psychologists, it is the responsibility of public school music administrators, music educators, and music teacher educators to provide the means for developing this unique aspect of humanity known as musical intelligence or music aptitude.

According to music faculty members, the children with special needs who have participated in the Rainbowtunes PreK–16 music education partnership are better prepared for the classroom music programs in the years to come. Faculty members report that Rainbowtunes participants are better able to match pitch and have a basic tonal and rhythm vocabulary as readiness for kindergarten. When compared to children who have not had the Rainbowtunes experience, the children who have come through the partnership program tend to be more comfortable singing tonal patterns and chanting rhythm patterns alone and with classmates. Faculty members observe that participants demonstrate the ability to think in music, or to audiate. There appears to be a correlation between the participants' ability to audiate and their success with classroom activities and life skills. The children who have participated in Rainbowtunes are able to express themselves though musical behaviors such as singing, movement, and basic improvisation.

PreK–16 music education partnerships enable school districts to address national, state, and district-wide curricular standards in arts education at the preschool level. Figure 4 provides information that pertains to the way in which the New York Arts Standards may be addressed in an early childhood music teaching and learning program for children with special needs.

Effective PreK–16 music education partnerships are designed to meet arts standards as well as district-wide literacy goals. Well-designed PreK–16 music education partnerships (a) strengthen whole language skills, phonics, and phonemic awareness skills; (b) increase vocabulary and listening comprehension; (c) support student participation and motivation; and (d) provide a means for self-expression.

Effect on Music Teacher Preparation. Clear and present musical, academic, and social learning benefits are a result of PreK–16 music education partnerships. PreK–16 music education partnerships also facilitate excellence in music teacher preparation by allowing preservice teachers to take ownership of one component of a comprehensive public school music program. As a student teacher, one may feel like an assistant, a helper, or a teacher-in-training. While the student teacher is all of these, preschool partnership programs provide an opportunity for preservice teachers and student teachers to participate as dignified partners in the music teaching and learning process. With the assistance of classroom teachers, the partnership process elevates preservice teachers and student teachers to "expert" status. As experts they are responsible for curricular development, lesson planning and delivery, and assessment.

Summary

Music teacher education programs that include PreK–16 music education partnership programs graduate teachers who are prepared to accommodate the individual musical, social, emotional, and academic needs of their future students. School districts that participate in PreK–16 music education partnership programs meet district, state, and national standards and empower preservice teachers to enter the workforce with an understanding of planning, presenting, and meaningful assessment. Children who participate in PreK–16 music education partnerships develop musicianship, literacy, social awareness, and life skills through a process that encourages self-expression and joyful participation.

As we shape effective music teacher training programs, it is important to consider that PreK–16 education is strengthened through music education partnerships that foster open communication and professional respect between public school administrators, collegiate faculty, classroom teachers, and preservice music teachers. Music teachers who possess the readiness to teach life's tasks through music and music through life's tasks are prepared to change the lives of exceptional children. While nothing can replace a mother's intuition about the special needs of her child, standards-based music teacher preparation programs that provide opportunities for preservice teachers to work with special populations graduate strong, caring, competent, and qualified teachers.

References

Circle, D. (2005). The future of music teacher education: Introduction. *Journal of Music Teacher Education, 14*(2,) 3–4. http://www.menc.org/journals.

Gardner, H. (1993). *Multiple intelligences: The theory in practice.* New York: Basic Books.

Gordon, E. E. (1997). *Learning sequences in music: Skill, content, and patterns.* Chicago: GIA.

Hammel, A. M. (2001). Preparation for teaching special learners: Twenty years of practice. *Journal of Music Teacher Education, 11*(1), 5–11. http://www.menc.org/journals.

Hogan, M. P.(Ed.). (2004, Fall). *Student teaching policy manual and forms.* (Available from the Office of Clinical Education and Department of Curriculum and Instruction, University A Campus, 720 Northern Boulevard, Brookville, NY 11548)

Madsen, C. K. (Ed.). (2000). *Vision 2020: The Housewright symposium on the future of music education.* Reston, VA: MENC.

O'Loughlin, R. A. (2000). Facilitating prelinguistic communication skills of attention by integrating a music stimulus within typical language intervention with autistic children [Abstract]. *Dissertation Abstracts International, 61* (03A): 947A.

Robbins, J., & Stein, R. (2005). What partnerships must we create, build, or reenergize in k–12 higher and professional education for music teacher education in the future? *Journal of Music Teacher Education,* 14(2,) 22–29. http://www.menc.org/journals.

Sobol, E., (2001). *An attitude and approach for teaching music to special learners.* Raleigh, NC: Pentland Press.

Valerio, W. H., Reynolds, A. M., Bolton, B. M., & Taggart, C. C., (1998). *Music play.* Chicago: GIA.

VanWeelden, K., & Whipple, J. (2005). The effects of field experience on music education majors' perceptions of music instruction for secondary students with special needs. *Journal of Music Teacher Education, 14*(2), 62–69. http://www.menc.org/journals.

Figure 1: A Three-Part Assessment Tool Designed to Measure Preservice Teacher Performance

Part I: INTASC Standards Inform Instructor Comments

STANDARD 1: CONTENT PEDAGOGY
The teacher understands the central concepts, tools of inquiry, and structures of the discipline he or she teaches and can create learning experiences that make these aspects of subject matter meaningful for students.

Instructor Comments:

STANDARD 2: STUDENT DEVELOPMENT
The teacher understands how children learn and develop and can provide learning opportunities that support a child's intellectual, social, and personal development.

Instructor Comments:

STANDARD 3: DIVERSE LEARNERS
The teacher understands how students differ in their approaches to learning and creates instructional opportunities that are adapted to diverse learners.

Instructor Comments:

STANDARD 5: MOTIVATION AND MANAGEMENT
The teacher uses an understanding of individual and group motivation and behavior to create a learning environment that encourages positive social interaction, active engagement in learning, and self-motivation.

Instructor Comments:

STANDARD 6: COMMUNICATION AND TECHNOLOGY
The teacher uses knowledge of effective verbal, nonverbal, and media communication techniques to foster active inquiry, collaboration, and supportive interaction in the classroom.

Instructor Comments:

Part II: Rubric for Converting Instructor Comments to Letter Grade

A (-)   Preservice teacher demonstrated clear and consistent understanding of all five pertinent INTASC standards.

B (+/-) Preservice teacher demonstrated clear and consistent understanding of at least three of the five pertinent INTASC standards.

C (+/-) Preservice teacher demonstrated clear and consistent understanding of at least two of the five pertinent INTASC standards.

D/F Preservice teacher demonstrated clear and consistent understanding of no more than one of the five pertinent INTASC standards.

Part III: Additive Rating Scale

Add one point for each observable criterion.

Musicianship
   The preservice teacher

   _____ performed with a steady sense of tempo while modeling the rhythmic chant.

   _____ performed the division patterns accurately.

   _____ performed the micro patterns accurately.

   _____ performed the rest patterns accurately.

   _____ performed the rhythmic chant with vocal inflection.

   _____ performed the rhythmic chant with dynamic variety.

Acculturation Activities
   The preservice teacher

   _____ performed the first verse of the text while tiptoeing around the room.

   _____ made eye contact with the children and encouraged children to follow, but did not expect them to tiptoe with accurate steady beat.

   _____ encouraged classroom teachers to join in.

   _____ performed second verse of the text while jumping on the word *jump* and hopping in place to the other macrobeats.

   _____ encouraged children to move as modeled, but did not expect them to do so with accuracy.

Total Points_____ (11 possible)

Figure 2: Lesson Plan Outline

Age/Grade Level for Lesson: Identify Pre–K, K–2, 3–5, 6–8, 9–12

Identify New York Arts Standards and National Standards that are met in this lesson

Goal	The students will experience ...
Objective	The students will perform, read, and write ...
Prerequisite Behavior	The students will demonstrate an understanding of ...
Classroom Materials	The teacher indicates materials, resources, and references.
Procedure	Introduction to Objective
	Core: Teacher outlines lesson steps
	Exploration: Students move through steps
	Summary: Students demonstrate understanding of objective
Classroom Management	The teacher clearly states the rules for lesson success, anticipates behavioral interruptions, and devises behavior modification solutions accordingly.
Lesson Assessment	The teacher designs a rubric that assesses student achievement of learning objective(s). The teacher indicates developmentally appropriate performance criteria such as "by teacher direction," "with prompt," and/or "without prompt."
Instructional Adaptations	The teacher ensures that the lesson accommodates students with:
	Learning Disabilities (processing)—short segments reinforced
	Communication Disorders (responding)—assessment tailored to include nonverbal ways that student can indicate understanding of lesson
	Visual and Hearing Impairments—lesson designed to reach minimum three senses simultaneously audio/visual/tactile
	Orthopedic or Other Physical Impairments
	Health Issues—lesson enforces Individualized Education Program (IEP) and makes sure classroom is handicap accessible
	Behavioral Issues—classroom management in place so student needs are served

Figure 3: Lesson Abstract and Accompanying Assessment Tool for Middle School Chime Ensemble

Fifteen elementary/lower middle school children with moderate to severe developmental disabilities will be taught to play the hand chimes. They will rehearse weekly for community and school performances. A music teacher will direct the ensemble in collaboration with a classroom teacher.

The Middle School Chime Ensemble will assist and motivate students to improve functional life skills and daily tasks including (a) literacy, (b) the ability to focus and follow directions, (c) listening skills and pitch recognition through "ear" training, (d) increased attention span, (e) fine motor skills, (f) self-care, (g) appropriate handling of instruments, and (h) the development of expressive and receptive communication through music. The Middle School Chime Ensemble will help the students develop confidence in their abilities while demonstrating improvement in their specific nonmusical IEP goals.

Assessment Tool: Middle School Chime Ensemble		
Student Name _____ Date _____		
Evaluation Criteria: Student achievement is evaluated at the end of each session. The students are evaluated on the following five performance goals. Progress is measured through the use of the following descriptors: 3 = frequently, 2 = evident, 1 = developing		
Goal #1	Student holds chime in one hand	_____
Goal #2	Student plays chime on cue with teacher direction	_____
Goal #3	Student stops chime playing with teacher direction	_____
Goal #4	Student reads letters A, B, C, D, E, F, G, on chime and musical staff with teacher direction	_____
Goal #5	Student arranges chimes in correct order, largest to smallest, in chime box at end of rehearsal with teacher direction	_____
	Weekly progress in total number of points:	_____

(Additional assessment tools are devised to measure each student's progress on obtaining greater independence with and without teacher prompt.)

Figure 4. State Standards Addressed in Early Childhood Music Programs

Standard 1. Creating, Performing, and Participating in the Arts
- Participants engage in singing, chanting, movement, and musical game-playing activities.
- They use the basic elements of music, including tonality, rhythm, and expressiveness, in their performances and musical creations.
- Students engage in individual and group musical and music-related tasks.

Standard 2. Knowing and Using Arts Materials and Resources
- Participants perform on traditional classroom instruments and a variety of nontraditional sound sources to create and perform music.
- They are provided various listening experiences, performance opportunities, and information about music.

Standard 3. Responding To and Analyzing Works of Art
- Participants demonstrate the capacity to listen to and comment on music.
- They use concepts from other disciplines to enhance their understanding of music, and music to understand concepts from other disciplines.

Standard 4. Understanding the Cultural Dimensions and Contributions of the Arts
- Participants develop a performing and listening repertoire of multicultural music that represents peoples of the world, including citizens of the United States.
- Participants explore the tonal and rhythmic vocabulary of culturally diverse musics and begin to understand the function and role that music plays in those cultures.

Perspectives
An Approach for Mentoring the Vocal Graduate Teaching Assistant
By Martha Rowe

Martha Rowe is an associate professor of voice at New Mexico State University in Las Cruces. She can be reached at mrowe@nmsu.edu.

The new vocal graduate teaching assistant (GTA) walks into her studio excited, naive, capable, insecure and—oftentimes—pretty clueless. She has had four to five years of university-level vocal training and perhaps a semester of vocal pedagogy. She is beginning to develop an understanding of her own vocal mechanism but has a very limited awareness of how to approach the voices of others. She isn't sure how to choose repertoire for her students, which vocalises to assign them, how to deal with attitude problems, or how to objectively grade each lesson. And how will she know if the students are making adequate progress for their level?

That was my experience as a GTA—and it is probably a common one. I was granted the position, told what my responsibilities were, handed a key to my studio and a list of my students, and then left to fend for myself for the next two years. The positive aspects of such an approach were feeling the faculty's confidence in my abilities and being free to develop my own curriculum and teaching style. The negative aspects included not really knowing if what I was doing was effective and not having the benefits of regular observations and feedback from a mentor.

The old adage states, "We teach as we were taught." I, too, have essentially handed my GTAs a key to their studio and left them to flounder for the next two years. Okay, I'm not that bad—but I don't have a program in place to help guide the development of teaching skills in my GTAs. Discussions with former and present GTAs regarding how their training (and, hence, their teaching) could have been more effective have led me to begin developing a strategy that will help future teaching assistants become better educators. The purpose of this article is to share that process. The article will address the four areas that I have found to be most useful in my own growth as a teacher and as aids in the mentoring process: (1) preparation of materials, (2) observation, (3) weekly discussion sessions, and (4) awareness of current research and other literature.

Preparation

The most practical of the four areas is that of preparation. As a teacher of 20-plus years, I still find that the amount and type of preparation I do affects my teaching. Novice teachers lack the knowledge of repertoire, pedagogical language, techniques, and analytical skills that a more seasoned teacher possesses, yet they are expected to just walk in, start teaching—and produce good results!

The role of a mentor could include the following: helping the GTAs know what to look and listen for in a student, learning how to interview and test a student, teaching the principles behind various vocalises and exercises, developing a varied repertoire of good literature appropriate to the level they will be teaching, and developing a strategy for objectively measuring students' work, to name a few.

Many of these areas are addressed in a good vocal pedagogy course, but it takes time and guidance to be able to incorporate and make practical the knowledge that such a course offers.

Help the GTAs design their own studio forms, such as student profiles and weekly lesson reports, or simply offer to share the format you use. Two publications that might prove especially useful are Joan Boytim's *The Private Voice Studio Handbook* (2005) and Rebecca Osborn's *The Private Music Instruction Manual* (2004). Both are directed to the independent studio teacher. The Osborn is more geared toward the younger student, but the teaching and organizational principles are excellent and useful at any level. Finally, encourage all graduate students to be quick to ask for help or advice but also to trust their own instincts.

Observation

The most popular assignment in my undergraduate vocal pedagogy course is a series of lesson observations. The students attend four 1-hour lessons, each in a different voice studio. Their assignment is simply to observe, report, and learn. This gives them the opportunity to note different teaching and learning styles and to begin to develop a set of their own teaching strategies. They observe beginning breathy sopranos, young tenors learning how to negotiate the *passaggio*, and graduate students preparing for auditions.

Our GTAs would benefit greatly from a program of weekly observations, not only of voice teachers but of other strong educators on the faculty as well. A flute professor might give the student new insights on breathing techniques. The cellist might open the student's ears to a new understanding of phrasing. Useful metaphorical as well as technical language and approaches can be gleaned from any number of sources. As a side note, let me offer that some of my most valuable pedagogical training came as a result of watching poor teachers teach. Even though the methods used were ineffective, I began to understand what *not* to do, which is of no small value.

Mutual observation is also valuable. I watch my GTAs teach as well as have them watch me. We then meet to compare notes, questions, observations and ideas, thus providing an ideal opportunity for mutual growth. Critical thinking and questioning are crucial aspects of such an activity, as is openness to new ideas and approaches. Such a technique would be even further strengthened by videotaping students as they teach and then watching and discussing those tapes together.

Weekly Discussions

Devote an hour each week to your GTAs for discussion and questions. Dialoguing and brainstorming are important elements in the development of a creative, independent teacher. Discuss specific students, pedagogical principles, repertoire, or whatever you and the student know would be most beneficial. Be prepared to offer reading lists and other source materials in the areas that are being addressed. This is also an excellent opportunity to mentor them in the development of professional deportment and attitudes. Help your GTAs gain insight into professional areas that go beyond subject matter, such as to how to avoid becoming a counselor, enabler, or buddy to their students. Most importantly, be prepared to listen. Allow your GTAs to express frustration about issues, such as a particularly difficult student, and offer ideas about how to address such situations.

Current Research

All voice teachers are called to stay abreast of developments and new understandings in the world of vocal pedagogy. It informs our teaching and broadens our understanding of our students and our art. Mentors can encourage the development of lifelong learning by incorporating such readings in their discussions with their GTAs. A wonderful and practical way to actively involve them in current research and findings is to assign them readings from recent journals or Web entries and then ask them to relate that information to one or more of their own students. The journals and Web sites of NATS, MENC, and the Voice Foundation are all excellent resources from which to draw current findings and new ideas.

I do not regret the fact that I was given such freedom in my early teaching years. But I do think that both my students and I paid a price for the lack of guidance. How much better might my teaching have been had I had intentional, organized guidance from a mentor who was willing to share his or her expertise with me? As a mentor, I look forward to seeing the results of incorporating these four principles in a more intentional manner. I suspect that my own teaching will improve as much as my GTAs.

References

Boytim, J. F. (2003). *The private voice studio handbook: A practical guide to all aspects of teaching.* Milwaukee, WI: Hal Leonard.

Osborn, R. (2004). *The private music instruction manual: A guide for the independent music educator.* Victoria, BC: Trafford.

Book Review
The Power of Questions
By Suzanne Burton

Suzanne Burton is an assistant professor of music education at the University of Delaware in Newark. She can be reached at slburton@udel.edu.

Falk, B., & Blumenreich, M. (2005). *The power of questions: A guide to teacher and student research.* Portsmouth, NH: Heinemann. (224 pages, softcover)

Teacher research is a type of inquiry that is designed to connect teaching practice with student learning outcomes. This type of inquiry has been noted for its ability to directly influence the process of teaching and learning and is an effective form of practical research for music educators. Through inquiry, teachers become empowered to address educational issues by active problem solving. In the 2005 book *The Power of Questions: A Guide to Teacher and Student Research,* Beverly Falk and Megan Blumenreich have provided an accessible framework for music educators to design and carry out inquiry within their own teaching contexts.

Overview

Ten chapters take the reader through the process of designing and conducting inquiry. While the milieu of the text is the general education classroom, transferring the material to any number of music education contexts is easily accomplished. The format of the 224-page book is clear and direct with a conversational tone. The authors have carefully considered how to represent the process of designing and conducting research to practitioners who may have little or no experience conducting inquiry. Emphasized throughout the book is the intersection of pedagogical content knowledge, practical application of theoretical constructs, and issues associated with the everyday act of teaching. Additionally, Falk and Blumenreich extend principles of conducting inquiry to students in the classroom and present questions to consider when designing inquiry-based projects for classroom work.

Included in the book are helpful examples, vignettes, outlines, exercises, and worksheets designed to put newly learned strategies into practice. Practical information, such as the "Handy Little Guide to Referencing in APA Format" and a sample literature review, is presented in the appendix. Furthermore, an online instructor's manual that includes rubrics for assessing professional development is available for teacher educators.

Contents

Falk and Blumenreich begin the book with a chapter titled "Making the Case for Teacher Research" in which they provide support for teachers to engage in inquiry within their own educational contexts. Citing constructivism as the premise upon which teacher research is built, they present inquiry as a primary means for powerful teaching and learning. The authors believe that central to conducting inquiry is the awakening of the learner's questions, which, when acted upon, become the driving force for learning.

Chapter 2 provides an explanation of experimental and naturalistic approaches for conducting research. Descriptions of teacher research, such as action research, personal narrative, case study, and ethnography, are supplied with related examples. While the reader is left to decide which approach is best for the questions that are being pursued, the main mode of inquiry presented throughout the chapter and in the discussion on reliability and validity is that of a naturalistic approach using qualitative methods.

In the third chapter, the authors give suggestions for finding a purpose and research questions for inquiry. Among the strategies discussed are becoming familiar with other teachers' research, keeping a journal on possible questions, considering how to improve teaching practice, observing how people interact in the workplace, and contemplating how policies and practices of schools affect students. The reader is then taken through the process of framing questions within a context, considering the biases that are brought to the study, and outlining the approach to study the question. This chapter extends inquiry to students by offering ways to guide and engage them in finding questions in the classroom. It concludes with an outline of exercises and a worksheet aptly designed to take the reader through this process.

Conducting a review of literature is the topic of chapter 4. In this chapter, Falk and Blumenreich discuss techniques of locating key words for conducting a search. They then walk the reader through the process of writing a literature review, from evaluating sources, taking notes, and analyzing articles, to sorting and synthesizing ideas. They conclude this chapter with a guide for writing a literature review.

In chapter 5, developing an action plan for inquiry is presented. As with preceding chapters, each step is presented in a cogent manner. Keeping the research questions at the fore, the authors explain how to design a study and move through important steps such as planning data collection and analysis, ensuring validity through triangulation of data sources, creating a time line for the research, and obtaining informed consent. Included is a framework of exercises for reviewing the research design and a plan for pursuing group inquiry with children.

Falk and Blumenreich explore an array of data-collection methods in chapter 6. These methods primarily yield qualitative data and range from maintaining a professional journal, taking field notes, conducting interviews, creating and administering surveys, and using audio and videotape, to sampling student work, using checklists, and accessing curricular or archival data. Exercises at the end of the chapter encourage the reader to explore these data-collection techniques in practical ways that are easily implemented in an educational context.

Throughout chapter 7, data analysis is presented as an ongoing aspect of teacher inquiry. Here the authors discuss how to organize data and go into detail regarding the process of emergent theme analysis and the coding and categorizing of data. Acknowledging bias is brought forth, followed by discussion of the necessity of reliability checks to the integrity of the research. Provided in this chapter are charts that the reader can use to assist with organizing and indexing data. Recommendations are also made for organizing and analyzing data with students.

Telling the story that best represents the research findings is the central theme of chapter 8. Key points covered in this chapter are how to decide on the best form for the presentation of findings, the importance of disclosing choices that were made regarding information that is included or left out of the study, how to address "messy" and inconclusive data, the importance of conducting member checks to ensure that the perspectives of the participants are accurately represented, and drawing viable conclusions and implications through reflection on the research process. The chapter also addresses the need to connect findings to existing literature. Finally, an outline for organizing a research report is furnished followed by tips on writing a good report. The authors conclude this chapter urging the reader to share what was learned with colleagues, and possible venues for disseminating research findings are discussed. At the end of the chapter, an outline for writing up research findings is given for a convenient reference.

Using children's questions to initiate inquiry is covered in chapter 9. The contents of this chapter may be the most difficult to extrapolate to the music education setting, due to the nature of music education curricula, the amount of instructional time afforded, the scheduling of classes, and available resources. However, the authors note that student-initiated inquiry leads to curricular practice that is developmentally appropriate at all levels of teaching and learning. In this chapter, ways to support and address the questions of students are provided along with accounts of how teachers have followed up on these inquiries. Falk and Blumenreich relate that teaching and learning in this fashion are time intensive and challenging in the general education curriculum. While daunting, this type of teaching and learning is beneficial for music educators to consider due to the richness it affords.

The final chapter addresses the "transformative possibilities" of teacher research. In this chapter, the reader is reminded of the power questions can have on teaching and learning if they are acted upon. Examples of how teacher research has influenced practitioners are given. The authors state, "Teachers and students are uniquely positioned to ask and find answers to questions of significance, especially questions related to learning" (p. 187). This, the premise underlying the book, brings the material full circle.

Conclusion

The power of questions: A guide to teacher and student research provides a clear, comprehensible path into conducting teacher research and is appropriate for use as a text for an entry-level course on teacher research methodology. While the book does not directly relate to music education, the material is easily transferred to a music education context. The primary disadvantage of this book is that it is situated in an elementary education perspective, perhaps making it difficult for the reader to readily make connections to music education in middle school and high school contexts. With everything considered, Falk and Blumenreich have presented a means of inquiry and reflection for educators of any discipline to learn more about their practice, further enabling powerful student learning.

Call for Papers, Panel Discussions, and Performances

Keokuk II: Centennial Symposium for MENC: The National Association for Music Education

May 31–June 2, 2007
Keokuk, Iowa

This symposium will commemorate the founding of MENC: The National Association for Music Education in Keokuk, Iowa in 1907. The symposium is being planned and administered by the History Special Research Interest Group (SRIG) of the MENC Society for Research in Music Education, with support from MENC and the City of Keokuk.

The symposium planning committee welcomes submissions for the following:
- Scholarly papers suitable for reading (complete)
- Panel discussions (an outline with names of participants)
- Performances (musical content, names of performers, and any equipment needs)

All topics should relate in some way to music education in the United States during MENC's first century (1907–2007).

Materials must be submitted electronically in any standard style format. Accepted scholarly papers will be considered for publication in the *Journal of Historical Research in Music Education*, which follows *The Chicago Manual of Style*, 15th ed. (Chicago: University of Chicago Press, 2003). Include the following information in the body of the electronic mail message: Name, address, telephone, affiliation, email address for further communication, and title of the paper or proposal. Send all information to Jere.Humphreys@asu.edu.

Complete papers and detailed proposals for other presentations must be received no later than **11:59 p.m., February 15, 2007**. Acknowledgment and notification (by March 15) will be sent via return e-mail.

Keokuk is accessible from airports in Burlington and Cedar Rapids, Iowa, Quincy, Illinois, and St. Louis, Missouri. The City of Keokuk hopes to provide ground transportation from Burlington and Quincy. The main housing and symposium venue will be the Holiday Inn Express in Keokuk.

The History SRIG, MENC, and City of Keokuk are planning several activities that should be of interest to symposium attendees, including tours, concerts, and an address on the geographical area and period.

For further information, contact:
Jere T. Humphreys
School of Music
Arizona State University
Tempe, AZ 85287-0405 USA
Jere.Humphreys@asu.edu

Call for Papers:

SDMENC/SCMEA Joint Conference Poster Session
Charleston, SC, February 8–10, 2007

The Southern Division of MENC and the South Carolina Music Educators Association will sponsor a joint research poster session at its conference in Charleston, SC on Saturday, February 10, 2007. We are accepting submissions of completed and in-progress studies being conducted by undergraduate students, graduate students, university faculty, and practicing teachers in public or private schools. This poster session is open to papers involving any aspect of scholarly research in music, including those that are philosophical, theoretical, or historical in nature, as well as reports that are qualitative or quantitative in design.

Deadline for submissions: December 1, 2006.

Submission procedures: All submissions should not have been published prior to the conference, and meet the Code of Ethics published in the Journal of Research in Music Education. Electronic submissions are encouraged (in MS Word or .pdf). Email the abstract and complete research report (if complete) to Dr. Jeremy S. Lane, SCMEA Research Chair, at jlane@mozart.sc.edu. Please indicate contact information including name, title, affiliation (if applicable), address, e-mail, phone, and fax numbers, on a separate title page. For those unable to send electronic copies, four copies of the abstract and report (if complete) may be mailed to:

> Dr. Jeremy S. Lane
> SCMEA Research Chair
> University of South Carolina School of Music
> 813 Assembly
> Columbia, SC 29208
> Ph. (803) 777-1501

Notification: Submitters will be notified on or before December 22, 2006.

If accepted, the primary or a listed co-researcher must register for and attend the conference to present the poster. If accepted, presenters will be expected to bring 40 copies of their abstract and 5 copies of the completed report to the session.

Call for Papers
Society for Research in Music Education
Research Symposium I
University of Kansas
July 5–7, 2007

The Society for Research in Music Education (SRME), with the co-sponsorship of MENC: The National Association for Music Education, is pleased to announce its first Research Symposium to be held at the University of Kansas, Lawrence, Kansas, July 5–7, 2007. This symposium is designed as a forum for the dissemination and discussion of new scholarship relating to music teaching and learning. Individuals are invited to submit proposals for presentation in which they may share new, unpublished research in music education. Submissions are invited for EITHER paper presentation OR poster presentation. Interested individuals are invited to attend the Symposium whether or not they present. Please direct inquiries about the Symposium to Martin Bergee, Music Education Research Council (MERC) Executive Committee Chair and Symposium Presider, at mencpapers@missouri.edu.

Those who wish to submit a report for consideration should comply with the following:

FOR PAPER PRESENTATION

Research submitted for paper presentation *must not have been presented at any other conference or forum, regardless of size or type of audience.* The paper may have been submitted for publication but must not have appeared in print prior to the Symposium.

FOR POSTER PRESENTATION

Research submitted for poster presentation must conform to the Code of Ethics published regularly in the *Journal of Research in Music Education* (also available at www.menc.org), in that (a) the paper should not have been presented at another major conference or other forum; and (b) the paper may have been submitted for publication but must not have appeared in print *in any forum* prior to the Symposium.
  Papers presented at other conferences will be considered for poster presentation if the audience was substantially different (e.g., a state meeting or a university symposium). A statement specifying particulars of presentation must be included with the submission.

FOR ALL PRESENTATIONS

1. The research may be of any type, but a simple review of literature will not be considered. Manuscript style of articles representing descriptive or experimental studies must conform to the most recent edition of the *Publication Manual of the American Psychological Association.* Authors of other types of studies may submit manuscripts that conform to the most recent editions of either *A Manual for Writers of Term Papers, Theses, and Dissertations* (Turabian) or *The Chicago Manual of Style.*

2. Only *electronic* submissions will be considered. Submit *one* file containing the full copy of your report, including an abstract not to exceed 250 words, with no title page. The full report should

contain no clues as to author identity or institutional affiliation. *In the body of the e-mail, please include the following information:* (a) the author's or authors' names, (b) current position(s) and institutional affiliation(s), (c) mailing address, telephone number, and e-mail address (submitter only), (d) the report's title, (e) the abstract, and (f) specifications of prior presentation as per Items 1 and 2 above. Also, in the body of the e-mail, please specify whether you want your submission to be considered for PRESENTATION ONLY, POSTER SESSION ONLY, or EITHER PRESENTATION OR POSTER SESSION. The full report with abstract should not exceed 6000 words in length. Send the file as an *attachment* in Word Document (.doc) or Portable Document (.pdf) format. Other formats will not be accepted. Incomplete submissions (e.g., projects in progress, reports without abstracts, requested information not present in the body of the e-mail, etc.) will be rejected.

3. Correspondence will be sent only to the submitter, and only by e-mail. The submitter should send the manuscript from the e-mail address he or she wishes to use for correspondence. You will be notified of receipt of the manuscript and the reviewers' decision exclusively by e-mail.

4. Send submissions to Martin Bergee at **mencpapers@missouri.edu**. Please use this e-mail address for all correspondence. Hard-copy submissions will not be accepted.

5. *Submissions must be received by 11:59 p.m. Central Daylight Savings Time, January 2, 2007.* Extensions will not be granted. If you have not received confirmation of your manuscript by January 10, please notify Martin Bergee at the above e-mail address.

6. A panel of qualified reviewers will screen all submissions.

7. Submitters will be notified of the reviewers' decision no later than February 15, 2007.

8. All presenters and attendees must be members of MENC and must register for the Symposium online at http://people.ku.edu/~cmj/mencresearchsymposium.html. Information about Symposium registration, lodging in the Lawrence area, and travel will appear on this site as the information is finalized.

9. All participants are expected to attend all sessions on July 6 and 7, including dinner on July 7.

An informal reception will be held the evening of Thursday, July 5. In addition, all attendees are encouraged to join the Organizing Committee for a breakfast on Sunday, July 8, at which discussion regarding plans for future symposia will take place.

A copy of this call can be viewed on MENC's Society for Research in Music Education page, http://menc.org/research.html, under "Announcements."

JOURNAL OF MUSIC TEACHER EDUCATION

Spring 2007　　　　　　　　　　　Volume 16, Number 2

Society for Music Teacher Education Executive Committee

Chairperson
Don P. Ester
Ball State University

Eastern Representative
Susan Conkling
Eastman School of Music

Southwestern Representative
Robin Stein
Texas State University–San Marcos

North Central Representative
Jane R. Barrett
Northwestern University

Southern Representative
Janet Robbins
West Virginia University

Northwest Representative
Tina Bull
Oregon State University

Western Representative
Marg Schmidt
Arizona State University

Immediate Past Chair
David Teachout
University of North Carolina–Greensboro

Chair-Elect
Linda Thompson
Lee University

Journal of Music Teacher Education Editorial Committee
William E. Fredrickson, Editor
Florida State University

Gail Barnes
University of South Carolina

Debra Hedden
University of Kansas

Colleen Conway
University of Michigan

Mitchell Robinson
Michigan State University

Alan Gumm
Central Michigan University

Cecilia Wang
University of Kentucky

Alice Hammel
James Madison University

Molly Weaver
West Virginia University

MENC Staff

MENC Executive Director
John J. Mahlmann

Deputy Executive Director
Michael Blakeslee

Director of Publications
Frances Ponick

Managing Editor
Linda C. Brown

The *Journal of Music Teacher Education* (ISSN 1057-0837) is published twice yearly by MENC: The National Association for Music Education, 1806 Robert Fulton Drive, Reston, VA 20191-4348.

This material is copyrighted by MENC: The National Association for Music Education. You can read or download a single print of an MENC online journal exactly as if you had purchased a subscription to a journal in print form. You do not have any other rights or license to this material. This material cannot be reproduced, retransmitted, or reprinted without permission from MENC. This means multiple copies for handout or library reserve cannot be made. Placing on Web sites or school broadcast systems is prohibited, and printing in full or part in other documents is not permitted. To make use of an article or a journal in any of the aforementioned circumstances, please send a request to our editorial department (caroline@menc.org), fax a request to Caroline Arlington at 703-860-9443, or call for more information at 800-336-3768, x238.

JOURNAL OF MUSIC TEACHER EDUCATION

Spring 2007   Volume 16, Number 2

CONTENTS

From the Chair
2007: A Year to Look Back—and Forward
Don Ester
3

Commentary
Improvisation
William E. Fredrickson
7

Importance of Various Professional Development Opportunities
and Workshop Topics as Determined by In-Service Music Teachers
Jeffrey E. Bush
10

Opinions of Music Teacher Educators and Preservice Music Students on the
National Association of Schools of Music Standards for Teacher Education
Jere L. Forsythe, Daryl W. Kinney, and Elizabeth L. Braun
19

An Exploratory Study of the Impact of Field Experiences on Music Education
Majors' Attitudes and Perceptions of Music for Secondary Students with Special Needs
Kimberly VanWeelden and Jennifer Whipple
34

Are They Ready to Student Teach? Reflections from 10 Music
Education Majors Concerning Their Three Semesters of Field Experience
Carol McDowell
45

If You Build It . . . : A Distance-Learning Approach for
Music Teacher Licensure Test Preparation
Gena R. Greher
61

Perspectives
Constructivism: Implications for Postsecondary Music Education and Beyond
James B. Morford
75

Announcements
84

From The Chair
2007: A Year to Look Back—and Forward

Don Ester
Chair, Society for Music Teacher Education

The year 2007 is a milestone in our profession. MENC: The National Association for Music Education celebrates 100 years of advancing music education, and SMTE observes the 25th anniversary of its founding. Perhaps there is no more appropriate time to reflect on the lessons of the past as we face the challenges of the present and plan for the future. Accordingly, MENC leaders, interested members, and other stakeholders in education will gather in Orlando this summer for the Centennial Congress to discuss shared goals for music education. Three months later, SMTE members will again converge on Greensboro, North Carolina, for the second biennial Symposium on Music Teacher Education; this symposium's theme is Collaborative Action for Change. As we approach these significant professional assemblies, it would be valuable for each of us to carefully consider the current educational policy environment that serves as the practical context for any proposed action plans.

Following a period that emphasized the development of subject content standards during the 1990s, we are well into a period that might be labeled "the age of assessment and accountability." With the passage of the No Child Left Behind Act (NCLB) in 2002, phrases such as "adequate yearly progress" and "highly qualified teachers" took on formal policy definitions—definitions that have had significant implications for schools and educators. In fact, these two elements of NCLB might serve as primary examples of the law of unintended consequences, and they are certainly worthy of our attention as we consider the future of music teacher education.

While NCLB does formally recognize the arts as one of the 10 core academic subjects, empirical evidence now points to a significant narrowing of the curriculum, including a loss of instructional time in arts education as a result of pressures related to Adequate Yearly Progress. Americans for the Arts (2007) reports the following:

> Despite there being 10 core subjects, NCLB currently requires schools to report student achievement test results for only reading and mathematics. The law requires that all students in the country meet state-determined standards in core subjects by the year 2014. Because of the amount of change schools must see in student achievement, there are many reports of decreasing instruction time for other subjects, such as the arts.
>
> The Council on Education Policy has recently completed a report entitled "From the Capital to the Classroom: Year Four of the No Child Left Behind Act." The report finds a majority of school leaders report gains in achievement, but 71 percent reported having reduced instructional time in at least one other subject to make more time for reading and mathematics. Elementary school leaders report a 22 percent decline in art and music

instruction because of No Child Left Behind. (Note: The Council on Education Policy report can be accessed at http://www.cep-dc.org/nclb/NCLBPolicyBriefs2005/CEPPB 3web.pdf.)

Simply stated, the same policy that unequivocally defined the arts as a core subject has led to the unintended consequence of decreasing the already limited instructional time dedicated to the arts at the elementary school level.

The NCLB principle of Highly Qualified Teachers exhibits a paradox similar to that of its principle of Adequate Yearly Progress. On the road to the well-intentioned goal of assuring that each child benefits from instruction by a highly qualified teacher in each subject area, some interesting detours have appeared. A variety of "alternative routes" to teacher licensing now exist, further confusing what actually constitutes highly qualified. Dr. Lee S. Shulman (2005), president of the Carnegie Foundation for the Advancement of Teaching and professor of education emeritus at Stanford University, addressed this topic:

> Teacher education does not exist in the United States. There is so much variation among all programs in visions of good teaching, standards for admission, rigor of subject matter preparation, what is taught and what is learned, character of supervised clinical experience, and quality of evaluation that compared to any other academic profession, the sense of chaos is inescapable. The claim that there are "traditional programs" that can be contrasted with "alternative routes" is a myth. We have only alternative routes into teaching. There may well be ways in which the teaching candidates of Teach for America or the New York City Fellows program meet more rigorous professional standards than those graduating from some "traditional academic" programs. Compared to any other learned profession such as law, engineering, medicine, nursing or the clergy, where curricula, standards and assessments are far more standardized across the nation, teacher education is nothing but multiple pathways. It should not surprise us that critics respond to the apparent cacophony of pathways and conclude that it doesn't matter how teachers are prepared. . . . Like our sibling professions, we must rapidly converge on a small set of "signature pedagogies" that characterize all teacher education. . . . If we do not converge on a common approach to educating teachers, the professional preparation of teachers will soon become like the professional education of actors. There are superb MFA programs in universities, but few believe they are necessary for a successful acting career. (p. 7)

The lack of standardization may be somewhat less of a concern in music teacher education than in some other subject areas, especially regarding subject matter preparation. Most music educators must complete a content major in music; however, many educators in other subject areas are not required to complete the specific content major.

Some legislative decisions can completely undermine the clear intentions of the NCLB guidelines. A specific example from my home state of Indiana is particularly instructive, although, regretfully, not unique. NCLB guidelines include the following statement:

> The law requires that all teachers of core academic subjects in the classroom be highly qualified. This is determined by three essential criteria: (1) attaining a bachelor's degree or better in the subject taught; (2) obtaining full state teacher certification; and (3)

demonstrating knowledge in the subjects taught. (United States Department of Education, 2006, p. 1)

In Indiana, however, teachers are "highly qualified" to teach elementary music if they "hold a valid Indiana teaching license appropriate for elementary school grades, AND PASSED THE REQUIRED PRAXIS II (#10011) LICENSING EXAM ENTITLED [emphasis in original] Elementary Education: Curriculum, Instruction, and Assessment" (Indiana Department of Education, 2006). This is true despite the fact that these elementary educators commonly have only minimal exposure to music content and methods—typically one course. The designated PRAXIS II exam (#10011) is *not* the music exam required of all music education graduates in Indiana. Rather, the elementary education PRAXIS II exam includes only 11 questions that collectively address "Arts and Physical Education Curriculum, Instruction, and Assessment" (Educational Testing Service, 2005). Needless to say, the level of required music knowledge is utterly insignificant. To compound the problem, Indiana music educators holding the Instrumental Music license (under Rules 46–47 of the Indiana licensing laws), as a result of completing an accredited undergraduate degree in music education, are not considered qualified—much less highly qualified—to teach elementary music in Indiana schools. They would need to complete the requirements for a General Music license by, at a minimum, taking classes in elementary music methods.

Clearly, the current emphasis on assessment and accountability presents some perplexing challenges. Dr. Marilyn Cochran-Smith (2002), John E. Cawthorne Millennium Professor of Teacher Education for Urban Schools and keynote speaker for the upcoming 2007 Symposium on Music Teacher Education, made the following observation regarding the accountability movement:

> As teachers—and teacher educators—we must be held accountable for our work. But policies intended to improve teaching quality can only be as good as the underlying conceptions of teaching, learning, and schooling upon which they are based. Teaching is complex. It is not simply good or bad, right or wrong, working or failing. Although absolutes and dichotomies like these are popular, they are limited in their usefulness. They tacitly assume there is consensus across our diverse society about the purposes of schooling and what it means to be engaged in the process of becoming an educated person as well as consensus about whose knowledge and values are of most worth and what counts as evidence of the effectiveness of teaching and learning. They ignore almost completely the nuances of "good" (or "bad") teaching in the context of particular times and places. They mistake reductionism for clarity, myopia for insight. And they fail to appreciate the institutional realities and complexities of the current accountability context. (Retrieved March 13, 2007, from Dr. Cochran-Smith's Web page, Lynch School of Education Web site: http://www2.bc.edu/~cochrans/)

Cochran-Smith's words offer a challenge to us as professional teacher educators—a challenge not only to dispel the simplistic dichotomies of the day but also to work at addressing the complexities inherent in our diverse society.

I am very pleased that Dr. Cochran-Smith has agreed to be the keynote speaker on the opening evening of the 2007 Symposium on Music Teacher Education. I hope you will be able to participate in this exciting three-day event, September 13–15 in Greensboro, continuing the momentum of the past five years: Since the 2002 MENC Conference Pre-session, we have seen participation in SMTE-sponsored events increase fourfold to over 220 at the 2006 MENC Conference Pre-session. Details regarding registration and the symposium program are available on the SMTE Web site: smte.us. I look forward to greeting you in Greensboro as we engage in "Collaborative Action for Change."

References

Americans for the Arts. (2007). *The impact of the latest federal education legislation on the arts.* Retrieved March 13, 2007, from http://www.americansforthearts.org/services/arts_education/arts_education_015.asp

Educational Testing Service. (2005) *The PRAXIS Series. Elementary education: Curriculum, instruction, and assessment (0011)*. Retrieved March 13, 2007, from http://www.ets.org/Media/Tests/PRAXIS/pdf/0011.pdf

Indiana Department of Education. (2006). *Highly qualified teacher requirements for elementary art & music school teachers.* Retrieved March 13, 2007, from http://www.doe.state.in.us/hqt/pdf/art-music_requirements.pdf

Shulman, L. S. (2005, Fall). Teacher education does not exist. *Stanford Educator*. Retrieved March 13, 2007, from http://ed.stanford.edu/suse/news-bureau/stanford-educator-newsletter.html

United States Department of Education. (2006). *Highly qualified teachers for every child.* Retrieved March 13, 2007, from http://www.ed.gov/nclb/methods/teachers/stateplanfacts.pdf

Commentary
Improvisation
William E. Fredrickson
Editor, Journal of Music Teacher Education

Watching wonderful teachers is always good for our preservice teachers, student teachers, and first-year teachers. It is good for all of us who teach and study the art and science of teaching. The only problem is that for the novice, watching a truly wonderful teacher may make the task look too easy. Good teaching often does not appear to be highly scripted. A good teacher takes advantage of events that occur in time that could not have been part of the original plan. Often really good teaching can appear as if it were simply happening organically, with little effort. This can leave novice teachers both highly impressed and grossly misinformed.

Recently I was watching three members of our jazz faculty playing in a combo setting with a musician who was applying for a position at our school. This combo "audition" appeared to be unscripted and highly improvisatory. For those of us who have trouble making music without a copy of our "part" in front of us, it was absolutely awe inspiring. When watching those musicians call a tune and then stage a terrific performance, all without anything but their instruments and personal experiences, observers might think that the music just happens. They might not think about the billions of notes, millions of scales, thousands of patterns, and hundreds of tunes each of those musicians practiced to perfection, or the many recordings and live performances they either participated in or heard, before ever getting together for this impromptu 20-minute concert. All that terrific music comes from a vast library of musical ideas they have carefully collected and archived in their minds (and fingers) over time, but it looks to us as if it all occurred to them on the spot.

When I was out of town recently, I set my graduate teaching assistant up to give a lecture to my class while I was gone. He did a lot of planning, prepared some interesting experiences for class participation, and videotaped his teaching for review after the fact. He told me that the class went well, but he was disappointed in the outcome. He said he wants to get to the point where he can do what I do when I walk into class, having just hurriedly left my office to get there on time, and apparently start talking about something that seems to just become a lesson. I realized at that moment that he sees what I do as magical, even after several years of his own very successful contractual teaching and most of a master's degree. Like most of us, I've spent years collecting thoughts and experiences, and many unseen hours planning how to weave them together into a syllabus that teaches about current philosophical thought and best practices, before I could rush out of my office at the last second and seem to just talk about whatever apparently occurred to me during the walk to the classroom. He doesn't see a lesson plan so he doesn't necessarily assume there is one.

A good friend of mine has suggested that experienced teachers, just like jazz musicians, have hundreds of lesson plans in their heads. Each has been developed and tested carefully over time, and it can be implemented and then modified as necessary to fit the circumstance. Novice teachers can't do this, nor should they try. But the temptation to think that they should, or can, is real. How many times have we seen undergraduate students in a conducting class, watching the top line of their scores and hoping someone will do something that they can identify, diagnose, and fix? We all know that this diagnostic challenge is only one small part of a rehearsal, but since that is what they see conductors do, it is understandable to think that a rehearsal plan has one item (the name of the tune for today), and the rest is magic. They also become frustrated because they may think we haven't shown them how it's done. It couldn't be hours of accumulated experiences and planning; there must be something else, a shortcut we haven't shared.

In truth, the vast majority of music education programs and music departments do a very good job of giving novice teachers the tools they need. The hard part is also helping them develop patience, time, and perspective. This semester I am teaching our version of the Introduction to Teaching class at my institution. There is a bunch of fresh-faced sophomores who are taking their first hard-core music education class, and they are ready to go. They are observing good teachers in the field, and my colleagues and I are working on getting them the things they need to know. But it occurred to me that I need to be better at making it look less like magic, or at least explaining the trick after I amaze them. I am beginning to talk with them about my own teaching as it unfolds in time, particularly if I can use it to make a point about something I think they should be able to do. At first it feels a bit like an actor violating the "fourth wall" and reminding the audience that they are just watching a play. I hope they find my pedagogical asides interesting and relevant, but more than that I hope they begin to understand that they can make magic too, after a whole lot of on-task practice.

As another variation on this theme, I would like to find ways to convince my applied music colleagues that private lessons are the perfect place to talk about the pedagogy of teaching an instrument to all their students. I asked a room full of highly experienced musicians (all of whom had doctorates in music) how many of them had ever taught a private music lesson. Everyone put up their hands. Then I asked how many of them had been systematically taught how to do that. This time there were no hands. I am beginning to think that I was just lucky. During both my bachelor's and master's degrees, my studio teachers talked to me regularly, and in some detail, about how to go about teaching others the things I was learning to do on my instrument. When I started taking on private students of my own, not only had I been exposed to a good deal of pedagogical information, but I also had the opportunity to discuss it and ask questions. I think that is quite different from being taught how to play, even at a very high level, and then simply trying to replicate that experience for someone else. There is probably a difference between real improvisation, stylistically knowledgeable and experientially informed performance, and simply doing whatever occurs to you. In the end, if it is done well, it will still look like magic.

Importance of Various Professional Development Opportunities and Workshop Topics as Determined by In-Service Music Teachers

By Jeffrey E. Bush

Jeffrey E. Bush is an associate professor of music education at Arizona State University in Tempe. He can be reached at Jeff.bush@asu.edu.

Professional development (PD) is an embedded aspect of the professional life of teachers (Bowles, 2003; Sparks & Hirsh, 1997). In-service workshops, conferences, meetings, seminars, small group work, residency programs, and classes typically constitute how PD is provided for public school music teachers. Music education topics tend to focus on working/expanding specific musical or other practical expertise, dealing with classroom management issues, improving students' critical thinking skills, developing curricula, exploring contemporary topics, or learning new competencies. At its best, PD refers to "the change in a teacher's knowledge base and actions" (Hookey, 2002, p. 888). However, all too often, it is a "demeaning, mind-numbing experience" (Sparks, 1997, p. 20) where lectures are presented by experts on topics that teachers may have little or no interest in.

Several researchers have identified conditions under which PD can be most effective. Sparks and Hirsh (1997) point out that effective PD is possible when it is results-based, centered on the curriculum or standards, rigorous, sustained and cumulative, and can be linked directly to what occurs in the classroom. Modification in practice after an in-service meeting was most common when the focus was relevant to everyday practice (Little & Hayes, 2003). Anderson and Wilson (1996), evaluating a discipline-based arts education program involving music specialists, classroom teachers, and administrators in a two-week professional development summer workshop, found that teachers, organizations, and institutions all need to be involved if educational change is to be successful.

Professional development should also be a shared responsibility of universities and schools, as both entities have a vested interest in the continued development of educators (Livneh & Livneh, 1999; Marsick, 1998). Examples of university involvement in PD activities include mentorship and professors acting as consultants for recent music education graduates (Fallin & Royse, 1994; Smith, 1995), leading a year-long seminar for in-service teachers (Keiny, 1994), and involvement in a multiyear in-service project for choral music teachers (Dolloff, 1994).

Reported benefits of successful PD are numerous. The results of a three-year PD evaluation by the Eisenhower Professional Development Program indicate that PD has the potential to change teachers' practice, particularly when the focus is on "specific, higher-order teaching strategies" (United States Department of Education [USDOE], 2000, p. 60). Professional development has been found to be transformative (Marsick, 1998), to provide teachers with advocacy tools (Kenreich, 2002), to promote inclusion of multiculturalism (Attah, 1991), and to be useful in motivating young educators to stay in the field (Cohen, 1987).

De l'Etoile (2001) found that music in-service sessions improved preschool caregivers' attitudes toward and their knowledge of developmentally appropriate music activities. Similarly, daycare workers who received music in-service training were found to have a higher response level from their students during music activities (Nichols & Honig, 1995). Takacs (1978) discovered that teachers' self-perception of their competency in music and other arts increased after they attended a two-week arts education seminar. Yarbrough, Price, and Bowers (1991) found that teachers were motivated to change their own rehearsal techniques when they learned about successful rehearsal-skills research. In a study of an Orff teacher training course, Robbins (1994/1995) learned that music teachers involved in a research group began to use reflective practices to further their own PD. Junda (1994) studied elementary general music teachers who were enrolled in a two-semester graduate course based on a Kodály approach. The researcher found that lesson planning, procedures (strategies to develop vocal, aural, inner-hearing, and sight-reading skills), teacher abilities (musical and instructional skills), and student abilities (musical skills and participation) improved with PD.

Colwell (1996/1997) reported on a PD residency program in Iowa. Sponsored by the state arts council, the state choral directors association, and a grant from the National Education Association (NEA), the program hired an experienced choral educator/workshop presenter to work with individual teachers in week-long residency programs. Results indicate that all participants profited, although there were differing opinions as to what the benefits were. Colwell also learned that when PD was individualized, all participants were pleased with the results, even though each saw different benefits.

Several studies have indicated that teacher choice and/or relevance are important aspects in PD success. In an investigation of predictors of voluntary participation in PD activities, Livneh and Livneh (1999) learned that self-motivation was the most predictive variable. Horsley (2002) found that teachers had both practical and personal/social reasons for voluntarily being involved in summer in-service workshops. Professional development is a personal matter and, to be effective, should be managed by the individual, according to Browell (2000). Bowles (2003) learned that the topics teachers were most interested in were technology, assessment, instrument/choral literature, standards, creativity, and grant writing.

Professional development has the potential to help teachers deal with change and improve their skills. However, research in PD has lagged behind many other topics in music education (Hookey, 2002). We know that delivery needs to be high quality (USDOE, 2000) and the focus needs to be on matters that are important to teachers (Colwell, 1996/1997). Since self-motivation is a predictor of involvement (Livneh & Livneh, 1999), it is prudent to ask teachers' opinions about PD opportunities and workshops. The purpose of this study was to determine the types of

PD opportunities and workshop topics that in-service music teachers think are important.

Methodology

A survey instrument was created to gather teacher biographical information, discover teachers' preferred ways of gaining PD, and determine the types of workshops they would like to attend. The profile questions solicited information about teachers' PD opportunities, what counts for recertification credit in their school districts, and whether they would be interested in local workshop opportunities sponsored by the state music educators association. Subjects were then asked to rate on 5-point scales the importance of eight PD elements: professional journals, Internet resources, discussions with fellow music teachers, discussions with nonmusic educators, summer or weekend courses/workshops, district-sponsored in-service/workshops, annual state music educators in-service conferences, and national in-service conferences. Subjects were asked, in the third section, to rate their interest in various workshop topics. This list consisted of 15 potential workshop topics: classroom management, music education for gifted/special learners, lesson planning, assessment, curriculum design based on state music standards, English as a second language, recruiting techniques, new music/repertoire, advanced instrumental techniques, conducting, festival information/preparation, grant writing, teaching methods for music classes they currently do not teach, technology, and cross-curricular integration. A final question asked respondents to add any potential workshop topic they would like to attend that did not appear on the list.

Questions were devised based on previously published literature and consultation with the music education faculty of a major university in the southwestern United States. Topics were excluded if they were not germane to all music education teaching areas being surveyed. Once constructed, the survey was pilot-tested by teachers enrolled in a graduate music education course. In addition, the questionnaire was given to the executive committee of the state music education association. Statements were modified based on input provided by both groups. The executive committee of the state music education association reviewed the survey for a second time; further modifications were made.

Subjects were randomly selected from a directory of all state music educators. Forty-two teachers were selected from each of the following teaching areas: band, strings, choral, and general music. Only educators who were listed as teaching in a single area were used; teachers listed as teaching in two or more areas (e.g., choral and general music) were excluded. Based on information contained in the directory, data on each individual's county, school type (elementary, junior high, high school, community school, or combinations), and school location (rural/urban) were also recorded.

Survey forms were mailed to all subjects. Three forms were undeliverable; consequently, three other individuals were selected who had similar characteristics (i.e., teaching area, rural/urban teaching location, school level). Individuals who did not return their surveys in the enclosed postage-paid reply envelopes by the due date were sent a second survey and return envelope.

Results

In the end, 108 surveys were returned, representing a return rate of approximately 65%, which is considered good for this type of survey research (Babbie, 1990). The numbers of respondents by teaching area were strings, 32; choral, 28; band, 24; and general music, 24. The breakdown by grade level was as follows: 55 subjects taught elementary school, 18 taught junior high school, 19 taught high school, 10 split teaching time between elementary and junior high school, 3 taught at both a junior and senior high school, 2 split time between elementary and high school, and 1 person taught at a community K–12 school. Approximately 82.5% of the respondents taught in urban settings and 17.5% worked in rural areas. The split between urban and rural teaching areas approximated the state's population distribution.

Due to an insufficient number of respondents in many categories (e.g., rural, certain types of schools), only descriptive statistics were used to review survey responses. Table 1 lists the rankings and means of statements dealing with the second and third section of the instrument: importance of various PD opportunities and types of workshops the respondents would like to attend. Overall rankings as well as rankings by teaching area (band, strings, choral, and general music) are also provided (Table 1).

Discussion

Many of the rankings come as no surprise to the experienced music educator. For instance, in the section on importance of various PD opportunities, most teachers ranked discussions with fellow music teachers and summer or weekend courses high. Likewise, it seems logical that workshops on new music repertoire would be of interest to those teaching performance ensembles. However, both sections of the survey revealed some intriguing results.

Most music teachers ranked district-sponsored PD in-service workshops near the bottom of the second section of the survey. This may suggest that many school administrators have little idea of what types of PD are most effective for music educators. This reinforces Brophy's (1993) concern that in-service activities designed for heterogeneous teacher groups, such as the entire teacher population in a single school, may not meet the specific needs of music teachers.

Similar to the Bowles study (2003), Internet resources were reported to be important to music teachers. This may be due to the accessibility of the Internet and the relative ease in using this tool. Bauer (1997) suggests that one of the Internet's greatest advantages is that it acts as a means of communication and can be used to ask questions of colleagues, to research materials, to connect to professional organizations, and to participate in continuing education. However, Richardson (2001) cautions that online learning should be held to the same high standards as traditional types of learning.

Respondents favored learning from those they identify as colleagues. This should remind us that peer coaching/delivery of PD has strong potential for success. School administrators should first look at the skills of and knowledge possessed by their own music faculty before bringing in outside clinicians. University music departments should create models to provide training for key district music teachers that includes not only music education instruction but also guidance on providing workshops for their colleagues. Bush and Browne (1999) report on a similar approach successfully used to implement a new curriculum in a Canadian province.

Differences between subjects in various teaching areas were largely minor. However, two differences in this section should be noted. General music specialists rated state music educators annual in-service conferences lower than any other group, and choral teachers ranked discussions with nonmusic educators higher than the other three groups. There are often more workshops for general music specialists than there are for band, strings, or choral teachers, possibly explaining the first difference. It may be that choral teachers have more in common with their nonmusic colleagues than with instrumental specialists, partially explaining the higher ranking. However, they rated this opportunity considerably higher than the general music specialists did, which is difficult to explain. More research is needed to explain this finding.

In the third section, there was general consensus that sessions on technology were welcome. These music teachers see the need for improving their skills in the practical use of music education technology. General music teachers reported different rankings than their performance ensemble colleagues for new music/repertoire, instrumental techniques, recruiting, and conducting, which is probably a result of the specifics of their teaching area. The differences found for student assessment, music education for gifted/special learners, cross-curricular subject integration, and English as a second language between general music teachers and performance ensemble specialists are also traditional. This suggests that school districts are not emphasizing these issues with their performance ensembles or that performance area teachers have received sufficient training to feel these areas are not major concerns to them. Individuals or organizations may argue for an increased emphasis in areas such as these, but performance teachers taking this survey do not feel the same concern. More study in this area would also be prudent.

Care should be taken in generalizing these results. However, they provide direction for both the design of teacher preparation programs and PD activities. The practitioner's voice needs to be recognized and addressed by universities in designing preservice teacher experiences. As well, attention in post-baccalaureate courses, workshops, and seminars should be directed at areas recognized as important by in-service teachers. State music educator associations and others responsible for professional development may also wish to consider these results when preparing workshops and in-service activities.

The results of this study suggest the need for additional work in several directions. It may be advisable to increase the types and numbers of workshops available to performance ensemble directors, similar to what is available for general music teachers. We need to learn more about what types of technology workshops are most useful to teachers and provide opportunities for them to receive what they need. District administrators and organization officials need to understand that performance ensemble specialists feel less strongly about some types of workshops than general music teachers do. If these areas (student assessment, music education for gifted/special learners, cross-curricular integration, English as a second language) are priorities for districts and organizations, performance area teachers may need to be led to understand their importance.

It would be interesting to determine the needs of music teachers with similar experience levels (beginning, experienced, and expert teachers). Determining what types of technology teachers want to learn about would also be useful. Finally, it would be prudent to replicate the present study in various regions of the country to determine if the results are nationally representative.

References

Anderson, J., & Wilson, B. (1996). Professional development and change communities. *Music Educators Journal, 83*(2), 38.

Attah, J. K. (1991). The principle of "Sankofa" in elementary music instruction in Southern Ghana: Selected school personnel's views of and their role in its implementation (Doctoral dissertation, University of North Texas, 1991). *Dissertation Abstracts International, 52*, 1245.

Babbie, E. (1990). *Survey research methods* (2nd ed.). Belmont, CA: Wadsworth.

Bauer, W. I. (1997). Using the Internet for professional development. *Music Educators Journal, 83*(6), 22–27.

Bowles, C. (2003). The self-expressed professional development needs of music educators. *Update: Applications of Research in Music Education, 21*(2). Retrieved April 26, 2005, from http://www.menc.org/publication/articles/journals.html

Brophy, T. (1993). *Evaluation of music educators: Toward defining an appropriate instrument.* (ERIC Document Reproduction Service No. ED375029)

Browell, S. (2000). Staff development and professional education: A cooperative model. *Journal of Workplace Learning, 12*(2), 57–65.

Bush, J. E., & Browne, N. (1999). Arts education in Saskatchewan: A study in cooperation. *Arts Education Policy Review, 100*(3), 31–35.

Cohen, V. W. (1987). Applied idealism: A proposed model of in-service training. *ISME Yearbook, 14*, 249–256.

Colwell, R. (1996/1997). Professional development residency program. *Quarterly Journal of Music Teaching and Learning, 7*(2–4), 76–90.

De l'Etoile, S. K. (2001). In-service training program in music for child-care personnel working with infants and toddlers. *Journal of Research in Music Education, 49*(1), 6–20.

Dolloff, L. (1994). Expertise in choral music education: Implications for teacher education (Doctoral dissertation, University of Toronto, 1994). *Dissertation Abstracts International, 56*, 2600.

Fallin, J., & Royse, D. (1994). Common problems of the new music teacher. *Journal of Music Teacher Education, 4*(1), 13–18.

Hookey, M. R. (2002). Professional development. In R. Colwell & C. Richardson (Eds.), *New handbook of research on music teaching and learning* (pp. 887–902). New York: Oxford University Press.

Horsley, S. (2002). Creating stronger music educators through group professional development. *Canadian Music Educator, 44*, 16, 21.

Junda, M. E. (1994). A model in-service music teacher education program. *Journal of Music Teacher Education, 3*(2), 6–19.

Keiny, S. (1994). Constructivism and teachers' professional development. *Teaching and Teacher Education. 10*(2), 157–167.

Kenreich, T. W. (2002). Professional development becomes political: Geography's corps of teacher leaders. *Theory and Research in Social Education, 30*(3), 381–400.

Little, P., & Hayes, S. (2003). Continuing professional development (CPD): GP's perceptions of post-graduate education-approved (PGEA) meetings and personal professional development plans (PDPs). *Family Practice, 20*(2), 192–198.

Livneh, C., & Livneh, H. (1999). Continuing professional education among educators: Predictors of participation in learning activities. *Adult Education Quarterly, 49*(2), 91–106.

Marsick, V. J. (1998). Transformative learning from experience in the knowledge era. *Daedalus, 127*(4), 119–136.

Nichols, B. L., & Honig, A. S. (1995). The influence of an inservice music education program on young children's responses to music. *Early Child Development and Care, 113*, 19–29.

Richardson, J. (2002). E-learning potential: Online staff development has great possibilities—and pitfalls. In A. Thorson (Ed.), *By your own design: A teacher's professional learning guide*. Columbus, OH: Eisenhower National Clearinghouse for Mathematics and Science Education. (ERIC Document Reproduction Service No. ED461517)

Robbins, J. (1994/1995). Levels of learning in Orff SPIEL. *Bulletin of the Council for Research in Music Education, 123*, 47–53.

Smith, M. V. (1995). The mentoring and professional development of new music educators: A descriptive study of a pilot program (Doctoral dissertation, University of Minnesota, 1995). *Dissertation Abstracts International, 55*, 2759.

Sparks, D. (1997). A new vision for staff development. *Principal, 77*, 20–22.

Sparks, D., & Hirsh, S. (1997). *A new vision for staff development*. Alexandria, VA: Association for Supervision and Curriculum Development and the National Staff Development Council.

Takacs, C. (1978). Measuring the impact of an in-service workshop on elementary teacher's self-perceptions as aesthetic educators. *Contributions to Music Education, 6*, 38–48.

United States Department of Education. (2000). *Does professional development change teaching practice? Results from a three-year study*. Retrieved June 21, 2006, from http://www.ed.gov/rschstat/eval/teaching/epdp/index.html

Yarbrough, C., Price, H. E., & Bowers, J. (1991). The effect of knowledge of research on rehearsal skills and teaching values of experienced teachers. *Update: Applications of Research in Music Education, 9*(2), 17–20.

Table 1. Rank and Means of Professional Development Questions by Teaching Area

Section Two	Overall		Band		Strings		Choral		General	
Importance of Various Professional Development Opportunities	Rank	Mean	Rank	Mean	Rank	Mean	Rank	Mean	Rank	Mean
Discussions with fellow music teachers	1	(4.76)	1	(4.92)	1	(4.75)	1	(4.89)	1	(4.46)
Summer or weekend courses/workshops	2	(4.21)	3.5	(4.17)	3	(4.03)	2	(4.48)	2	(4.25)
State music educators annual in-service conference	3	(4.10)	2	(4.21)	2	(4.14)	3	(4.15)	6	(3.83)
Internet resources	4	(3.97)	6	(3.96)	5	(3.77)	5	(4.08)	3	(4.17)
Professional journals	5	(3.95)	3.5	(4.17)	4	(3.84)	6	(4.00)	4	(3.88)
National in-service conferences	6	(3.73)	5	(4.00)	6	(3.55)	7	(3.62)	5	(3.87)
Discussions with non-music educators	7	(3.70)	7	(3.50)	8	(3.45)	4	(4.12)	7	(3.78)
District-sponsored PD in-service/workshops	8	(3.49)	8	(3.42)	7	(3.52)	8	(3.52)	8	(3.48)

Section Three	Overall		Band		Strings		Choral		General	
Workshops Teachers Would Like to Attend	Rank	Mean	Rank	Mean	Rank	Mean	Rank	Mean	Rank	Mean
New music/repertoire	1	(4.29)	1	(4.48)	1	(4.31)	1	(4.65)	8	(3.71)
Technology	2	(4.03)	3	(4.14)	3	(3.94)	2	(4.25)	3	(3.92)
Student assessment in music	3	(3.87)	4	(4.13)	5.5	(3.74)	6	(3.72)	1	(4.04)
Curriculum design based on state music standards	4	(3.78)	7.5	(3.82)	5.5	(3.74)	5	(3.75)	4	(3.91)
Recruiting techniques/methods	5	(3.72)	5	(4.00)	4	(3.81)	3	(4.08)	13	(2.95)
Music classroom management	6	(3.69)	10.5	(3.67)	8	(3.71)	7	(3.56)	5	(3.90)
Conducting	7	(3.65)	6	(1.32)	9	(3.61)	4	(4.00)	12	(3.13)
Music education for gifted/special learners	8	(3.59)	10.5	(3.67)	7	(3.73)	13	(3.21)	6	(3.82)
Lesson planning in music	9	(3.58)	9	(3.68)	12	(3.43)	11	(3.36)	2	(4.00)
Cross-curricular subject integration	10	(3.45)	14	(3.35)	14	(3.32)	10	(3.38)	7	(3.78)
Grant writing	11.5	(3.44)	7.5	(3.82)	10	(3.55)	12	(3.28)	12	(3.14)
Advanced instrument techniques for teachers	11.5	(3.44)	2	(4.35)	2	(3.97)	15	(2.58)	14	(2.73)
Teaching methods for music classes not currently teaching	13	(3.37)	13	(3.36)	13	(3.39)	8	(3.52)	9	(3.26)
Festival information and preparation	14	(3.32)	12	(3.55)	11	(3.52)	9	(3.50)	15	(2.68)
English as a second language in music classrooms	15	(2.98)	15	(2.82)	15	(3.13)	14	(2.75)	10	(3.23)

Opinions of Music Teacher Educators and Preservice Music Students on the National Association of Schools of Music Standards for Teacher Education

By Jere L. Forsythe, Daryl W. Kinney, and Elizabeth L. Braun

Jere L. Forsythe is associate professor of music education at The Ohio State University in Columbus. He can be reached at forsythe.1@osu.edu. Daryl W. Kinney is assistant professor of music education at the same institution. He can be reached at Kinney.61@osu.edu. Elizabeth L. Braun is director of the Athens Community Music School at Ohio University in Athens. She can be reached at braune@ohio.edu.

The purpose of music teacher education is to develop competent music educators for schools and other settings. Although the process of becoming a teacher begins before preservice music students enter the program and does not end on its completion, the teacher education program represents the most intensive and formal effort to prepare music teachers for teaching. The music teacher education curriculum contains a broad range of requirements established collectively by music and music education faculty, university general education committees (liberal studies), education departments (education courses), and state legislative bodies acting through state departments of teacher education (state mandates). The resulting program includes experiences, required courses, and electives thought to be essential to the preparation of competent teachers. After completing all requirements, preservice music students normally receive both a degree and a teaching license—the formal credentials necessary for employment.

The content and control of music teacher education is the subject of some controversy, and opinions among interested parties vary considerably across the nation. Some music teacher education programs seem to function with considerable autonomy while others are closely governed by the local college of education. When programs are periodically evaluated for accreditation purposes, standards and governance of teacher education are inevitably reconsidered. During this process, confusion may exist about which agency is the governing authority because several groups and institutions are usually involved. There is little doubt, however, that the principal national governing body for teacher education is the National Council for Accreditation of Teacher Education (NCATE). The majority of teacher education institutions belong to this organization and must meet its standards for accreditation. NCATE has established cross-disciplinary standards for teacher education. However, with respect to the content standards for subject matter taught, NCATE normally defers to the learned society of a discipline. For music education, that learned society is the National Association of Schools of Music (NASM), the accrediting agency for music and music-related disciplines.

The standards for NASM accreditation include a wide range of expectations that must be met for an institution to be accredited. The standards and procedures are described in the *NASM Handbook*, a publication that is updated annually and published and distributed to Association members biannually. The *Handbook* contains rather extensive and somewhat detailed descriptions of required experiences as well as music and music teaching competencies that programs must be designed to develop. It also contains descriptions of teacher attributes that are considered desirable for effective teaching. Located in two sections of the *Handbook 2002–2003*, the first description lists "competencies common to all professional baccalaureate degrees in music and to all undergraduate degrees leading to teacher certification" (p. 81); the second includes the requirements for the baccalaureate degree in music education as well as a description of "desirable attributes, essential competencies, and professional procedures" (p. 93). The distinction between the terms "attributes" and "competencies" is both interesting and appropriate considering that some of the items listed are more general in nature, describing personal characteristics and attitudes rather than specific behaviors. Thus, the items range from rather specific, observable competencies (e.g., the ability to read music at sight with fluency) to desirable traits (e.g., a personal commitment to the art of music).

The competencies and teaching attributes included in the *NASM Handbook* have been approved, cumulatively, over many years by NASM members; they represent a work in progress, reflecting changes made in response to the needs of current music teacher education. During NASM accreditation evaluations, compliance with these standards receives its closest scrutiny. However, it is difficult to determine the extent to which these standards are given serious consideration by teacher education faculty when they develop courses and experiences for music teacher education programs. Obviously, when a competency is closely associated with the objectives of a required course, the relevance of the standard is clear (e.g., conducting skills are developed in conducting classes). However, due in part to the more general nature of some of the standards, as well as a shifting of language in the *Handbook* between the terms "should" and "must," it is less clear whether the NASM standards influence course content of music education programs in any pervasive fashion.

Some teacher educators apparently do not see NASM as an important source of objectives for teacher preparation. For example, Asmus (2000) asserts, "the profession, not NASM, needs to determine those competencies expected of our future music educators" (p. 5). Yet if the standards serve as a basis for program accreditation, albeit indirectly from NCATE through deferral to NASM, consensus among music teacher educators concerning the standards would seem to be important. However, it is not known how familiar music teacher educators are with the standards or to what extent they agree with them. No study of the opinions of music teacher educators concerning the standards has ever been undertaken. Thus, it is not known if the NASM standards influence the curriculum of teacher education or whether music teacher educators even agree that the competencies listed are important to successful music teaching. Undoubtedly, the NASM standards have been developed with input from music teacher educators over the years, yet no research has been conducted on this issue.

Moreover, the specific theoretical or research underpinnings of the NASM standards are not clear, but the competencies and attributes described in the *Handbook* seem to correspond with much of what is found in recent literature. The principal focus of the NASM standards is on musical and music teaching behaviors, which would be expected. While a number of generic teacher behaviors are included (e.g., the capability to inspire others), the emphasis of the NASM standards is on subject-matter competence developed through course work. It is assumed that competencies described in the standards are embedded in curricular offerings, yet verification of this notion has not been confirmed through research.

Research literature on the topic of standards for competent teaching is far-reaching and includes studies of cross-disciplinary, generic teacher behaviors as well as specific music teaching competencies. The competency-based teacher education movement that began some 30 years ago led to numerous studies aimed at developing descriptions of essential competencies for effective teaching (Beazley, 1981; Brophy & Good, 1986; Taebel, 1980; Taebel & Coker, 1980). Grant and Drafall (1991) summarized and reviewed an extensive history of studies and theoretical approaches to the study of teacher effectiveness. Investigators have attempted to define the content of and to measure the qualities and competencies associated with effective music teaching (Brand, 1984; Brophy, 1993; Hamann, Lineburgh, & Paul, 1998). Studies have also focused upon perceptions and conceptions of preservice and in-service teachers concerning various dimensions of teacher effectiveness (Butler, 2001; Cassidy, 1993; Duke & Madsen, 1991; Henninger, 2002; Madsen, Standley, & Cassidy, 1989). The basis for developing competencies has been rooted in theoretical models (Rosenshine & Furst, 1973), observations and descriptions of master teachers (Baker, 1981; Farmilo, 1981), and opinions of experts and practitioners (DePugh, 1987). Teachout (1997) compared the views of preservice and experienced teachers concerning effective teaching behaviors and found that 7 of the top-10-ranked behaviors overlapped between the two groups. He also found that many of the top-ranked characteristics were more generic in nature (e.g., enthusiastic, energetic) and that more musical behaviors (e.g., display a high level of musicianship) were ranked higher by preservice teachers than by experienced teachers.

Beyond issues of music teacher competency, another aspect of the current study about which little research has been conducted concerns the extent to which behaviors described in teacher education standards are considered "learnable." The "nature-nurture" debate (i.e., teachers are "born" not "made") is relevant to teacher education in that both prospective teachers and teacher educators may feel that some behaviors are more learnable than others. While no research has directly addressed this topic, rather extensive research has been done on the related issue of teacher efficacy (a teacher's belief or conviction that he or she can influence how well students learn). This line of research has sought to determine whether teachers' predispositions toward change in learners can influence their efforts (Bandura, 1977). In general, the research has shown that teacher attitudes are an important aspect of bringing about change in learners (Barnes, 1998; Shahid & Thompson, 2001). No research has examined efficacy in relation to learnability of teacher behaviors associated with music teaching, yet if teacher educators and preservice students do not believe that a certain competency or attribute is learnable, this could have implications for teacher education.

The purpose of the current study was to determine the views of music teacher education faculty and preservice music students concerning the NASM standards for music teacher education. The study was designed to determine, first, whether these respondents think that each standard is important for competent music teaching, and second, whether they believe that each standard is learnable during and as a result of the teacher education program.

Method

The survey instrument contained 45 items taken from the *NASM Handbook* available when the survey was developed (2002–2003); 38 of the items are common to all specializations, and the remaining items are specific to vocal/general and instrumental music education. While most of the questionnaire items described teacher competencies/attributes taken verbatim from the *Handbook*, several items had to be adapted slightly to be appropriate for the questionnaire. Items were organized by categories corresponding to those in the NASM standards, including those common to all baccalaureate degrees in music: (1) performance (7 items), (2) aural skills and analysis (3 items), (3) composition and improvisation (2 items), (4) history and repertory (2 items), (5) technology (2 items), and (6) synthesis (4 items); and those required for the baccalaureate degree in music education: (1) desirable attributes (7 items), (2) music competencies (5 items), (3) vocal/choral or general music teaching specialization (4 items), (4) instrumental music teaching specialization (3 items), and (5) teaching competencies for all specializations (6 items). Respondents were asked to rate the level of agreement or disagreement with each item using a 5-point Likert scale extending from strongly disagree (1) to strongly agree (5). A group of teacher educators and preservice music students responded to each item, rating its importance for both effective teaching and learnability through a teacher education program. Demographic information was also requested of all respondents. The survey took approximately 20 minutes to complete.

For purposes of the survey, teacher educator was defined as anyone directly involved in the teaching of required music education courses who was also considered to be a music education faculty member. The teacher educator respondents were recruited during three professional meetings. In the first, the survey was distributed to willing participants at a meeting of the Committee for Institutional Cooperation (CIC), a consortium of music teacher educators from the Big Ten athletic conference (University of Illinois, University of Minnesota, University of Michigan, University of Wisconsin, University of Iowa, Northwestern University, Indiana University, Pennsylvania State University, Michigan State University, and The Ohio State University). The meeting took place in October 2002 on the campus of the University of Illinois. Approximately 35 questionnaires were distributed; some attendees took forms back to their home campuses for colleagues who did not attend the CIC meeting. Questionnaires were also distributed at a meeting of the Ohio Society for Music Teacher Education ($n = 15$), a consortium of music teacher educators from teacher education institutions in the state of Ohio, and at a Research in Music Behavior Symposium held in March 2003 ($n = 20$), a research symposium of music teacher educators from across the United States. Thus, 70 questionnaires were distributed across the three conferences. Each participant received the questionnaire and a stamped return envelope addressed to the investigator. This approach resulted in a return of 27 questionnaires (38.5%).

The preservice music student respondents were defined as either undergraduate music students seeking a degree or postbaccalaureate students seeking initial licensure for music teaching. Subjects were students enrolled in the Introduction to Music Education courses at two major midwestern universities. All students in attendance on the day the questionnaire was distributed and who were willing to participate completed the questionnaire ($n = 52$).

Demographics were summarized descriptively, and rating responses were analyzed using SPSS statistical analysis software. Responses on the 1–5 scale were averaged for each item, resulting in mean ratings that were then ranked from highest to lowest for importance and learnability. In addition, independent t-tests were computed to compare mean ratings of teacher educators and preservice students on importance and learnability.

Results

Results of the demographic information of those surveyed revealed that the teacher educators ($n = 27$) had an average of 21 years of experience as teacher educators, ranging from 4 to 50 years. The areas of specialty were 52.6% general music, 15.8% choral, and 31.6% instrumental. For gender and race, 52.6% were women and 47.4% were men, with 89.5% categorizing themselves as White and 10.5% as Black. The preservice music students ($n = 52$) were 4.3% freshmen, 65.2% sophomores, 17.5% juniors, and 13% postbaccalaureate. Areas of specialization were 78.3% instrumental, 13.0% choral, and 8.7% general music. For gender and race, 56.5% were women and 43.5% were men, with 87.0% categorizing themselves as White, 10.8% as Black, and 2.2% as Hispanic.

The opinions of both teacher educators and preservice music students concerning the importance of each item for competent music teaching showed some variability, though most items received ratings of 4.0 or above (agree/strongly agree). The range of responses for teacher educators on the 38 common items was 3.80 to 4.89 (see Table 1), yet 24 of the items were rated 4.5 or higher; standard deviations were lower on the highest rated items than on the lowest rated items. Preservice music students' responses ranged from 3.82 to 4.93 (see Table 2), with 27 of the items being rated 4.5 or higher; standard deviations were lower on the highest rated items among students as well. Only two items received ratings below 4.0 from the students. It appears that both faculty and students consider these standards important for competent music teaching.

Table 1 and Table 2 show that the highest-ranked item was identical for both faculty and students ("personal commitment to the art of music"), and one low-ranked item ("the ability to compose …")

was the same for both (ranked 37th). This highest-ranked item is a very summative item, containing broad generalizations of attitudes, values, and behaviors. Given its comprehensive nature, it should perhaps come as no surprise that this is a highly rated item. Two of the three top-rated items were the same for both groups, yet students rated "conducting" as the third highest rated competency whereas it was ranked 22nd by faculty. Perhaps it would be expected that at this point in the curriculum (65.2% sophomores) and from this specialization (78.3% instrumental) that students would place a high premium on conducting. It is not uncommon for students to aspire to performance-oriented secondary teaching at this level, and this may account for the highly positive rating of the importance of conducting. Moreover, faculty categorized themselves primarily in the general music specialization (52.6%), which may also account for the somewhat lower rating of conducting compared to the students.

The relatively low rating of composing and improvising (see Table 1 and 2) was an interesting result. Given the fact that this is an objective of music education included in the *National Standards for Arts Education* (1994), a comprehensive description of what everyone should know and be able to do in music, it is somewhat surprising that faculty and students did not rate this item as being more important. However, when looking at ratings rather than rankings, a better perspective is perhaps gained since this and most other items were highly rated by all respondents.

Independent *t*-tests computed on the factor of importance for each item revealed only two items that had a significantly different rating from faculty and students. For the first, students rated "understanding basic interrelationships and interdependencies among the various professions and activities that constitute the musical enterprise" at 4.31, whereas faculty rated this at 3.80 ($p < .05$). For the second, "*Performance*. In addition to the skills for all musicians, functional ability in keyboard and other classroom instruments appropriate to the student's future teaching needs is essential," students rated this item significantly higher ($p < .05$) than did faculty (4.80 to 4.36, respectively).

A number of other items received interesting differential results with respect to means and variability. For example, the long tradition of requiring the development of keyboard skills continues today. Yet, compared to other items, this item received relatively low mean ratings and rankings from both faculty (4.30 rating and 25th ranking) and students (4.30 rating and 32nd ranking). The standard deviation for this competency was among the highest of all items for faculty ($SD = 1.03$), indicating a range of views on this traditional requirement. This finding parallels the results found in the Teachout (1997) study.

Another surprising finding with respect to traditional curriculum offerings concerned the importance of music teachers having "a basic knowledge of music history through the present time." The mean rating of faculty was 4.31 (31st ranking) with a standard deviation of 1.05, again indicating a wider range of responses. Student mean rating of this item was 4.39 (ranking 28th) with a standard deviation of .61. Again, the importance of these items does not seem to be in serious question, but opinions vary, and ratings compared to other items were surprisingly low.

Turning to the issue of learnability, respondents indicated the extent to which they agreed (5 = strongly agree) or disagreed (1 = strongly disagree) that each item described something that is learnable during and as a result of the teacher education program. Opinions concerning the learnability of each competency/attribute varied considerably among respondents. As can been seen from Table 3 and Table 4, the faculty generally tended to rate items higher (more learnable) than students, with the lowest-rated item being 3.94 for faculty and 3.50 for students. As can be seen, standard deviations, even for the highest-rated items, were considerably greater for learnability than importance for both groups, suggesting that views on this factor were less cohesive. No highest-rated or lowest-rated items were the same when comparing students' responses to those of the faculty. From Table 4 it can be seen that the closest agreement was for "the ability to place music in historical, cultural and stylistic contexts," rated third highest by students and fourth highest by faculty.

Faculty members rated performance skills and theoretical knowledge as very learnable (see Table 3), whereas some of the more general behaviors associated with teaching (e.g., the capability to inspire others) were rated lower. Students rated conducting as the most learnable competency, whereas faculty ranked it in 26th place (see Table 4). The other two items highly rated as learnable by students concerned learning music history. However, students seemed to doubt that composing and improvising are very learnable behaviors in that they gave the lowest ratings to two items addressing this aspect (Table 4).

Table 5 summarizes all items for which independent t-tests revealed significant differences ($p < .05$) between students and faculty on the factor of learnability. Further substantiating the fact that students are less optimistic about the learnability of these behaviors is the fact that, in every case, the mean ratings of these items were significantly lower for students. Moreover, students rated 14 items below 4.0, yet faculty rated only two items below this level. Apparently, faculty's perceptions of efficacy concerning a number of these behaviors are higher than those of students.

Discussion

This study of the NASM standards for music teacher education has indicated that a substantial majority of the teacher competencies and attributes described in the *NASM Handbook* are regarded as important for music teaching competence by both teacher education faculty members and preservice music students. Few of the 38 items listed received a mean rating lower than 4 points on the scale from 1 (strongly disagree) to 5 (strongly agree). Moreover, only two items showed significantly different opinions between faculty and students on the issue of importance. Apparently NASM has succeeded in providing a set of expectations that are considered important for successful teaching. However, an examination of comments from teacher education faculty suggests that these standards may be considered necessary but not sufficient. One respondent commented, "I'd add competencies in interpersonal relationships, leadership ability, and sufficient self-confidence to provide 'teacher presence'"; another added that it is important for teachers to learn "communication with parents/community"; and still another wrote, "These are pretty comprehensive. The only omission I see is 'Delivery of Instruction,' such as rapidly engaging learners, providing appropriate feedback and correction of errors, development of the 'teacher presence,' designing instruction that results in good classroom management, rapport with students (eye contact, vocal projection and enthusiasm), etc."

There were somewhat surprising results for some of the traditional requirements in the music curriculum. Keyboard competency received mixed opinions and was not rated as high as were many other items in the survey. While there is no way to compare these results to views from years past, it may well be that this attitude reflects changes in technology. Perhaps the demands for keyboard skills were more prevalent in years past, whereas the use of sequencing and other software has raised questions concerning the necessity of traditional keyboard skills, especially for certain specializations (e.g., instrumental). More surprising was the relatively low rating of basic knowledge of music history. It is difficult to interpret this response. The reference to knowledge of history "to the present time" may have affected those who feel that more contemporary music history is not as important. This potential for confusion and open interpretation plagues this and many other items. Moreover, it may well be that respondents took this to mean the study of Western classical music, and perhaps with the growing emphasis upon non-Western (world) music, this item received less enthusiasm. In fact, the rating of another item suggests this is the case. Under the main heading of "music competencies" and the item heading "analysis/history/literature," a clearer reference to "the literature of diverse cultural sources" is included. This item was rated and ranked higher than the aforementioned music history item among faculty and students.

These overall positive responses to most items perhaps should be expected considering the very general nature of the descriptions. Many of the items contain multiple demands, any one of which may be the principal factor influencing the response. Different and more discriminating results might well occur if an item were broken down into more discrete parts. For example, a requirement that is often at issue when programs are undergoing accreditation review concerns functional knowledge of wind, string, percussion, and voice for all specializations. With so many items included, respondents were not allowed to agree with some and disagree with others. Moreover, lack of clarity of some items may also affect opinions. Rather high standard deviations occurred for a number of items suggesting perhaps a range of views or perhaps a lack of understanding of the item. For example, "the ability to read [music] at sight with fluency" received a mean rating of 4.50 from both faculty and students, yet the standard deviation for faculty was .98 and for students was .69. Because this item is under the "performance" category, presumably the item refers to fluency in sight reading on one's principal instrument. If it were to fall under the heading of "aural skills and analysis," it might be interpreted to mean sight-singing ability, which is an altogether different competency. Interestingly, sight singing and dictation (melodic, harmonic, or rhythmic) are never directly listed as competencies, yet these are major components of the music curriculum in schools of music.

Importance received higher ratings than learnability for all items (overall mean of 4.58 for importance compared to 4.19 for learnability). The issue of learnability generated interesting and varied results, and the most disagreement between students and faculty occurred in the ratings of this factor. Teacher educators were notably more optimistic about the learnability of these behaviors than were preservice music students. In fact, the overall mean rating of learnability for all factors was 4.44 for faculty and 4.09 for students. The more positive attitudes of teacher educators may reflect a kind of teacher efficacy for teacher education, an affirmation that their professional raison d'etre is not in question. Students, on the other hand, appear somewhat skeptical about certain behaviors. Even their highest-rated behavior (conducting) was rated lower than the highest behavior of the faculty (performance skills) with respect to learnability. This may be a result of the level of the students involved in this survey (65.2% sophomores); perhaps by the time they are seniors, their views of learnability will change. In the meantime, teacher educators may need to transmit some of their optimism and to help students believe that these important aspects of successful teaching are learnable and that the curriculum, in time, will help them develop these competencies.

References

Asmus, E. (2000). Foundation competencies for music teachers. *Journal of Music Teacher Education, 9*(2), 5–6.

Baker, P. J. (1981). *The development of music teacher checklists for use by administrators, music supervisors, and teachers in evaluating music teacher effectiveness.* Unpublished doctoral dissertation, University of Oregon, Eugene.

Bandura, A. (1977). Self-efficacy: Toward a unifying theory of behavioral change. *Psychological Review, 84*(2), 191–215.

Barnes, G. (1998). *A comparison of self-efficacy and teaching effectiveness in preservice string teachers.* Unpublished doctoral dissertation, The Ohio State University, Columbus.

Beazley, H. V. (1981). Development and validation of a music education competency test. *Journal of Research in Music Education, 29*, 5–10. Brand, M. (1984). *Music teacher effectiveness research.* Houston, TX: Author. (ERIC Document Reproduction Service No. ED253 443)

Brophy, T. (1993). *Evaluation of music educators: Toward defining an appropriate instrument.* (ERIC Document Reproduction Service No. ED375029)

Brophy, J., & Good, T. L. (1986). Teacher behavior and student achievement. In M. Wittrock (Ed.), *Handbook of research on teaching* (3rd ed.) (pp. 328–375). New York: Macmillan.

Butler, A. (2001). Preservice music teachers' conceptions of teaching effectiveness, microteaching experiences, and teaching performance. *Journal of Research in Music Education, 49*, 258–272.

Cassidy, J. W. (1993). A comparison between students' self observation and instructor observation of teacher intensity behaviors. *Bulletin of the Council for Research in Music Education, 115*, 15–29.

Consortium of National Arts Education Associations. (1994). *National standards for arts education.* Reston, VA: MENC.

DePugh, D. L. (1987). *Characteristics of successful senior high school choral directors in the state of Missouri: A survey of teacher self-perception and student and administrator assessment.* Unpublished doctoral dissertation, University of Missouri, Columbia.

Duke, R. A., & Madsen, C. K. (1991). Proactive versus reactive teaching: Focusing observation on specific aspects of instruction. *Bulletin of the Council for Research in Music Education, 108*, 1–14.

Farmilo, N. R. (1981). *The creativity, teaching style, and personality characteristics of the effective elementary music teacher*. Unpublished doctoral dissertation, Wayne State University, Detroit, Michigan.

Grant, J. W., & Drafall, L. E. (1991). Teacher effectiveness research: A review and comparison. *Bulletin of the Council for Research in Music Education, 108*, 31–48.

Hamann, D. L., Lineburgh, N., & Paul, S. J. (1998). Teaching effectiveness and social skill development. *Journal of Research in Music Education, 46*, 87–101.

Henninger, J. C. (2002). The effects of knowledge of instructional goals on observations of teaching and learning. *Journal of Research in Music Education, 50*, 37–50.

Madsen, C. K., Standley, J. M., & Cassidy, J. W. (1989). Demonstrations of high and low contrasts in teacher intensity. *Journal of Research in Music Education, 37*, 85–92.

National Association of Schools of Music handbook (2002–2003). Reston, VA: National Association for Schools of Music.

Rosenshine, B., & Furst, N. (1973). The use of direct observation to study teaching. In R. M. W. Travers (Ed.), *Second handbook of research on teaching* (pp. 122–183). Chicago: Rand McNally.

Shahid, J., & Thompson, D. (2001, April). *Teacher efficacy: A research synthesis*. Paper presented at the annual meeting of the American Educational Research Association, Seattle, WA.

Taebel, D. K. (1980). Public school music teachers' perceptions of the effect of certain competencies on pupil learning. *Journal of Research in Music Education, 28*, 185–197.

Taebel, D. K., & Coker, J. G. (1980). Teaching effectiveness in elementary classroom music: Relationships among competency measures, pupil product measures and certain attribute variables. *Journal of Research in Music Education, 28*, 250–264.

Teachout, J. D. (1997). Preservice and experienced teachers' opinions of skills and behaviors important to successful music teaching. *Journal of Research in Music Education, 45*, 41–50.

Table 1. Highest and Lowest Mean Ratings of Importance by Teacher Educators (*n* = 27)

Attribute/Competency	Mean	SD
Highest		
1. Personal commitment to the art of music, to teaching music as an element of civilization, and to encouraging the artistic and intellectual development of students, plus ability to fulfill these commitments as an independent professional. (PMS Rank 1)*	4.89	.32
2. The ability to work productively within specific education systems, promote scheduling patterns that optimize music instruction, maintain positive relationships with individuals of various social and ethnic groups, and be empathetic with students and colleagues of differing backgrounds. (PMS Rank 5)	4.84	.38
3. The capability to inspire others and to excite the imagination of students, engendering a respect for music and a desire for musical knowledge and experiences. (PMS Rank 2)	4.84	.50
Lowest		
36. *Arranging*. The prospective music teacher should be able to arrange and adapt music from a variety of sources to meet the needs and ability levels of school performing groups and classroom situations. (PMS Rank 25)	4.16	.71
37. The ability to compose, improvise, or both, at a basic level in one or more musical languages. For example the imitation of various musical styles, improvisation on preexisting materials, the creation of original compositions, experimentation with various sound sources, and manipulating the common elements in nontraditional ways are essential. (PMS Rank 37)	4.05	.52
38. Understanding basic interrelationships and interdependencies among the various professions and activities that constitute the musical enterprise. (PMS Rank 33)	3.80	.96

* Preservice Music Students' Rank of Same Item

Table 2. Highest and Lowest Mean Ratings of Importance by Preservice Music Students ($n = 52$)

Attribute/Competency	Mean	SD
Highest		
1. Personal commitment to the art of music, to teaching music as an element of civilization, and to encouraging the artistic and intellectual development of students, plus ability to fulfill these commitments as an independent professional. (TE Rank 1)*	4.93	.33
2. The capability to inspire others and to excite the imagination of students, engendering a respect for music and a desire for musical knowledge and experiences. (TE Rank 3)	4.91	.28
3. *Conducting.* The prospective music teacher must be a competent conductor, able to create accurate and musically expressive performances with various types of performing groups and in general classroom situations. They must be competent in score reading and the integration of analysis, style, performance practices, instrumentation, and baton techniques. (TE Rank 22)	4.87	.34
Lowest		
36. Working knowledge of the technological developments applicable to the area of specialization. (TE Rank 34)	4.06	.98
37. The ability to compose, improvise, or both, at a basic level in one or more musical languages. For example, the imitation of various musical styles, improvisation on preexisting materials, the creation of original compositions, experimentation with various sound sources, and manipulating the common elements in nontraditional ways are essential. (TE Rank 37)	3.88	.86
38. Rudimentary capacity to create derivative or original music both extemporaneously and in written form. (TE Rank 35)	3.82	.90

* Teacher Educators' Rank of Same Item

Table 3. Highest and Lowest Mean Ratings of Learnability by Teacher Educators (*n* = 27)

Attribute/Competency	Mean	SD
Highest		
1. Technical skills requisite for artistic self-expression in at least one major performance area at a level appropriate for the particular musical concentration. (PMS Rank 6)*	4.72	.46
2. An understanding of the common elements and organizational patterns of music and their interaction, and the ability to employ this understanding in aural, verbal and visual analyses. (PMS Rank 16)	4.66	.59
3. The ability to read at sight with fluency. (PMS Rank 19)	4.66	.49
Lowest		
36. The capability to inspire others and to excite the imagination of students, engendering a respect for music and a desire for musical knowledge and experiences. (PMS Rank 35)	4.05	.78
37. The ability to work within specific education systems, promote scheduling patterns that optimize music instruction, maintain positive relationships with individuals of various social and ethnic groups, and be empathetic with students and colleagues of differing backgrounds. (PMS Rank 31)	3.94	.85
38. Understanding basic interrelationships and interdependencies among the various professions and activities that constitute the musical enterprise. (PMS Rank 28)	3.94	.97

* Preservice Music Students' Rank of Same Item

Table 4. Highest and Lowest Mean Ratings of Learnability by Preservice Music Students (*n* = 52)

Attribute/Competency	Mean	*SD*
Highest		
1. *Conducting.* The prospective music teacher must be a competent conductor, able to create accurate and musically expressive performances with various types of performing groups and in general classroom situations. They must be competent in score reading and the integration of analysis, style, performance practices, instrumentation, and baton techniques. (TE Rank 26)*	4.57	.56
2. A basic knowledge of music history through the present time. (TE Rank 12)	4.45	.66
3. The ability to place music in historical, cultural and stylistic contexts. (TE Rank 4)	4.43	.62
Lowest		
36. Forming and defending value judgments about music. (TE Rank 30)	3.64	.93
37. Rudimentary capacity to create derivative or original music both extemporaneously and in written form. (TE Rank 34)	3.58	.86
38. The ability to compose, improvise, or both, at a basic level in one or more musical languages. For example, the imitation of various musical styles, improvisation on preexisting materials, the creation of original compositions, experimentation with various sound sources, and manipulating the common elements in nontraditional ways are essential. (TE Rank 22)	3.50	.94

* Teacher Educators' Rank of Same Item

Table 5. Significant Differences ($p < .05$) of Mean Ratings of Learnability by Groups

Attribute/Competency	Teacher Educators ($n = 27$)		Preservice Students ($n = 52$)	
	M	*SD*	*M*	*SD*
Technical skills requisite for artistic self-expression in at least one major performance area at a level appropriate for the particular musical concentration.	4.72	.46	4.32	.60
The ability to read (music) at sight with fluency.	4.66	.48	4.06	.83
An understanding of the common elements and organizational patterns of music and their interactions, and the ability to employ this understanding in aural, verbal and visual analyses.	4.66	.59	4.15	.92
The ability to compose, improvise, or both, at a basic level in one or more musical languages. For example, the imitation of various musical styles, improvisation on preexisting materials, the creation of original compositions, experimentation with various sound sources, and manipulating the common elements in nontraditional ways are essential.	4.37	.50	3.50	.94
Working independently on a variety of musical problems by combining one's capabilities in performance, aural, verbal and visual analysis, composition and improvisation, and history and repertory.	4.73	.56	4.31	.73
The ability to lead students to an understanding of music as an art form, as a means of communication, and as a part of their intellectual and cultural heritage.	4.42	.96	3.91	.81
An understanding of child growth and development and an understanding of principles of learning as they relate to music.	4.57	.68	4.17	.71
The ability to assess aptitudes, experiential backgrounds, orientations of individuals and groups of students, and the nature of subject matter, and to plan educational programs to meet assessed needs.	4.52	.96	3.80	.78
An understanding of evaluative techniques and ability to apply them in assessing both the musical progress of students and the objectives and procedures of the curriculum.	4.47	.70	4.04	.70

An Exploratory Study of the Impact of Field Experiences on Music Education Majors' Attitudes and Perceptions of Music for Secondary Students with Special Needs

By Kimberly VanWeelden and Jennifer Whipple

Kimberly VanWeelden is an associate professor of music education at Florida State University in Tallahassee. She can be reached at kvanwee@garnet.acns.fsu.edu. Jennifer Whipple is legislative policy analyst in the Office of Program Policy Analysis and Government Accountability for the Florida legislature. She can be reached at jenniferwhipple@comcast.com.

Researchers have found that the single most important variable in the success of mainstreaming is the attitude of the teacher toward students with special needs (Stone & Brown, 1987). Studies investigating attitudes toward special learners in music have found music educators generally have positive attitudes toward the concept of mainstreaming (Brittin, 1995; Hawkins, 1992; Sideridis & Chandler, 1995; White, 1981–1982; Wilson & McCrary, 1996). However, many music educators have expressed reluctance to work with students with special needs due to increased challenges of classroom management (Hawkins, 1992), the need to acquire new skills and competencies to adapt instruction (Sideridis & Chandler, 1995), and the need to create a successful learning environment for all students (Gfeller, Darrow, & Hedden, 1990). These concerns have become the impetus for greater training within music education undergraduate curricula so as to prepare preservice teachers to meet the current challenges of the profession.

Descriptive research examining institutions that offer undergraduate degrees in music education has found that many of them require coursework designed to prepare preservice music teachers to work with special learners (Colwell & Thompson, 2000; Heller, 1995; Schmidt, 1989). It is reasonable to assume that these courses are included in teacher training programs to help foster positive attitudes toward working with students with special needs as well as to provide information to assist with challenges preservice teachers may encounter while working with special learners in music. However, Colwell and Thompson (2000) recommend further investigation of the nature of this coursework to determine what content is covered and whether these courses offer future music educators field-based experiences working with students with special needs in music settings.

While several studies have investigated in-service music educators' attitudes toward students with special needs, to date little research has been conducted investigating the effects of field experiences with special learners on preservice teachers' perceptions of music for these students. Two studies, however, relate closely to the current paper. In the first, Kaiser and Johnson (2000) examined the effect of an interactive experience on music majors' perceptions of music for deaf students. A pretest questionnaire was administered to all participants, followed by a 30-minute description of the experience and a one-time interaction with the students. The interaction consisted of a performance by the university students; visual-tactile demonstrations of sound vibrations and pitch; and opportunities for the children to feel, play, and conduct the instruments. At the conclusion of the study, a posttest was administered for comparison analysis. Results revealed positive changes in music majors' perceptions of music for deaf students and in their confidence in their ability to work with deaf children in music settings.

In the second study, VanWeelden and Whipple (2005) examined the effect of field experiences on music education majors' perceptions of music instruction for secondary students with special needs. A pretest questionnaire was administered to all preservice teachers followed by one week of preparation for the field experience, then by 10 general music experiences with middle school students with special needs. The preservice teachers were divided into two groups: one to work with students with emotional and/or behavioral disorders and one to work with students with acute cognitive delays. All preservice teachers were given the responsibility of planning, preparing, and teaching specific music concepts from an adaptive secondary general music curriculum within their assigned classrooms over the course of 5 weeks. At the end of the field experience, preservice teachers completed a posttest questionnaire for comparison analysis. Results revealed preservice teachers felt significantly more positive about using music in the education of secondary students with special needs after the field experience.

Both field experience studies revealed that preservice teachers' perceptions of music for the populations served became more positive after the interaction (Kaiser & Johnson, 2000; VanWeelden & Whipple, 2005). However, because preservice teachers worked with only one subpopulation of students with special needs, the question whether preservice teachers would display differences in their attitudes and perceptions if they worked with more than one subpopulation of students with special needs within a field experience has yet to be answered. Therefore, the purpose of the current study was to compare the effect of a long-term field experience on music education students' attitudes and perceptions of music for secondary students with special needs within two subpopulations. Three attitude and two perception questions were examined. The attitude questions were (a) Do field experiences change preservice teachers' attitudes about their *personal comfort* when working with persons with physical, mental, and emotional disabilities? (b) Do field experiences change preservice teachers' attitudes about their *professional comfort* when working with students with special needs? and (c) Do field experiences change preservice teachers' attitudes about their *willingness* to work with students with special needs? The perception questions were (a) Do field experiences change preservice teachers' perceptions of whether their educational training prepared them to work with students with special needs? and (b) Do field experiences change preservice teachers' perceptions of behavior and learning of students with special needs? Additionally, comparisons were made between preservice teachers who worked with one subpopulation of students with special needs in a previous study (VanWeelden & Whipple, 2005) and those who worked with two subpopulations in the present study.

Method

The subjects ($N = 59$) were undergraduate music education majors at a large university enrolled in a course titled Assessment and Teaching Music: Secondary. This course was part of the undergraduate music education curriculum and included students focusing on choral, instrumental, or general music. Music education majors ($n = 31$) who worked with two subpopulations of students with special needs had 9 weeks of in-class instruction (Monday, Wednesday, and Friday every week) and 6 weeks of field-based secondary general music lab experience (working with secondary students with special needs on Monday and Friday) during the spring 2004 ($n = 16$) and fall 2004 ($n = 15$) semesters. Music education majors ($n = 28$) who worked with one subpopulation of students with special needs in the previous study had 10 weeks of in-class instruction (Monday, Wednesday, and Friday every week) and 5 weeks of field-based secondary general music lab experience (working with secondary students with special needs on Monday and Friday) during the fall 2002 ($n = 13$) and spring 2003 ($n = 15$) semesters (VanWeelden & Whipple, 2005).

In-class Instruction

The in-class instruction encompassed activities pertaining to various aspects of teaching general music within secondary schools. Specifically, five broad areas were covered: (a) song leading, Orff instrumental orchestrations, world music and dance, and Western art music microteaching; (b) music listening; (c) musical games; (d) issues within secondary schools; and (e) assessment and evaluation procedures. The first three areas gave the preservice teachers an opportunity to plan and teach various musical activities that would be appropriate for a secondary general music class. No accommodations for special learners were required for these activities. The last two areas included multiple assignments, lectures, and readings for accommodating and grading students with and without special needs in secondary general music class settings.

Work with Students with Special Needs

The field-based secondary general music lab experience entailed working with students with special needs at a local middle school. These students were primarily educated within a self-contained, special education setting and were divided into two classrooms based on the students' special needs. The first class consisted of students with emotional and/or behavioral disorders (EDBD), whose special needs often result in academic delays. The second class contained students who exhibited acute cognitive delays (ACD), such as autism, Down syndrome, mental retardation, and extensive learning disabilities. Each classroom had 11 to 15 students representative of standard middle school ages.

Field-Based Experiences

During the spring and fall 2004 semesters, preservice music educators worked with students in both the EDBD and ACD classrooms. The classes were taught at the same time but in separate locations. Preservice teachers were divided into two groups of eight. Each group was assigned to work with students in one of the classrooms for the first 3 weeks of the experience, then moved to the other classroom for the remaining 3 weeks. In the previous study during the fall 2002 and spring 2003 semesters, the preservice teachers were also divided into two groups. However, preservice teachers worked only with students in either the EDBD or ACD classroom for the entire experience. During all semesters, each classroom was supervised by one of the researchers. Additionally, all the preservice teachers were grouped based on their gender and major emphasis (choral, instrumental, or general) to create roughly the same preservice teacher demographics within each classroom. Preservice teachers were further divided into teaching groups of three or four persons, creating two teaching groups per classroom, using the same demographic considerations. The researchers determined all divisions prior to the field experiences.

The researchers created four secondary general music curricula, one for each semester, that were used as the foundation for the field teaching experiences. The curricula contained the same types of activities found in the in-class portion of the course, specifically, song leading, Orff instrumental orchestrations, world music and dance, Western art music, music listening, and musical games. Because most of the students with special needs participated during multiple field experience semesters (i.e., both when preservice teachers taught one subpopulation and when they taught two subpopulations), different curricula were needed to provide new variations of these activities for the students. The only exceptions to this were the opening and closing songs sung by all students and preservice teachers during all semesters.

The week immediately prior to the field experience was devoted to explaining logistics, dividing the preservice teachers into teaching groups, discussing the curriculum, and giving the teaching groups time to plan and prepare for their first teaching experience. During the first week of the field-based experience, preservice teachers introduced themselves, created name tags for each student, sat interspersed with the students, and participated as teaching assistants while the researchers taught the lessons. The purpose of this first week was to give the preservice teachers time to acclimate to the experience and students without the additional responsibilities of teaching.

Beginning in the second week, the preservice teacher groups were given responsibility for preparing and teaching all aspects of the lessons. Since there were two preservice teaching groups per classroom, the groups alternated lesson responsibilities every other lesson (spring 2004/fall 2004) or every other week (fall 2002/spring 2003). Each lesson contained four activities from the curriculum, giving each member of a teaching group the opportunity to plan and lead the class during the lesson. Additionally, preservice teachers were required to teach a different part of the curriculum every lesson. When groups were not actively involved teaching the lesson, they acted as teaching assistants to help students individually. During the last teaching experience for each group, preservice teachers were responsible for planning and preparing the lesson without guidelines provided by the researchers. The researchers guided individual preservice teachers and teaching groups in preparing lessons as needed to capitalize on strengths of the students within the classrooms to which they were assigned.

Additionally, the researchers met with the preservice teaching groups immediately after each teaching session to aid their self-evaluation. At the end of the spring and fall 2004 semesters, each preservice teacher had taught twice within both the EDBD and ACD classrooms, taught in four different general music curricular areas, and assisted individual students with various musical tasks during 12 class periods. Preservice teachers involved in the field experience during the fall 2002 and spring 2003 semesters taught four times in different general music curricular areas and assisted individual students with various musical tasks during 10 class periods in either the EDBD or ACD classroom.

The Survey Instrument

The dependent variable was a survey comprising 17 questions about the preservice teachers' attitudes and perceptions of music for secondary students with special needs, including how comfortable, willing, prepared, and perceptive they were in working with special learners. This questionnaire was fashioned after a similar survey instrument used by Kaiser and Johnson (2000), who investigated the effect of an interactive experience on music majors' perceptions of music for deaf students, and was piloted by the authors in previous studies with a comparable population of preservice teachers teaching students with special needs (VanWeelden & Whipple, 2005). Prior to any in-class discussion relating to students with special needs or general music lab experience, teacher-subjects for all semesters were asked to complete the pretest questionnaire. At the conclusion of the field experience, teacher-subjects were asked to complete the same questionnaire, creating a pretest-posttest design. All survey questions used a 5-point Likert-type scale ranging from "strongly disagree" to "strongly agree" to ensure all participants interpreted the rating scale in the same direction. Questions are listed in Figure 1.

Results

To begin the analysis, questions were grouped according to the following categories: personal attitudes (questions 1, 2, 3, and 4); professional attitudes (questions 5, 9, 10, and 11); attitudes of willingness (questions 12, 13, and 14); perceptions of teacher preparation (questions 6, 7, and 8); and perceptions of student behavior and learning (questions 15, 16, and 17). A one-way ANOVA comparing the pretest scores of the preservice teachers who worked with one population of students with special needs to those who worked with two populations of students with special needs was completed for each category. No significant differences were found between the two groups of preservice teachers for any category. Another one-way ANOVA was conducted to compare the posttest scores of the preservice teachers who worked with one population to those who worked with two populations of special learners. Again, no significant differences were found between the two groups of teachers within any attitudinal or perception category.

To determine whether preservice teachers' attitudes and perceptions changed over the course of the two types of field experiences, one-way ANOVAs for both preservice teacher groups were conducted. Significant increases from pretest to posttest were found for both teacher groups. For the group of preservice teachers who worked with two populations of students with special needs, scores significantly increased after the field experience within the categories of personal attitudes [$F(1, 60) = 34.41, p < .001$], professional attitudes [$F(1, 60) = 11.03, p = .002$], and perceptions of teacher preparation [$F(1, 60) = 9.79, p = .03$]. Significant increases were also found when all categories were combined, creating an overall pretest and posttest score [$F(1,60) = 20.60, p < .001$]. Attitudes regarding willingness and perceptions of student behavior and learning both increased, though not significantly.

For the group of preservice teachers who worked with one population of students with special needs, scores significantly increased after the field experience within the categories of personal attitudes [$F(1, 54) = 6.20, p = .016$], professional attitudes [$F(1, 54) = 11.34, p = .001$], and perceptions of teacher preparation [$F(1, 54) = 18.46, p < .001$]. Significant increases were also found when all categories were combined, creating an overall pretest and posttest score [$F(1, 54) = 9.58, p = .003$]. Attitudes regarding willingness and perceptions of student behavior and learning both improved, though not significantly. Refer to Table 1.

Discussion

The field experiences described in this study gave preservice teachers an opportunity to work with students with special needs in self-contained, special education classrooms. Neither field experience structure (i.e., teaching one versus two subpopulations) gave the preservice teachers the opportunity to work with students with and without special needs together in one classroom. This may explain why preservice teachers' perceptions of the behavior and learning capabilities of the students with special needs, compared to other children of the same age, did not change significantly after either type of field experience. However, the personal attitudes of the preservice teachers, when interacting with persons with physical, mental, and emotional special needs, did become more positive after the field experience, regardless of whether they worked with one population or two populations of students with special needs. Similar results were found within the professional attitudes category where both preservice teacher groups' attitudes toward working with students with special needs in music settings improved. Positive teacher attitudes, both personal and professional, are important components in the successful inclusion of special learners in music classrooms (Stone & Brown, 1987).

Research has found that music educators generally have positive attitudes toward the concept of mainstreaming (Brittin, 1995; Hawkins, 1992; Wilson & McCrary, 1996), yet they have expressed negative attitudes regarding the actual integration of students with mental, emotional, and behavioral disabilities in general music classrooms (Sideridis & Chandler, 1995). The personal and professional attitudes of the preservice teachers within this study, however, became more positive after interacting with students with special needs in the general music lab experience. Thus, it seems, combining knowledge and teaching skills acquired in class with direct hands-on application with either one or two populations of special learners can alter preservice teacher attitudes, since both types of field experiences achieved comparable outcomes.

The preservice teachers' perceptions of educational preparation to work with students with special needs in music education settings were rated significantly higher at the end of the field experience. A major factor of working in the field during preservice training is to practice and prepare for "real-life" experiences. Since this field experience was designed to prepare preservice teachers to successfully work with students with special needs in music, the results of the study indicate this goal was met.

Willingness to work with students with special needs in the future also showed increases for both groups of preservice teachers (either one or two populations), though neither was significant. This was the only category of questions that asked preservice teachers to predict future activities. Because most preservice teachers do not know what type of position they will take after their internship, speculation could have been difficult for the teachers. However, the preservice teachers did have significant improvement in their personal and professional attitudes and when all categories were combined. Therefore, a longitudinal study during the preservice teachers' internship and/or after they are working within the profession could be used to investigate whether attitudes regarding willingness to work with students with special needs in their specific music education setting have changed. In addition, the use of interviews and observations could further help answer the research questions found herein and may be beneficial in future study.

It is interesting to note that both field experiences produced the same outcomes. Creating and arranging a successful field-based experience can be a time-consuming and logistically challenging endeavor for the university music education faculty. We believed that the more diverse experiences that were provided for preservice teachers to work with various subpopulations of students with special needs, the better prepared they would be for later employment situations. However, the results of this study indicate preservice teachers' attitudes and perceptions improved regardless of how many populations they worked with during the field experience. Ultimately, it seems that any experience working with students with special needs may be beneficial because it is impossible to prepare preservice music teachers for every situation. Furthermore, good teaching is good teaching, regardless of the presence or absence of student disabilities. In regular, inclusive, and self-contained classrooms, the goal is to break down the task in whatever way necessary to best meet student needs. Therefore, future teacher trainers may not need to incorporate numerous subpopulations of students with special needs within their field experiences in order for preservice teachers to benefit.

References

Brittin, R. V. (1995, November). *Changing music educators' attitudes toward inclusion of students with disabilities.* Poster session presented at the annual meeting of the National Association for Music Therapy, Houston, TX.

Colwell, C. M., & Thompson, L. K. (2000). "Inclusion" of information on mainstreaming in undergraduate music education curricula. *Journal of Music Therapy, 37*(3), 205–221.

Gfeller, K., Darrow, A. A., & Hedden, S. K. (1990). Perceived effectiveness of mainstreaming in Iowa and Kansas schools. *Journal of Research in Music Education, 38*, 90–101.

Hawkins, G. D. (1992). Attitudes toward mainstreaming students with disabilities among regular elementary music and physical educators (Doctoral dissertation, University of Maryland, College Park, 1991). *Dissertation Abstracts International, 52*, 3245A.

Heller, L. (1995). Undergraduate music teacher preparation for mainstreaming: A survey of music education teacher training institutions in the Great Lakes region of the United States (Doctoral dissertation, Michigan State University, 1994). *Dissertation Abstracts International, 56*, 858A.

Kaiser, K. A., & Johnson, K. E. (2000). The effect of an interactive experience on music majors' perceptions of music for deaf students. *Journal of Music Therapy, 37*(3), 222–234.

Schmidt, C. P. (1989). An investigation of undergraduate music education curriculum content. *Bulletin of the Council for Research in Music Education, 99*, 42–56.

Sideridis, G. D., & Chandler, J. P. (1995). Attitudes and characteristics of general music teachers toward integrating children with developmental disabilities. *Update: Applications of Research in Music Education, 14*(1), 11–15.

Stone, B., & Brown, R. (1987). Preparing teachers for mainstreaming: Some critical variables for effective preservice programs. *Educational Research Quarterly, 11*(2), 7–10.

VanWeelden, K., & Whipple, J. (2005). The effect of field experiences on music education majors' perceptions of music instruction for secondary students with special needs. *Journal of Music Teacher Education, 14*(2), 62–69.

White, L. D. (1981–1982). A study of attitudes of selected public school music educators toward the integration of handicapped students in music classes. *Contributions to Music Education, 9*(5), 36–47.

Wilson, B., & McCrary, J. (1996). The effect of instruction on music educators' attitudes toward students with disabilities. *Journal of Research in Music Education, 44*, 26–33.

Figure 1. Survey Instrument Questions

1. I am comfortable interacting with middle school students.

    Strongly Disagree   Strongly Agree
        1   2   3   4   5

2. I am comfortable interacting with people with physical disabilities.

    Strongly Disagree   Strongly Agree
        1   2   3   4   5

3. I am comfortable interacting with people with mental disabilities.

    Strongly Disagree   Strongly Agree
        1   2   3   4   5

4. I am comfortable interacting with people with emotional disabilities.

    Strongly Disagree   Strongly Agree
        1   2   3   4   5

5. I believe music education should be a part of the curriculum for students with special needs.

    Strongly Disagree   Strongly Agree
        1   2   3   4   5

6. I feel my educational training has prepared me to work with students with special needs in a secondary general music class setting.

    Strongly Disagree   Strongly Agree
        1   2   3   4   5

7. I feel my educational training has prepared me to work with students with special needs in a music ensemble setting.

    Strongly Disagree   Strongly Agree
        1   2   3   4   5

8. I feel my educational training has prepared me to work with students with special needs in a private music studio setting.

    Strongly Disagree   Strongly Agree
        1   2   3   4   5

9. I would be comfortable working with students with special needs in a secondary general music classroom.

 Strongly Disagree   Strongly Agree
  1   2   3   4   5

10. I would be comfortable working with students with special needs in a private studio for music lessons.

 Strongly Disagree   Strongly Agree
  1   2   3   4   5

11. I would be comfortable working with students with special needs in a music ensemble.

 Strongly Disagree   Strongly Agree
  1   2   3   4   5

12. I would be willing to provide music experiences to students with special needs in a secondary general music classroom.

 Strongly Disagree   Strongly Agree
  1   2   3   4   5

13. I would be willing to provide music experiences to students with special needs in a secondary performance ensemble.

 Strongly Disagree   Strongly Agree
  1   2   3   4   5

14. I would be willing to provide music experiences to students with special needs in a special education classroom.

 Strongly Disagree   Strongly Agree
  1   2   3   4   5

15. I believe students with special needs behave in class the same as other students their age.

 Strongly Disagree   Strongly Agree
  1   2   3   4   5

16. I believe students with special needs can learn the same musical material as other students their age.

 Strongly Disagree   Strongly Agree
  1   2   3   4   5

17. I believe lesson adaptations for students with special needs should be stated on the lesson plan.

 Strongly Disagree   Strongly Agree
  1   2   3   4   5

Table 1. Pretest and Posttest Mean Scores and Standard Deviations by Category and Teacher Group

Category	Pretest		Posttest	
	M	SD	M	SD
Personal Attitudes				
1 Population	15.07	3.10	16.75*	1.75
2 Populations	14.71	2.03	17.61**	1.85
Professional Attitude				
1 Population	15.64	2.42	17.60**	1.91
2 Populations	16.19	1.72	17.68*	1.79
Attitudes regarding Willingness				
1 Population	14.00	1.56	14.25	1.48
2 Populations	14.00	1.48	14.13	1.17
Perceptions of Teacher Prep				
1 Population	9.89	2.42	12.28**	1.67
2 Populations	10.32	2.44	12.16*	2.17
Perceptions of Students				
1 Population	10.75	1.93	10.82	2.10
2 Populations	9.84	1.82	10.77	2.04
All Groupings				
1 Population	65.35	9.23	71.71*	5.73
2 Populations	65.06	6.17	72.17**	6.04

* $p \leq .05$
** $p \leq .001$

Are They Ready to Student Teach? Reflections from 10 Music Education Majors Concerning Their Three Semesters of Field Experience

By Carol McDowell

Carol McDowell is associate professor of music education at Southeast Missouri State University in Cape Girardeau. She can be reached at cmcdowell@semo.edu.

An often heard American proverb states, "Experience is the best teacher." Teacher preparation programs must provide their students with the best knowledge and experiences possible so that their students can become successful, productive educators. Many teacher-training programs now attach a field-experience component to their methods courses to allow preservice teachers to apply their knowledge to a "real" classroom situation.

Cruickshank and Armaline (1986) traced the origins of field experience and revealed that as far back as 1839, Cyrus Pierce, principal of the first public normal school (an institution for the training of teachers) in Lexington, Massachusetts, required his 20 female students to teach each other while he observed. At the same time, Richard Edwards, first president of Illinois Normal University, agreed with Pierce that some kind of practice teaching was an essential normal-school requirement. These practice teachings could occur in the normal-school classroom where normal-school students taught each other, assumed the role of children, or instructed children in an outside school, either permanently or for a stated period of time, such as one or two weeks (as reported in Cruickshank & Armaline, 1986, p. 34).

Field experience, or practice teaching, has been defined in many different ways. Cutietta (2000) defines field experience as one of three types:

Type #1
• Any experience which happens in a school setting instead of the college classroom, including observation, tutoring, mini-teaching, and doing non-instructional tasks
Type #2
• Any "hands-on" task related to teaching including operating media, planning instruction, designing instructional materials, peer teaching/conducting
Type #3
• Student teaching (p. 6)

Cruickshank and Armaline (1986) categorize field experience as (a) direct (the preservice teacher is the teacher); (b) indirect (the preservice teacher watches someone else teach); or (c) third-hand (an experience that the preservice teacher has heard about from a third party). This study will use the indirect (observation) and direct (actual teaching) definitions of Cruickshank and Armaline.

The question of how much field experience to include in a curriculum for music teacher training has long been discussed. Rozmajzl (1992) reports that in many programs, students encounter their first field experiences during an introduction to music education course, which usually occurs during the sophomore year. The suggestion that field experience begin during the sophomore year corresponds with a report by Davidson (2003). In this indirect phase of field experience, preservice teachers may observe elementary, instrumental, and choral music educators in action and then submit an observation report. The report includes how the cooperating teacher delivers instruction, maintains discipline, and motivates students. These observations can occur individually on students' own time as well as during class time with a group.

Following the introductory music education course, preservice teachers become involved in teaching children (preschool through secondary school) as part of their methods classes. University faculty often arrange practice teachings and then observe and critique students' lessons. If a faculty member is unavailable to observe, preservice teachers may videotape their lessons for later viewing. The cooperating teachers may also give feedback so that preservice teachers receive another viewpoint concerning their lessons.

Cuttieta's (2000) research found that the amount of feedback included in one's field experience corresponds with the success of one's student teaching. Scherer (1979) explains that one of the general goals for an early field experience is to make an easier transition into student teaching (pp. 208–209). The field-experience component of methods courses forms the bridge from classroom learning into student teaching, which is considered by many to be the most important part of teacher preparation (Legette, 1997). Student teaching normally occurs in the senior year after all professional course work and field experiences are completed.

Does the amount of field experience affect the success of student teaching? Grossman (1980) found that extensive early field experience did not result in a more successful student teaching performance. Additionally, field experience that did not include feedback resulted in poor student teaching performance (Cutietta, 2000).

Although field experience has been added to teacher preparation programs, the research supporting field experience as an essential component is contradictory. Music field experiences vary widely between universities, making it difficult to form any broad-based conclusions. This research study traces one class of 10 music education majors through their field experiences at a Missouri university. Preservice teachers at this university must participate in 60 hours of field experience prior to student teaching (Southeast Missouri State University course syllabi for Secondary Blocks II & III Field Experience, 2002). The state of Missouri mandates two credit hours of field experience prior to student teaching, but there is no state rule on the number of contact hours (D. Adams, personal communication, January 11, 2005).

These university students encounter their first stage of field experience as part of their Introduction to Music Education (ME 222) course (Introduction course) during the second semester of their sophomore year, which is also referred to as Block I in the secondary education department. The students meet in class for 1 hour on Tuesday mornings, and have 2 hours on Thursday mornings for field experience, with 1 hour allotted for travel and 1 hour for observation. This introductory course is worth 2 credit hours and includes approximately 10 hours of indirect field experience (observation). The observation environments for this study included two orchestras (one beginning and one high school), two high school bands, one beginning band, two high school choirs, and one elementary general music class. Students in the Introduction course also taught one 15-minute instrument demonstration for elementary students at a local school.

Block II occurs in the first semester of the junior year, when preservice students have three courses that require field experience. In Theories of Learning and Management (ME 271, two credit hours), students are required to keep an 8-week private teaching log for an individual student or a small group of students. In Teaching Reading in the Content Area of Music (ME 272, two credit hours), students observe four different classroom settings (high school choir, junior high jazz band, sixth-grade band, and elementary general music) and develop five lesson plans on the music concepts of rhythm, melody, harmony, form, and tone color. They teach a 25-minute practice lesson to the music-academy students and then teach that same 25-minute lesson at an area elementary school. This course is conducted more as a workshop than as a lecture class. Finally, in General Music Methods–Elementary and Secondary (ME 371, four credit hours), students observe seven different classroom settings (two elementary general music classes, one middle school general music class, sixth-grade guitar, high school handbells, preschool music, and a Suzuki group violin class), and then develop and teach two 30-minute elementary-music lessons and one 30-minute secondary lesson at multiple school sites. Block II contains approximately 20 hours of field experience. Unlike Block I, Block II students enroll in a separate, nongraded three-credit hour field experience course (ME 270). Teaching sites were all within a 40-minute driving distance and were chosen primarily for their full-time, cooperating teachers.

Block III is the secondary school portion of music education majors' field experience. Students observe four secondary classroom settings. Students then find their own sites for their practice teaching in private lessons, beginning band, middle and high school bands, and a soloist or group who is participating in a music contest. Block III Field Experience (ME 370) requires 30 hours of teaching time and is a one-credit hour, nongraded course (Southeast Missouri State University course syllabi, 2002). A summary of all the education blocks is shown in Table 1.

Table 1. Summary of Music Education Blocks

	Course Title	Number of Credit Hours	Number of Observations	Number of Practice Teachings
Block I	Introduction to Music Education	2	8	One
Block II	Theories of Learning and Management	2	0	Eight-week private teaching log
	Teaching Reading in the Content Area of Music	2	4	One 25-minute elementary music lesson
	General Music Methods Elementary & Secondary	4	7	Three 30-minute general music lessons
Block III	Instrumental Teaching Techniques or	3	4	Arranged by student
	Techniques of Teaching Choral Literacy	2	4	Arranged by student
Block IV	Student Teaching	12		

Procedure

At the end of each education block, class members were asked to reflect upon their field experiences for that particular semester. I teach the Block I introductory course and all the Block II courses except Theories of Learning and Management. I also observed all of the students' practice teachings, provided feedback, and had them write reflections for their MoStep Teaching Portfolio. The State of Missouri, through the Department of Elementary and Secondary Education, mandates programmatic assessment through the MoStep portfolio. This document is required for all education majors at this university and asks them to reflect upon their teachings by answering the following questions (College of Education, 2001): What happened during the lesson? What did your students learn from the lesson? What did you as the teacher learn? and What do you still need to learn?

Participants in this study comprised 10 music majors, 9 instrumentalists, and 1 vocalist (students observe the same classes and have the same field-experience schedule regardless of major). Participants were enrolled in Block I (Introduction to Music Education) during spring 2003, Block II (Elementary and Secondary General Music Methods) during fall 2003, and Block III (Secondary Methods) during spring 2004. The purpose of this study was to record 10 music education majors' perceptions of their field experiences during their methods courses. Subjects were asked to reflect upon five general areas: (a) How did you view your field experience? (b) Do you feel your field experience has prepared you to teach in the next education block? (c) What specific types of teaching activities did you do in your field experience? (d) What were five things that prepared you to go out and teach in your block classes? and (e) What concerns do you have about your next field-experience component? Subjects took from 1 to 10 weeks to complete their reflections, but not everyone completed the response papers. A copy of all reflection questions is included in Appendixes A, B, and C.

Results

This study included only 10 students, but results correspond with findings from previous studies. A content analysis of the responses indicated that students were basically satisfied with their three semesters of field experience. Eight of the 10 students responded to the Block I (spring 2003) survey questions given below.

Do you feel you had enough field experience in your music education course? Why or why not?

All 8 music education majors agreed that they received enough field experience, but 3 students responded that they would like to have observed more choir directors. (Many area choirs do not meet within the allotted field-experience time.) Other comments included the following:

"I found out through Block I that I really do want to teach and that I can do it. Being able to actually go and deal with students first-hand is a priceless experience! Block I was everything I'd hoped it to be" (#1).

"We got our feet wet.... We had great lessons in learning how to teach, and we had a chance to see what we learned by applying it.... I learned that it isn't that easy.... I feel that by getting my feet wet last year, I will not be so nervous and more prepared this [next] semester" (#2).

"I definitely had ample time to observe different [teaching] styles with different ages of students to give me ideas to teach, but not really enough time to try out these ideas" (#7).

"Seeing what music teachers do every day in the flesh was a wake-up call to me. I now know that teaching music is what I want to do for the rest of my life. Without field experience, learning to be a teacher (well, a successful and efficient one) would be completely pointless" (#10).

Do you feel your field experience has prepared you to teach in Block II? Why or why not?

The students felt that they were as prepared as they could be to teach in Block II (elementary) coursework. One student wrote, "If nothing else, it's [Block I] made me more anxious to teach" (#1), while another did not know if she was quite prepared because she barely had any teaching experience outside this class (#4). Another student thought he was prepared for Block II from a paperwork standpoint, but the emotional and communicative demands of the job seemed to be somewhat of a mystery to him (#9). Three students wanted even more teaching experience at this beginning level.

What specific types of teaching activities did you do in your field experience?

In addition to their eight classroom observations, students in the Introduction course also taught one 15-minute instrument demonstration for elementary students at a local school. Students described their instrument demonstration for this question. The instruments shown were the French horn, piano, voice, euphonium, trumpet, trombone, and two flutes. One student expressed concern about taking control of the class and keeping everyone interested (#9), while another student said that she learned a lot from this experience because it made her realize how silly students can be (#8).

What were five (5) things that you feel most prepared you to go out and teach in Block II?

The answers for this question varied widely. Some of the most common responses were (a) the observations themselves, (b) reading philosophies and writing their own music education philosophy, (c) the advocacy project, and (d) the 15-minute teaching experience.

What concerns do you have about Block II teaching? Are there any particular skills that you want to learn or develop?

Three students expressed concern about classroom management, behavioral issues, and dealing with children with special needs. Also listed were student-teacher interactions, comfort and/or nervousness in front of students, and lesson planning. One student had no major concerns about teaching in Block II.

Answers after Block II

This class of music education majors was given the same list of questions to answer after they finished the Block II (elementary) portion of their field experience. The Block II coursework occurs during the first semester of the junior year. Students have 2 days (2 hours each day) allotted for their field experience teaching during this semester. Six of the 10 students provided answers to these questions. Their responses to each Block II (fall 2003) survey question are given below.

Do you feel you had enough field experience in your music education courses? Why or why not?

All 6 subjects said that they had enough field experience in Block II. One even stated that it would be "hard to fit any more in with our busy music major schedules" (#1). But another student wrote that he "didn't think you could ever have enough field experience" (#2). One student expressed that he would have preferred to work with one teacher throughout his elementary experience (#1), while two others (#5, #6) felt that their experiences were positive because they had the opportunity to observe and work with a variety of teaching styles and strategies. (Due to the rotating schedule of the local public school elementary music teachers, it is impossible for preservice teachers to see the same class at the same time every week.)

Do you feel your field experience has prepared you to teach in Block III? Why or why not?

Unanimously, the music education majors felt prepared to move into their secondary field experience (Block III). Feeling more comfortable in front of children and having experience in dealing with a wide variety of situations and planning lessons were listed as benefits of their previous teaching. One student described his fears on going in to teach a kindergarten class during Block II. "Were they going to run around crazy like in the movie *Kindergarten Cop* or would they be bored to tears and fall asleep? When I taught a young beginning band class this semester, I wasn't as nervous as I used to be" (#2).

What specific types of teaching activities did you do in your field experience?

University students developed and taught two 30-minute elementary music lessons and one 30-minute secondary lesson at multiple school sites. Two music majors worked with students with special needs—a deaf student and a student in a wheelchair. Block II contained approximately 20 hours of field experience, which included 11 classroom observations. This was twice the amount of field experience time as in Block I.

What were five (5) things that you feel most prepared you to go out and teach in Block III?

Again, the answers for this question were quite varied. Some mentioned the handouts that were given for the class notebook, activities in class, design of lesson plans (linking the different parts together), collaborative work with other university students on lessons and teachings, and the different teaching styles of Dalcroze, Suzuki, Kodály, and Orff. "The Block II binder was good for me because I've learned to be much more organized. This has helped in organizing my teachings and observations for Block III." This student also had a touching reaction: "Working with other university students on lessons and teachings was also an excellent opportunity for me, because I've found that anytime I have questions or need help to prepare a certain lesson I can ask my colleagues and they can help with anything and provide valuable input. The relationships I built with my classmates in Block II will be ongoing throughout my professional career and are priceless" (#1). Another wrote that he is "beginning to understand the work required to plan a lesson and that teaching general music looks a lot easier than it is" (#5).

What concerns do you have about Block III teaching? Are there any particular skills that you want to learn or develop?

Handling a disruptive student, assigning grades, dealing with inadequate conducting time in front of large ensembles, applying some of the concepts learned in Block II and reformatting them to Block III (older age group), and disciplining students were listed as concerns for the next field experience step. In general, the music education majors felt that Block II prepared them for the future and made them excited about teaching lessons. "Not really being educated in [the elementary] area provided a challenge to educate myself before being able to help the students. I think this was a valuable experience in retrospect" (#6).

Answers after Block III

This class of music education majors was again given the same list of questions to answer after they finished the Block III (secondary) portion of their field experience. Block III course work occurs during the second semester of the junior year. Students again have 2 days (2 hours each day) allotted for their field experience teaching during this semester. Five of the 10 students provided answers to these questions. Their responses to each Block III (fall 2003) survey question are given below.

Do you feel you had enough field experience in your music education courses? Why or why not?

Most preservice teachers wrote that they were provided with enough field experience, but again, they felt they could have used even more time with students if their schedules had allowed. Unlike previous field experiences, the professor did not arrange Block III teaching sites. One student saw this as an advantage because "it made you get into contact with teachers" (#5). Another responded that his field experience gave him a realistic look at teaching and helped him to decide that this is really what he wants to do (#6). One person (#8) enjoyed teaching the same group of students during Block III. Another expressed dissatisfaction with this block because it did not give him enough time to observe and teach. There was "more time in lecture talking about the 'real' world than actually seeing the real world for myself" (#7).

Do you feel your field experience has prepared you to student teach? Why or why not?

This question exposed some insecurity in these music majors. Although their field experiences had prepared them as well as they could have, one student expressed, "it is time for me to step up to the plate. . . . it is just those first time jitters that are already getting to me" (#5). The opportunity to teach a little vocal music, just for the experience, was suggested for improvement (#6). Two students expressed that they had not found their teaching styles yet, but this was not necessarily a bad thing (#3, #8). One student wrote that he "had hoped to have a more hands-on approach because that's what is going to happen in the spring when I student teach" (#7). Another replied that she could not answer this question until she was actually student teaching (#3).

What specific types of teaching activities did you do in your field experience?

Students observed four secondary classroom settings and then found their own practice teaching sites for private lessons, beginning band, middle and high school bands, and a soloist or group who was participating in a music contest. Block III Field Experience (ME 370) requires 30 hours of teaching time. I was not the instructor for Block III courses.

What were five (5) things that you feel most prepared you to go out and student teach?

Again, answers varied widely. Methods courses, conducting, the Teaching Music Reading course, elementary methods, Block II field experience, all ensembles, and all instrumental techniques courses were mentioned.

What concerns do you have about student teaching? Are there any particular skills that you want to learn or develop?

Classroom management and working with children with special needs were skills that students wanted to develop. There were also concerns about keeping the flow and direction of the lesson and not being able to hear mistakes in the music. One person wrote, "Student teaching really scares me. I am as prepared to go as I can be, I just don't feel that I am ready. There is nothing more that this institution could have done, it is just a personal feeling of dismay that I have" (#5).

Discussion

Teacher training programs are site specific, which makes it difficult to form any general conclusions. Verrastro and Leglar (1992), however, synthesized results of 55 teacher-education programs between 1955 and 1985. Half of their studies expressed some common concerns regarding student teaching and field experience:

(1) More time should be spent in applying theory to practice; field experiences, and possibly student teaching, should occur earlier in the curricular sequence. (2) Supervision of student teaching should be improved; the student should receive more feedback from both the college supervisor and the cooperating teacher, and there should be more coordination among members of the triad. (3) During the field experiences, more time should be spent in teaching and less time in observing. (p. 687)

Verrastro and Leglar's findings correspond partially to this study.

The indirect portion of these preservice teachers' field experience was observing music teachers in a variety of settings and teaching one 15-minute instrument lesson. Students expressed that these observations and writing their own music education philosophies were the most helpful activities during Block I. This is their first step toward applying what they have learned in the classroom as well as what they perceive as valuable in a child's musical education. One preservice teacher wrote that there was too much time spent talking about the real world in Block III rather than experiencing it (#7).

Field experience begins for these university students in the second semester of their sophomore year. This is the same recommendation given by Davidson (2003) and Rozmajzl (1992). Introducing field experience any earlier into the music education undergraduate program can be difficult because preservice teachers have not completed their music theory and history courses, nor have they developed their conducting skills. On the other hand, while they may not have their teaching skills polished at this point, the indirect (observation) portion of their field experience could begin earlier should the curriculum allow (i.e., without giving students an excessive number of hours).

Supervising field experience and student teachers can be problematic for the university faculty. Public school schedules and university schedules seldom match, so coordinating the teaching times can be extremely complex. Field experience and student teaching observations by music education faculty are time consuming and are often not included in a faculty member's teaching load. Sometimes the faculty member conducting the observations is not always the person who taught the students in their methods courses (nor even a music educator), making it difficult to transfer course work into the teaching situation. Faculty time and travel expenses can also provide obstacles and can make observations less frequent (Hoffer, 1987). This university does allow travel time and reimbursement for the instructors of methods courses so that they may supervise field-experience and student-teaching observations.

The subjects for this study all wrote that they would welcome more field experience to prepare them for their student teaching. According to practicing elementary and general music educators who are trained in Orff, Kodály, Dalcroze, and Gordon, student teachers are coming to them poorly prepared (Spurgeon, 2004). Part of the reason for this poor preparation is that there is usually only one elementary/general music course in the undergraduate curriculum. Course content is not standardized among university music schools due to the wide variety of education and background of the college instructors. Unless the college instructor has had additional training in any of the above methodologies, they are only briefly mentioned in the methods course. One Block II student noted the benefit of these methods.

The subjects for this study noted some weak areas in which they needed more practice before continuing their educational sequence. Classroom management and working with students with special needs were mentioned at all three levels of their fieldwork. Practicing music teachers expressed these same concerns in research by Taylor (1970). Taylor's subjects also felt that they needed more keyboard work, wider exposure to materials, and improved teaching methods that were interesting and realistic to schoolchildren. Today, 35 years after Taylor, preservice teachers still feel unprepared in the latter three areas. Perhaps teacher training programs could revise or add curricula to address classroom management and students with special needs.

Preservice teachers in Wolfgang's (1990) research highly valued their field experience. These university students did, also. Their 60 hours of field experience placed them in many different teaching situations, which was considered an advantage by one student: "I think this early in the game it doesn't matter who you teach with because you're going to learn something from that teacher, only because you have never been in that particular situation" (#8).

Although this study was limited in scope, the experiences of these 10 subjects can increase our sensitivity to the issues highlighted by their concerns. Teacher preparation programs need to question students in order to know how to lead them, serve them better, and move music education forward. This research focused on one university's field-experience program. Questions for further investigation include

  (a) How will these students' field experiences affect their student teaching?

  (b) How will these students' student teaching affect their first year of teaching?

  (c) How can this music teacher training program change to meet the students' needs?

  (d) How does the music department's field experience component at this university compare to other universities of the same size or to other Missouri universities?

There are many variations in teacher preparation programs, but perhaps after further research, more general conclusions can be made. Having preservice teachers reflect upon their feelings and concerns can contribute to the improvement of music teacher training programs.

References

College of Education. (2001). *MoStep Training Portfolio manual*. Unpublished manuscript, Southeast Missouri State University, Cape Girardeau.

Cruickshank, D. R., & Armaline, W. D. (1986). Field experiences in teacher education: Considerations and recommendations. *Journal of Teacher Education, 37*(3), 34–40.

Cutietta, R. A. (2000, March). *Cloning Holly through field experiences: Do field experiences help us create the ideal teacher?* Paper presented at the meeting of the Music Educators National Conference, Washington, DC.

Davidson, M. C. (2003, March). *Undergraduate music education courses for the 21st century*. Paper presented at the meeting of the Organization of the American Kodály Educators, Minneapolis, MN.

Grossman, G. C. (1980). *A comparison of the effectiveness of student teachers who have had extensive early field experience with those who have not*. (ERIC Document Reproduction Service No. ED207943)

Hoffer, C. R. (1987). Tomorrow's direction in the education for music teachers. *Music Educators Journal, 73*(6), 27–31.

Legette, R. M. (1997). Enhancing the music student-teaching experience: A research review. *Update: Applications of Research in Music Education, 16*(21), 25–28.

Rozmajzl, M. (1992). Preparatory field experiences for elementary education majors. *Update: Applications of Research in Music Education, 10*(1), 19–24.

Scherer, C. (1979). Effects of early field experience on student teachers' self-concepts and performance. *Journal of Experimental Education, 47*(3), 208–214.

Spurgeon, A. (2004). Proposed changes for the undergraduate elementary music education curriculum. *General Music Today, 17*(3), 28–32.

Taylor, C. H. (1970). Opinions of music teachers regarding professional preparation in music education. *Journal of Research in Music Education, 18*, 330–339.

Verrastro, R. E., & Leglar, M. (1992). Music teacher education. In R. Colwell (Ed.), *Handbook of research on music teaching and learning* (pp. 676–696). New York: Schirmer Books.

Wolfgang, R. E. (1990). Early field experience in music education: A study of teacher role socialization (preservice teachers) (Doctoral dissertation, University of Oregon, 1990). *Dissertation Abstracts International, 52*(1), 137A.

Appendix A
Music Education Block II
A Reflection of Block I Field Experience

Our goals affect our actions, expectations, and perceptions. This happens even when we are not explicitly aware of our goals. By expressing our goals, we can examine them and decide whether they are useful for us at this time.

You have expressed your goals for music education through your philosophy papers. Now I would like you to reflect back on your field experiences and coursework during your Block I Principles of Music Education (ME 222) course. Please answer each question thoughtfully and thoroughly on a separate piece of paper. You may complete these answers in your own handwriting, but please make sure your writing is large and legible.

1. During the spring 2003 semester (ME222), you observed eight (8) different classrooms. These classrooms were:

    A. Sixth-Grade Orchestra   E. Elementary Music
    B. High School Band I   F. High School Band II
    C. High School Choir I   G. Sixth-Grade Low Brass
    D. Freshman Orchestra   H. High School Choir II

You also had one mini-teaching experience on tone color to elementary students.

Do you feel you had enough field experience in your music education course? Why or why not? As you answer this question, consider what your goals for field experience are/were. Your answer may include goals such as:

    A. To find out what teaching is really like (career exploration)
    B. To see if I like teaching (personal preferences)
    C. To see if I can really do it (self-testing)
    D. To learn some skills and modify certain habits and characteristics (training)
    E. To develop my own approach or style of teaching
    F. To apply what I am learning in college to real students and to real classrooms (putting theory into practice)

What do you conclude? How do you view your field experience?

2. Do you feel your field experience has prepared you to teach in Block II? Why or why not?
   - If not, are there some specific kinds of teaching situations you would like to explore?
   - Would you like to have worked with or under a particular type of teacher, one with a certain philosophy, approach, type of training, or background?
   - Was there some particular subject matter you would like to have tried teaching before going out to student teach?
   - Were there some specific kinds of learners about whom you wanted to learn more or with whom you wanted to have more teaching experience?

3. What specific types of teaching activities did you do in your field experience (leading discussions, giving a lecture, setting up a role play, one-to-one tutoring, helping a child with personal problems, discussing a controversial issue with a class, dealing with a disruptive child, dealing with a child with disabilities, assigning grades, meeting with a parent, designing and teaching a lesson, setting up a classroom and teaching a lesson, or doing a demonstration)?

4. What were five (5) things that you feel most prepared you to go out and teach in Block II?

5. What concerns do you have about Block II teaching? Are there any particular skills that you want to learn or develop?

The answers to these questions will help prepare you for your portfolio reflection writings, particularly questions of "What have I learned?" and "What do I still need to learn?" The ME 222 course was an introduction to music education course. This class was designed to let you observe different styles of teaching and various teaching situations as well as make you think about "why" you are studying music education.

Appendix B
Music Education Block III
A Reflection of Block II Field Experience

Our goals affect our actions, expectations, and perceptions. This happens even when we are not explicitly aware of our goals. By expressing our goals, we can examine them and decide whether or not they are useful for us at this time.

You have expressed your goals for music education through your philosophy papers. Now I would like you to reflect back on your field experiences and coursework during your Block II courses: Theories of Learning & Management (ME 271), Teaching Reading in the Content Area of Music (ME 272), and General Music Methods—Elementary & Secondary (ME 371). Please answer each question thoughtfully and thoroughly on a separate piece of paper. You may complete these answers in your own handwriting, but please make sure your writing is large and legible.

1. During the fall 2003 semester, you observed many different classrooms. These classrooms were:
   - A. Elementary Music I
   - B. Elementary Music II
   - C. High School Choir
   - D. Fifth-Grade General Music
   - E. Jazz Band
   - F. Elementary Music III
   - G. Sixth-Grade Band
   - H. Handbell Choir
   - I. Preschool Music
   - J. Suzuki Group Violin Lessons
   - K. Sixth-Grade Guitar

You also had one practice teaching experience, one elementary teaching experience on rhythm or melody at elementary school I, one music teaching experience on a music concept of your choice at elementary school II or III, and one secondary teaching experience at a middle school. In addition, you kept an eight-week private teaching log for an individual student or small group of students.

Do you feel you had enough field experience in your music education courses? Why or why not? As you answer this question, consider what your goals for field experience are/were. Your answer may include goals such as

   A. To find out what teaching is really like (career exploration)
   B. To see if I like teaching (personal preferences)
   C. To see if I can really do it (self-testing)
   D. To learn some skills and modify certain habits and characteristics (training)
   E. To develop my own approach or style of teaching
   F. To apply what I am learning in college to real students and to real classrooms (putting theory into practice)

What do you conclude? How do you view your field experience?

2. Do you feel your field experience has prepared you to teach in Block III? Why or why not?
   - If not, are there some specific kinds of teaching situations you would like to explore?
   - Would you like to have worked with or under a particular type of teacher, one with a certain philosophy, approach, type of training, or background?
   - Was there some particular subject matter you would like to have tried teaching before going out to student teach?
   - Were there some specific kinds of learners about whom you wanted to learn more, with whom you wanted to have more teaching experience?

3. What specific types of teaching activities did you do in your field experience (leading discussions, giving a lecture, setting up a role play, one-to-one tutoring, helping a child with personal problems,

discussing a controversial issue with a class, dealing with a disruptive child, dealing with a child with disabilities, assigning grades, meeting with a parent, designing and teaching a lesson, setting up a classroom and teaching a lesson, or doing a demonstration)?

4. What were five (5) things that you feel most prepared you to go out and teach in Block III?

5. What concerns do you have about Block III teaching? Are there any particular skills that you want to learn or develop?

The answers to these questions will help prepare you for your portfolio reflection writings, particularly questions of "What have I learned?" and "What do I still need to learn?" The Block II courses provided the elementary portion of your field experience. These classes were designed to let you observe different teaching styles and various teaching situations in an elementary music classroom as well as develop lesson plans and actually teach elementary music classes.

Appendix C
Music Education Block III B
A Reflection of Block III A Field Experience

Our goals affect our actions, expectations, and perceptions. This happens even when we are not explicitly aware of our goals. By expressing our goals, we can examine them and decide whether they are useful for us at this time.

You have expressed your goals for music education through your philosophy papers. Now I would like you to reflect back on your field experiences and coursework during your undergraduate training before you begin your student teaching. Please answer each question thoughtfully and thoroughly on a separate piece of paper. You may complete these answers in your own handwriting, but please make sure your writing is large and legible.

Consider your field experiences for Instrumental (ME 372) and Choral Techniques (ME 373) courses.

1. Do you feel you had enough field experience in these music education courses? Why or why not? As you answer this question, consider what your goals for field experience are/were. Your answer may include goals such as

    A. To find out what teaching is really like (career exploration)
    B. To see if I like teaching (personal preferences)
    C. To see if I can really do it (self-testing)
    D. To learn some skills and modify certain habits and characteristics (training)
    E. To develop my own approach or style of teaching
    F. To apply what I am learning in college to real students and to real classrooms (putting theory into practice). What do you conclude? How do you view your field experience?

2. Do you feel your field experience has prepared you to student teach? Why or why not? If not, are there some specific kinds of teaching situations you would like to explore?
    - Would you like to have worked with or under a particular type of teacher, one with a certain philosophy, approach, type of training, or background?
    - Was there some particular subject matter you would like to have tried teaching before going out to student teach?

- Were there some specific kinds of learners about whom you wanted to learn more, with whom you wanted to have more teaching experience?

3. What specific types of teaching activities did you do in your field experience (leading discussions, giving a lecture, setting up a role play, one-to-one tutoring, helping a child with personal problems, discussing a controversial issue with a class, dealing with a disruptive child, dealing with a child with disabilities, assigning grades, meeting with a parent, designing and teaching a lesson, setting up a classroom and teaching a lesson, or doing a demonstration)?

4. What were five (5) things that you feel most prepared you to go out and student teach?

5. What concerns do you have about student teaching? Are there any particular skills that you want to learn or develop?

The answers to these questions will help prepare you for your portfolio reflection writings, particularly questions of "What have I learned?" and "What do I still need to learn?"

If You Build It . . . : A Distance-Learning Approach for Music Teacher Licensure Test Preparation

By Gena R. Greher

Gena R. Greher is the coordinator of music education and an assistant professor of music education at the University of Massachusetts in Lowell. She can be reached at Gena_Greher@uml.edu.

Introduction

Our public education system is currently engulfed by the No Child Left Behind Act (NCLB) of 2001 (2002), which forces American public schools to place greater-than-usual emphasis on standardized testing. This focus on high-stakes testing has implications not just for K–12 students and their teachers, but for teachers-in-training and their professors as well. Whether one believes in the educational benefits of high-stakes testing or not, the fact remains that those of us who are involved in the training of teachers are greatly affected by NCLB. As teacher educators, we need to incorporate our state's learning standards into the curriculum and focus on effective methodologies based on developmentally appropriate learning theories, as well as advocate alternative assessment strategies. Yet the irony of this is that institutions of higher learning and their professors will be judged by how their students, and ultimately their future students, perform on standardized tests. In her commentary regarding the contradictions inherent in basing accountability on standardized testing, Martha Casas (2003) stated,

> Teacher educators spend countless hours teaching students the importance of using authentic assessments and how to design assessment alternatives. Via coursework, preservice educators learn about portfolios, rubrics, holistic scoring, and the need for using anecdotal records, particularly for younger children. Nevertheless, upon completion of the teacher education program, students soon realize that their understanding of the content will be assessed only by a paper and pencil test.

The Department of Education's Test for Educator Licensure in the state where I teach is one such test by which my students will be judged. To ensure that new teachers are highly qualified in their respective subject areas, this state's exam, which consists mainly of multiple-choice questions, is designed to test students for subject-matter knowledge as well as educational theory and methodology. While there is no question that teachers should have command of their subject matter, there is also no question that a teacher's ability to apply that knowledge in the classroom is of equal importance. Whether one's ability to effectively apply content knowledge can be gleaned from a multiple-choice test is debatable; nonetheless, this is the method currently used in our state.

In our music department, which has a 5-year dual-degree program in music education, students preparing for careers in teaching spend the bulk of their freshman and sophomore years ensconced in music theory, history, and performance classes. In addition to this emphasis on learning subject content, in their junior and senior years our music education students are also learning how to build on children's innate musicality in their various pedagogy and methods classes. Much of the work in these pedagogy classes involves the study of learning theories and effective methodologies for applying content knowledge in a classroom situation. By the time these students are ready to take the exam needed for teacher certification, their memory of what was studied in their theory and history classes is rather sketchy. Past exam results showed that our students encountered the most difficulty with the theory, aural skills, and music literature and history portions of the state licensure test. As with many students, unless they have been applying facts learned in previous classes on a regular basis, the information is generally stored into memory, released for the test, and erased from memory shortly after the test, especially if the course in question is given earlier than 11 a.m. before their junior year. Although a review process for passing the licensure exam would help increase the pass rate of our students, the dilemma is how to prepare these students for the licensure test without taking away precious class time from learning the educational theories, philosophies, and methodologies that will help them to become highly qualified and effective teachers. Our department's initial response was to add a review class taught by one of our graduate assistants for upperclassman music education majors. However, given everyone's already overcrowded schedules, this created a host of logistical problems.

Rationale for a Distance-Learning Solution

Due to the difficulty of scheduling teacher-preparation seminars that are convenient for most of our students, distance learning seemed to offer a solution to our scheduling dilemma for a variety of reasons. Today's students are used to constant connectivity; they are more comfortable reading from a computer screen and more used to writing via a keyboard than with paper and ink (Frand, 2000). As suggested by Oblinger, Barone, and Hawkins (2001), we now live in an era where the Internet has always been a part of life for many of our students. By not being constrained by either location or time, distance learning affords people the opportunity for time-shifting and place-shifting as well as for engaging in synchronous and/or asynchronous learning opportunities (Frand; Cohen, 2002; Levine & Sun, 2002; Natriello, 2005; Oblinger et al.).

In a study of student attitudes toward Web-based instruction in a music methods class, Bauer (2001) found that his students liked the asynchronous aspects of Web-based instruction. He did, however, find a strong correlation between student attitudes and whether they had access to the Internet from home, in that those with access were more positive about this method of instruction. He also found that students with less technology experience were more apt to find this mode of instruction more impersonal. Bauer's study, though small in scope, suggests that some combination of a traditional class and Web-based instruction can complement each other.

Many institutions of higher learning now offer some form of distance learning, either through Web discussion boards and chat rooms in traditional classrooms, or by offering whole or parts of classes online (Frand, 2000; Levine & Sun, 2002; Natriello, 2005; Oblinger et al., 2001). While there is no doubt that a distance-learning option is convenient for the students, it is a labor-intensive proposition for faculty (Levine & Sun; Oblinger et al.). According to Levine and Sun, with few exceptions, there is very little guidance or training for faculty in the preparation of teaching in an online environment. These authors also note that older or part-time students are more apt to embrace distance learning than are younger, more traditional college-bound students (Levine & Sun).

The distance-learning site as I envisioned it would not be a course per se, but a resource for our students to use to augment their learning experience. The students in my classes are all used to the weekly Web discussions and reading assignments that form a major part of our class work. In addition, our technology class is virtually paperless, with all assignments posted and turned in through the class Web. It did not seem that I was asking my students to participate in an activity that would be completely foreign to them. However, over the 5 years I have been conducting my classes in this manner, I have observed that just about half the students in each of my classes willingly participates in the Web discussions on a regular basis. The other half needs to be prodded and cajoled in spite of the fact that the syllabus clearly states that weekly participation in the Web discussion will count toward their grade. In addition, I have observed that when assignments are turned in through Web postings, more than two-thirds of the students will post assignments past their due dates, whereas this is not the case when students physically hand me their assignments. Therefore, before committing to a task that was sure to be labor-intensive, I conducted an informal poll of students in my classes. Given the choice between attending a review class at specific times and clicking a mouse at their own convenience, students expressed enthusiastic support for the development of a Web-based preparation site, with assurances that they would definitely participate on a regular basis.

Project Scope

In the winter of 2003, I applied for and received a technology-related professional development grant sponsored by my university. This was a collaborative project with one of my colleagues from our computer science division. My colleague oversaw the computer programing aspects of the site, assisted by one of his students. The graphic look of the site was developed by one of our university's graphic design students. I oversaw the planning, implementation, and content, aided by one of my teaching assistants. She was responsible for gathering questions and audio and graphic files and getting these to my colleague and his student.

Our state's licensure exam in music relies on aural excerpts and score reading, which made the multimedia capabilities of the Web a natural fit for this kind of test preparation. While the overall plan was to have both a remedial section and a diagnostic section, due to time and budget constraints, we have concentrated on developing just the diagnostic portion at this time. We use a password-protected login and faculty can access a results page to monitor the progress of our students to ensure that they are fully prepared to take the exam. Students have the option of taking a simulation of the entire test or a practice test in which they can focus on a specific area of study.

The format of our site was based on the music content guidelines outlined by our state on its Web site. They are as follows:

Music Content Areas

    Multiple Choice
    I. Music Theory and Analysis = *33%*
       A. Music Theory
       B. Aural Analysis
    II. Music History and Literature = *33%*
       A. Music History and Literature
       B. Aural Analysis
    III. Music Education = 14%

    Open Response Essay
    IV. Integration of Knowledge and Understanding = *20%*

Each content area was divided into a variety of content-specific subareas. Various members of the music faculty, based on their area of expertise, came up with questions for each subarea (see Appendix A for sample questions). These questions were randomized to ensure that each time a person took our Web-based test, the questions would be different. It was and continues to be an enormous undertaking.

Through the development of this Web site, I was looking to answer the following questions:

1. Is it possible to design a Web site that would adequately replicate the content and conditions of the actual music teacher test our students will eventually take?
2. If there were a Web site to help students prepare for the exam, would they actually use it?
3. Is the Web site preferable to the on-campus review classes?

Pilot Study—Issues Encountered

According to the terms of the grant, we had a year to develop the site and get it into a useable state. We had just barely completed the preliminary student testing and debugging of the site by the end of the grant period in June 2004. While the people on the computer programming side of this collaboration were creating the software structure and physical layout of this site, those of us on the music side were creating the content. On the programming side, there were many technical issues regarding Internet browser sensitivity, sound-file size, and operating system compatibility. Once we opened the site up for student use, there was the possibility of overburdening the server, which did happen initially. A newer and more powerful server was eventually installed during the summer of 2004.

Due to the search and retrieval aspect of the Web site under development, the underlying structure of the site was written using Extensible Markup Language (XML), which describes data. One of the issues we encountered early on was the initial failure of the audio clips to play when tested on a Macintosh (Mac) platform. My colleague did some research into the difficulties he encountered and discovered that Macs are browser-sensitive and that several of the earlier browser versions did not support the use of XML. Therefore, for this particular site to work on a Mac, the user would need to work in Netscape's 7.1 browser. We decided to inform Mac users that Netscape 7.1 would be needed to run the program and to put a download link on the home page of our site.

It was a rather daunting task to coordinate all of the questions and apply them to the correct subsection, not to mention coaxing the various faculty members to submit their questions in a timely manner. The contributing faculty voluntarily undertook this task in addition to their already massive workloads. We fell behind schedule due to content and technical issues and couldn't actually begin preliminary testing until the beginning of May 2004, with a report deadline looming at the beginning of June 2004. Students were also involved in finals during this time.

Pilot Study—Findings

Our computer lab is equipped with Power Mac G4 computers, but there were some compatibility issues with regard to Macs and the OS X operating system, which was new to our lab. Many students had problems playing the audio files, yet many others encountered relatively little difficulty. We believed that the new server due for installation over the summer would rectify this situation. We later discovered that many of the large audio files hadn't yet been replaced by the smaller reviewed audio files, and the file size discrepancies caused the inconsistencies in playback.

Of the approximately 30 students who were asked to do so, 11 students actually went through the program in both practice and test modes and e mailed me their issues and suggestions, as well as filled out a 5-point Likert survey (see Appendix B). With the exception of one student who had philosophical issues with the site being browser-specific, most students felt the site would be useful for preparing for the exam ($M = 4.2$). Given the technical difficulties some users experienced, the students were mostly positive in preferring this method to the test preparation classes we had been holding ($M = 3.7$). They all said that the site was easy to navigate ($M = 4$), liked the convenience of doing this on their own time ($M = 3.6$), and thought the questions provided were of a balanced variety ($M = 3.6$).

With regard to the types of questions that were included, one student wrote, "They were balanced, some were harder than others. . . . some were totally over my head, but it's a good thing because I probably need to know this stuff." Another student commented, "I enjoyed the wide variety of musical examples . . . I also found my own strengths put to the test." While half the respondents encountered technical difficulties, which centered mainly on the playing of audio samples, they found the graphic examples clear and helpful. They liked knowing how they did at the end of the Web-based test ($M = 4.7$), but would like a breakdown of the areas where they are weak ($M = 4.6$). All students felt this was a positive addition to our program ($M = 4.2$).

During this time, several students could not attend the test-prep seminars, but were either involved with developing this site or used this site in its preliminary phase in their own test preparation. Through e-mail exchanges with me, they reported that the information from the site was very useful and that they passed the actual test. Most of the students, while quick to point out errors during the debugging phase, have been very supportive of this project. While this may not be a perfect solution, it seemed that this approach had the potential to alleviate the dilemma of having to "teach to the test" without taking the focus away from the goal of teaching our students how to teach for musical understanding.

The Test Prep Site Goes Live

By summer 2004, the new server was installed. Several faculty members reviewed our questions and made suggestions for changes. Many of the initial questions had been revised, and all of the sound files had been replaced with smaller MP3 files. We were now ready for students to use the program and assist with the final phase of debugging, if necessary. Rather than eliminate the review classes entirely, we decided to scale them back to fewer meetings where our graduate assistant could concentrate solely on preparing for the essay-writing portion of the state licensure exam, since this was not yet covered by our Web site. I asked my music methods class, which consisted of 11 seniors who would be preparing for the actual state test in the spring, to log in several times in practice mode and several times in the simulated test mode. I also asked four of my graduate students who still needed to take the test to participate in the debugging process. They were asked to e-mail my colleague and me if they encountered any problems. Given the fact that questions were randomized, they were all sent an e-mail telling them that e-mailing us the question number was meaningless and they would need to e-mail us a screen shot of any questions that had typos, questionable answers, or audio problems.

Of the 15 people who were asked to participate, 3 undergraduate and 3 graduate students actually did so on a regular basis. Five students claimed they encountered problems but either failed to send us e-mails or just verbally complained every now and then. One of the 5 sporadic users used a completely different browser than the one specified, and the other 4 students never bothered to get past their initial issues. Of the 6 students who were in regular e-mail contact with us, only 1 of them ever followed the procedure of sending us the screen shots, so we were never quite sure of the specific issues raised. What we gathered from their e-mails was that there were still some isolated cases of audio problems, there were several questions with typos, and there were a couple of questions where the answers were suspect. Therefore, over the winter of 2005, I went through all of the code and made a list of every question that needed to be changed. It was at this time that I discovered an entire section where the larger audio files hadn't been replaced with the smaller MP3 files.

Findings

At the start of the spring 2005 semester, my colleague and I met to clear up all the issues. The site was ready for my students to prepare for the exam. Like the previous semester, only a handful of students actually logged in. Since I have the ability to log in to the results page, I can get a readout of who has logged in, when they logged in, and whether they logged in to the practice section or the simulated test. I discovered that as it got closer to when each student was scheduled to take the actual licensure exam, his or her Web-site activity increased. Based on e-mails concerning the actual exam, 7 students took the licensure exam over the spring and summer of 2005, 4 in the spring and 3 in the summer. All 4 students who took the exam in the spring passed. Of these 4 students, 3 used the site often. The student who didn't e-mailed me the following explanation:

> Well to be honest my usage was limited. I used it only once in practice mode. The system requirements were so stringent that it was too much of a hassle for me to be faithful with it. The one time I did use it, it helped me to understand what my strengths and weaknesses were. In preparing for the test, I focused on my weaknesses.

The stringent requirement this student refers to is the need to use a specific browser, which he obviously didn't want to download and install.

The first student to pass told me she found the site helpful and harder in some ways than the actual licensure exam. Two other students e-mailed me their thoughts. By using this site, one of the students was able to figure out a strategy for her test preparation:

> I definitely used your Web site. Although I regularly got repeat questions, it got me looking into the subjects I knew the least about (i.e., music history). I didn't go through with taking the real test on there, but doing the practice tests over and over allowed me to figure out exactly what I needed the most help on. From there I made my own sort of study material and researched the answers.

The other student wrote the following:

> I did use the program a bit in preparing for my exam. I found it helpful mostly in the test and found that much of the material that was covered on the prep course Web site was either actually on the test or very closely related. The theory portion was helpful in the sense that it helped me review the material that I felt I needed to know, though the test itself was actually quite light on Theory.

Of the 3 students who took the exam in the summer, 2 students used the site. The student who didn't use the site was the one who kept having trouble with the login. Though he did not pass the actual exam, this student participates regularly in our Web discussions and is generally highly motivated. He stated, "I tried using the Web site a few times but it never ended up working properly for me. I'm not sure if my computer was set wrong or what but I didn't bother with it too much anyway." The other 2 used the site often. One of the students had taken a prep class elsewhere and had this to say:

> I must admit that it fell short in comparison to yours. . . . One of the biggest advantages of your site is the layout and how it's organized (i.e., theory, history, education). It's tailored toward "preparation for music licensure" and not just unnecessary questioning. . . . Once we got over the audio & technical hurdles for the listening samples, the site worked out smoothly.

She also mentioned that this site most closely replicated the actual exam. The other student wrote the following:

> I did use it, especially a few days before I took the exam. The only feature I would like to see added is a way to see what the correct answer is. . . . Besides that, I found it very helpful. I think many of the questions are a lot harder than on the actual test.

With one exception, all the students who took the licensure test and contacted me are self-regulated learners who respond often and regularly to our class Web discussions. They also e-mail me regularly when there is a question about a reading assignment or project.

Discussion

Compared to previous years, we had a higher proportion of students who passed the exam, though at this point I would hesitate to attribute that solely to the addition of the Web site. While admittedly this is too small a sample to be able to generalize to a larger population, I believe these students' reactions to using the Web site are consistent with other research (Bauer, 2001; Flor, 2002; Greher, 2003; Zdzinski, 2001). As indicated by the student responses after taking the licensure exam, our site was useful and it adequately prepared students for the format and content of the actual exam. This corresponds to the first research question concerning whether it was possible to design a Web site that would adequately replicate the content and conditions of the actual music teacher licensure exam.

Concerning the third research question about whether the Web site was preferable to the on-campus review classes, those students who used the site preferred the flexibility afforded by distance learning to the on-campus review. Answering the second question pertaining to whether students would use a Web site to prepare for the exam is the most challenging. The biggest issue was the distance-learning medium itself. No matter how perfectly one plans, technology can fail, and as with any system, there is no guarantee that students will actually use it.

While there clearly are technical issues that we can take control over and fix, there will always be situations that are out of one's control, such as an Internet provider's server malfunction. As students and educators, we need to get comfortable with the idea that when using technology there will be situations we cannot control. I have been experimenting over the years with distance-learning courses and using Web boards to enhance class discussions with middle school, high school, college, and graduate school students, and there have always been situations where no matter how well I planned, there were times when the students couldn't access the Internet. So while the distance-learning format offers a great deal of flexibility in both time and location, one also needs to build in some flexibility when it comes to due dates.

I have observed that the self-motivated students will participate on a regular basis even in the absence of such participation being tied to a grade. The less-motivated students will barely participate, if at all, even if it means receiving an F for that portion of their work. As indicated by the research, merely putting the information out there doesn't necessarily mean students will actually use it (Oblinger et al., 2001; Cohen, 2002; Flor, 2002; Greher, 2002; Levine & Sun, 2002; Natriello, 2005). A general assumption is that most college students, who consider computer use fairly commonplace, will naturally prefer a computer-based learning environment. The reality is closer to the findings of Frand (2000), Cohen, and Natriello in that merely replicating an existing educational paradigm may not be enough to lure the average learner, and this type of learning environment needs to be mediated in some way.

The fact that I chose to replicate a test type of situation works to the strengths of the medium but also highlights a major flaw in much of the thinking about the design of distance learning. As pointed out by Natriello (2005), most distance learning tries to re-create classroom-like environments, and at the moment, we are only achieving modest educational changes. He believes the potential is there for radical change in how we think about education and how we deliver it (Natriello). As stated by Frand (2000), "The outlook of those we teach has changed, and thus the way in which we teach must change." Frand also points out that the way our students interact with technology is different from the way our more mature population interacts with it. Our students are more apt to take a trial and error approach (Frand). However, I have observed that many of my college students are less willing to experiment with technology than Frand's research would suggest. There is a group who is just interested in knowing what the right answer is and would rather be told the quickest way to get there.

On the positive side, this project indicates that it is possible to create a test environment that is completely asynchronous and can provide instant feedback for both the student and the teacher without taking time away from class. This approach can have important implications for the future of test preparation and perhaps ease the burden teachers now feel about having to teach to the test at the expense of teaching for understanding. The negative side is that if we only seek to replicate existing modes of traditional instruction electronically, we are missing the greater potential of this highly interactive medium. Therefore, if and when I get to work on the remediation portion of this Web site, I will need to think about a format that builds on approaches to learning that allow for student exploration, problem-solving, and experimentation consistent with the ways most students are already interacting with their technology, and build in questions that will help guide the student's exploration without a total replication of a test situation.

Many of us in higher education are beginning to deal with campus-based realities that necessitate the inclusion of online courses and online components to our courses. We need to reassess the purpose of technology in music education and to better reflect how students actually use it, rather than focusing solely on technology as an efficient medium for the dissemination of content. Training educators to incorporate technology in a manner that encourages purposeful exploration while placing the emphasis on creative thinking might provide a framework for a more student-centered approach to teaching with technology.

References

Bauer, W. I. (2001). Student attitudes toward web-enhanced learning in a music education methods class: A case study. *Journal of Technology in Music Learning, 1*(1), 20–30.

Casas, M. (2003, October 12). The use of standardized tests in assessing authentic learning—a contradiction indeed. *Teachers College Record, 105*. Retrieved June 27, 2004, from http://www.tcrecord.org/Content.asp?ContentID=11211

Cohen, D. E. (2002, January). *Teaching jazz appreciation online: An examination of course design and online moderating techniques.* Paper presented at the Ninth International Technological Directions in Music Learning meeting of the Institute for Music Research, San Antonio, TX. Available from http://music.utsa.edu:16080/tdml/

Flor, J. W. (2002, January). *Relationships among attitude, motivation, and interface design during a college on-line course.* Paper presented at the Ninth International Technological Directions in Music Learning meeting of the Institute for Music Research, San Antonio, TX. Available from http://music.utsa.edu:16080/tdml/

Frand, J. L. (2000). The information-age mindset: Changes in students and implications for higher education. *EDUCAUSE Review, 35*(5), 14–24.

Greher, G. R. (2002). Picture this!© 1997: An interactive listening environment for middle school general music. *Dissertation Abstracts International, A63*(05), 1760. (UMI No. 3052881)

Greher, G. R. (2003). Multimedia in the classroom: Tapping into an adolescent's cultural literacy. *Journal of Technology in Music Learning, 2*(2), 21–43.

Levine, A., & Sun, J. C. (2002). Barriers to distance education. In *Distributed education: Challenges, choices and a new environment* (pp. 1–22). Washington DC: American Council on Education Center for Policy Analysis and EDUCAUSE.

Natriello, G. (2005). Modest changes, revolutionary possibilities: Distance learning and the future of education. *Teachers College Record, 107*(8), 1885–1904.

No Child Left Behind Act, 20 U.S.C. § 6301 et seq. (2002). Retrieved from http://www.ed.gov/policy/elsec/leg/esea02/107-110.pdf

Oblinger, D. G., Barone, C.A., & Hawkins, B. L. (2001). Distributed education and its challenges: An overview. In *Distributed education: Challenges, choices and a new environment* (pp. 1–47). Washington DC: American Council on Education Center for Policy Analysis and EDUCAUSE.

Zdzinski, S. F. (2001, January). *Developing reflective pre-service music educators using blackboard course info software.* Paper presented at the Eighth International Technological Directions in Music Learning meeting of the Institute for Music Research, San Antonio, TX. Available from http://music.utsa.edu:16080/tdml/

Appendix A. Sample Questions from Web Site

Music Theory and Analysis

1. To play from an oboe part, a B-flat trumpet must transpose
    - ☐ one whole tone lower
    - ☐ a minor third lower
    - ☐ a major third lower
    - ☐ one whole tone higher
2. In a melodic analysis, which is not usually considered?
    - ☐ rhythm
    - ☐ dynamics
    - ☐ contour
    - ☐ interval structure
3. Which is not a compound meter?
    - ☐ 3/8
    - ☐ 9/4
    - ☐ 6/4
    - ☐ 12/2
4. The following excerpt is
    - ☐ monophonic
    - ☐ homophonic
    - ☐ polyphonic
    - ☐ monophonic and polyphonic
5. The excerpt is what chord progression?
    - ☐ vi–ii–V–I
    - ☐ vi–IV–V–I
    - ☐ VI–11°–iv–I
    - ☐ VI–11°–iv–i
6. The pitch error occurs in what measure?
    - ☐ M 2
    - ☐ M 4
    - ☐ M 6
    - ☐ M 8

Music History and Literature

7. A "cantus firmus" is
   - ☐ a repeating rhythmic pattern
   - ☐ a bass ostinato
   - ☐ an early sonata form
   - ☐ a preexisting melody or series of notes of any type
8. Typically, sonata-allegro form can be found in
   - ☐ the concerto da camera
   - ☐ the second movement of a romantic concerto
   - ☐ the first movement of a classical symphony
   - ☐ the third movement of a string quartet
9. A twentieth-century composer who delved extensively into East-European folk music was
   - ☐ Béla Bartók
   - ☐ Alban Berg
   - ☐ Paul Hindemith
   - ☐ Arnold Shoenberg
10. William Billings was the first American singing master to
    - ☐ teach singing schools in Boston
    - ☐ compose his own music
    - ☐ both of the above
    - ☐ neither of the above
11. *Einstein on the Beach* is representative of what style of music?
    - ☐ neoclassicism
    - ☐ pointillism
    - ☐ early Ives compositions
    - ☐ minimalism
12. This excerpt is
    - ☐ a mass
    - ☐ a sonata
    - ☐ a chant
    - ☐ a madrigal

Music Education

13. The preparation beat must convey
    - ☐ tempo
    - ☐ dynamics
    - ☐ style
    - ☐ all of the above
14. *Con sordino* is
    - ☐ somewhat fast
    - ☐ with mutes
    - ☐ with accents
    - ☐ very soft
15. The tessitura is
    - ☐ a vocal phenomenon that results from a freely functioning total instrument
    - ☐ a changing male voice
    - ☐ the area within the range where the voice sits most comfortably
    - ☐ a cluster of high energy partials or overtones

16. Movement should be included in the music classroom for all of the following reasons but one
    - ☐ It's a developmentally sound approach to motor coordination.
    - ☐ It's an important means for helping children achieve musical skills and understanding.
    - ☐ It can replace a physical education program during a budget crisis.
    - ☐ It's a form of play, which is how children understand their world.
17. Singing is a cornerstone of the _____ philosophy.
    - ☐ Orff
    - ☐ Suzuki
    - ☐ Dalcroze
    - ☐ Kodály
18. Which is not an aspect of the Suzuki method?
    - ☐ Delay music reading until musical skills and technique have developed.
    - ☐ Involve parents in lessons and home practice.
    - ☐ Use of a mnemonic rhythmic system
    - ☐ Development of listening skills at an early age

Appendix B. Web Site Questionnaire

SA (Strongly Agree) = 5, A (Agree) = 4, N (No Opinion) = 3, D (Disagree) = 2, SD (Strongly Disagree) = 1

Ques. #	QUESTION	Mean	Median	SD
1	I found this site easy to use.	4	4	0.94
2	This site will be useful in preparing for the MTEL exam.	4.2	4	0.67
3	I knew the answers to most of the questions.	3	3	0.67
4	This site will help me identify my areas of weakness.	4	4	0.82
5	I prefer the test-preparation classes.	3.2	3	0.98
6	I found the questions to be challenging.	4.2	4	0.6
7	The aural examples were helpful.	3.3	4	1.56
8	The graphic musical examples were helpful.	4.5	4	0.52
9	This site was confusing to navigate.	4.2	4	0.6
10	I found it useful to work in the practice mode.	3.9	4	0.7
11	There were too many technical problems with the site.	3	3	1.34
12	It was hard to hear the aural examples.	3.2	4	0.79
13	I prefer this online preparation over the test-prep seminar.	3.7	4	0.63
14	I don't think this site will be helpful.	4	4	0.81
15	I found that the practice mode prepared me for the test mode.	3.6	4	1.21
16	I like the convenience of preparing for the test on my own time.	3.6	4	0.81
17	I found the variety of questions to be balanced.	3.6	4	1.22
18	There were relatively few technical problems in using this site.	3.1	4	1.19
19	It was easy to download the necessary browser to use the site.	3.3	3	1.14
20	I think I will use this site often in preparation for the MTEL exam.	3.9	4	1.14
21	I didn't find this site to be convenient to use.	3.9	4	1.03
22	This site provided a necessary review.	3.6	4	0.79
23	I found this site to be too complicated to use.	4.3	4	0.67
24	I would like the site to also have a review area.	4.4	4	1.03
25	I don't think I will use this site much.	3.6	4	0.69
26	The graphic examples were very clear.	4.5	5	1.19
27	The web site is a good addition to the Music Studies program.	4.3	5	0.47
28	I liked knowing how I did at the end of the test.	4.7	5	0.67
29	I would like a breakdown of what areas I am weak in.	4.6	5	0.93
30	I would like more help with essays.	3.5	3	0.94

Perspectives
Constructivism: Implications for Postsecondary Music Education and Beyond

By James B. Morford

James B. Morford is a graduate assistant for the World Music Center, West Virginia University, in Morgantown. He can be reached at jmorfor2@hotmail.com.

The manner in which music should be taught is a source of continual—and often heated—debate. Scholars have suggested that the practices that dominate current teaching may not represent the most desirable method of instruction, particularly when addressing subjects such as music, which involve the "affective domain" of learning (Abeles, Hoffer, & Klotman, 1994). If music educators are to update their methods, then the challenge is to develop a viable alternative to current practices, which may in turn require implementation of a fundamentally new philosophy of music education.

Some of the current trends in music education stem from the aesthetic philosophy, which gained popularity in scholarly discourse in the 1970s and 1980s, most notably through the writings of Bennett Reimer. Reimer (1989) suggested that the primary goal of music education was to develop emotional "responsiveness to the power of the art of music," and that any nonartistic functions of music were secondary and only to be addressed when helpful. A significant response to the aesthetic philosophy occurred with the introduction of the praxial philosophy of music education in the 1990s. Championed by David Elliott (1996–1997), the praxial philosophy stressed that the importance of music is in doing rather than responding, and that the "full range of attributes, meanings, expressions, references, and cultural-ideological aspects" (p. 25) must be considered at all times.

While these developments served to update the practices of music educators through the reexamination of *what music is*, and by extension, how it should be taught, the philosophy of constructivism has concurrently developed into a possible source of fresh practices in music education through the exploration of *what learning is*. Much of the music teacher training in America occurs within highly structured postsecondary educational bodies (i.e., universities and colleges); therefore, it may be within these institutions that the implementation of a new teaching philosophy is most needed. This essay will discuss some fundamental aspects of the constructivist theory and explore the implications of constructivism for educational design to illuminate existing and proposed applications in postsecondary music instruction.

Constructivism exists in multiple manifestations in education; however, some general themes exist for constructivist educators (Broomhead, 2005). Jackie Wiggins (2004), a leading practitioner and advocate of constructivism in postsecondary music education, provides the following list of the basic tenets of constructivist teaching:

- People learn through constructing their own understanding as a result of their experiences and interactions with others.
- Each individual constructs his or her own reality through experiences and interactions. The ways we perceive the world are colored by our personal collection of experiences.
- All ways of knowing and interpreting the world are valid—each for the individual who holds them.
- To learn, people must have opportunities to construct their own understanding of what is being taught.
- People are best able to construct understanding when new information is presented in a holistic context—one that enables them to understand how parts connect with the whole.
- Learning occurs in a social context. Teaching and learning are social processes.
- School learning experiences should be real-life experiences that include ample opportunity for meaningful interaction with peers and teacher.
- Within these experiences, both teacher and peers provide scaffolding that enables the individual to succeed.
- Students need to understand the goals of the experience and have sufficient grounding in the processes and understandings necessary to achieve the goals.
- Learning experiences should be highly contextual, rooted in genuine (musical) experience. The context, goal, processes, and understandings necessary for reaching the goal must be evident to the student.
- The ideal teaching/learning experience enables students to engage in the solution of genuine (musical) problems rooted in genuine (musical) contexts. Good problems are structured in ways that enable students to find and seek solutions to new problems.
- Problems for learning should be designed in ways that foster multiple solutions—and the various solutions should be considered and valued for their uniqueness, creativity, and originality. This is a particularly important aspect of problem solving in the art. (pp. 88–89)

This contemporary summary can be understood more thoroughly through an investigation of the historical foundations and educational concepts of constructivism. The implications of these tenets for postsecondary music education can then be investigated through exploration of the issues of relevance and curricular design. Examples of practical applications of the theory can then be examined within the context of the applied studio.

Historical Foundations of Constructivism

Constructivism is a theory of knowledge and learning derived primarily from the works of the cognitive psychologist Jean Piaget and the social psychologist Lev Vygotsky. The term "constructivism" is derived from Piaget's proposition that an individual's knowledge is not limited to a collection of isolated pieces of information, but is constructed from the cumulative information derived from experiences into an overall perspective of the operational aspects of the environment (Ormrod, 2003).

More precisely, Piaget's epistemology avoids the concept of knowledge as a copy of reality; instead, it provides an explanation of knowing as the use of "schemas" (Stendler-Lavatelli, 1970). This term refers to the mental symbols and structures associated with particular patterns of behavior. It is the individual's use of these representations, which function as internal operators that direct a person to act on or transform a given set of abstract or concrete objects, that defines knowing (Adler, 1970). If schemas exist within the mind and knowledge exists through the use of schemas, where does knowledge exist? Constructivists look to Vygotsky's sociocultural perspective to gain insight.

Vygotsky's theory of cognitive growth indicates that complex mental processes begin as social interactions with more knowledgeable others. Further, Vygotsky suggests that the individual dimension of consciousness is ancillary to the social dimension (Cobb, 2005). From this perspective, it could be proposed that knowledge of an object exists, not within the mind of the knower, but externally, as the complex interaction of all knowers' perspectives.

Contemporary constructivism combines the views expressed by Piaget and Vygotsky to formulate a comprehensive understanding of knowledge. Catherine Twomey Fosnot (2005) states that the constructivist theory "describes knowledge not as truths to be transmitted or discovered, but as emergent, developmental, nonobjective, viable, constructed explanations by humans in meaning making in cultural and social communities and discourse" (p. ix).

Fosnot's (2005) use of the word "explanations" serves as the connective tissue between the "individual constructivism" of Piaget's theory and the "social constructivism" of Vygotsky's theory by articulating the active nature of knowledge (Ormrod, 2003). Knowledge is not a set of data, but rather a way of acting upon reality (Barros, 1971).

This concept of knowledge necessitates an abandonment of the traditional definition of learning as the passive reception of directly transmitted information (Lord, 1993). A concise explanation of the constructivist view of learning is given by Wiggins' (2004) statement that "each individual constructs his or her own reality through experiences and interactions. The ways we perceive the world are colored by our personal collection of experiences" (p. 88).

Piaget's epistemology frames learning in two complementary forms of adaptation: "assimilation" and "accommodation." In assimilation, an existing schema is used successfully to act upon an object that deviates slightly from previously known objects within the same domain. If assimilation fails, that is, if the object encountered deviates sufficiently from the norm, then the individual must accommodate by modifying the existing schema. To determine its applicability, this new schema, constructed through accommodation, might then be applied to the objects in the domain that were known according to the old schema. Marilynne Adler (1970), perhaps to imply that Piaget's dualistic conception of learning is a more comprehensive model than that of the behaviorists, stresses that "the only real *change in behavior*, and thereby in mental structure, occurs in accommodation" (p. 3) [emphasis in original].

For Piaget, learning is governed by the assimilative or accommodative adaptation of the individual through the resolution of cognitive dissonances that occur between newly encountered objects and existing schemas. Given constructivism's use of Vygotsky's perspective in its description of knowledge, how do sociocultural aspects figure into the constructivist explanation of learning?

Whereas sociocultural theorists emphasize the concept of "distributed cognition" (Ormrod, 2003), many constructivists believe "the conceptual structures that constitute meanings or knowledge . . . are constructs that each user has to build up for him- or herself" (Glasersfeld, 2005, p. 5). Fosnot (2005) describes learning from a constructivist perspective as

> a self-regulatory process of struggling with the conflict between existing personal models of the world and discrepant new insights, constructing new representations and models of reality as a human meaning-making venture with culturally developed tools and symbols, and further negotiating such meaning through cooperative social activity, discourse, and debate in communities of practice. (p. ix)

Society and culture can thus be seen to provide both the sources of the building blocks of new schemas and the point of interaction for existing schemas. Thus, we have Wiggins' (2004) statement, "People learn through constructing their own understanding as a result of their experiences and interactions with others" (p. 88).

Educational Concepts

While a comprehensive theory of instruction based on the assumptions of the constructivist epistemology has not been established, it is necessary to illuminate a few concepts that such a theory might address before arriving at any possible implications of constructivism for postsecondary music education and teacher training.

Jerome S. Bruner (1979b) states that "the structure of knowledge—its connectedness and the derivations that make one follow from another—is the proper emphasis in education" (p. 120). From this idea it follows that "the relationship between the learner and the subject matter should be the focus of teaching rather than the content itself" (Rinaldo, 2004, p. 32). This suggests that "high-road learning" (Maclellen, 2005), which emphasizes conceptual understanding, is the proper focus of educators.

Constructivists focus most prevalently on the understanding of concepts and are interested in performance "only insofar as it springs from, and thus demonstrates, such understanding" (Glasersfeld,

1995, p. 5). The specific variety of performance that is most indicative of conceptual understanding is problem solving, which requires a "conceptual repertoire . . . not only of certain abstract building blocks, but also a variety of relationships that can be posited between them" (Glasersfeld, p. 5). If this repertoire is to be constructed by the student, as constructivism suggests, then what is the role of the teacher in the educational process?

Wiggins (2004) states, "To learn, people must have opportunities to construct their own understanding of what is being taught" (p. 88), suggesting that the teacher's role might be to act as the provider of opportunities for the student. The constructivist perspective on the role of the teacher may be further understood from John Dewey's (1938/1950) proposal of the way that a teacher can appropriately involve subject matter in the classroom:

> The way is, first, for the teacher to be intelligently aware of the capacities, needs, and past experiences of those under instruction, and, secondly, to allow the suggestion made to develop into a plan and project by means of the further suggestions contributed and organized into a whole by members of the group. The plan, in other words is a co-operative enterprise, not a dictation. The teacher's suggestion . . . is a starting point to be developed into a plan through contributions from the experience of all engaged in the learning process. . . . The essential point is that the purpose grow and take shape through the process of social intelligence. (p. 85)

This interpretation of the role of the teacher agrees with Bruner's (1979a) "hypothetical mode" of teaching. In this mode, the students and teacher assume a cooperative role in manipulating the content of the material that is explored. Bruner (1968) asserts that "instruction must facilitate and regulate the exploration of alternatives on the part of the learner" (p. 43). It follows that the teacher "needs to take account of what learners bring to the learning situation—their purposes and ideas" (Driver, 1995, p. 399). Constructivists demonstrate their adherence to these concepts by "promoting an environment in which pupils can acquire knowledge through investigation of relevant questions" (Avriham, 2000, p. 476).

The Problem of Relevance

The concept of "relevance" is a point of ambiguity in the constructivist framework. Relevance can be content oriented or motivationally oriented, and the apparent lack of distinction between these two definitions indicates a subtle but important problem that exists for teachers who wish to incorporate constructivism within the current educational system. Following a discussion of several constructivist projects that have been implemented throughout Israel, Aharon Avriham (2000), of the Center for Futurism in Education at Ben Gurion University of the Negev, articulates the problem:

> Almost all of the above mentioned projects and similar ones have been carried out in schools teaching **compulsory** conventional **disciplinary** (or interdisciplinary) curricula.

> But there is an inherent necessary contradiction between the Constructivist approach that emphasizes active and inquisitive learning which in turn requires **real interest** of the learners in the object of inquiry on the one hand, and a **coerced disciplinary** curriculum which cannot be of interest to most learners at the same time, on the other hand. (pp. 476–477) [emphasis in original]

Learning experts have suggested that a constructivist classroom is the most productive environment for fostering a high level of engagement in students (Wiggins, 2004), but conflict arises when the subject matter is deemed relevant by anyone other than students (i.e., teachers, administrators, or bodies of government). Intent engagement necessitates internal motivation on the part of the student, and this motivation can only be guaranteed when the subject matter to be addressed is chosen by the student because of his or her existing concept of its relevance.

Constructivism and Curricular Design

Undergraduate music programs in America appear to employ the traditional approach to curricular design mentioned by Avriham. Students are required to successfully complete courses that address music appreciation, theory, history, and individual and ensemble performance. Further requirements may exist that relate to a student's chosen area of emphasis; for example, music education students are often required to complete courses that address particular methods of instruction. Each of these courses contributes in a different way to a student's ability to interact with music.

Even in the ideal traditional curriculum, where individual courses are coordinated to facilitate the creation of cognitive structures that interrelate the multiple manifestations of music being presented to the students, the problem of relevance persists for constructivists. A coordinated curriculum satisfactorily addresses Wiggins' (2004) belief: "People are best able to construct understanding when new information is presented in a holistic context—one that enables them to understand how parts connect to the whole" (p. 88). However, it does not resolve the issue of motivation-oriented relevance. Herein lies the primary implication of constructivism for postsecondary music programs.

From a strictly constructivist perspective, curricula should not be predetermined by an authoritative entity; instead, they might exist as a self-constructed, active expression of the subject matter with which the student chooses to engage. Thus, if constructivism is to be wholly embraced as the appropriate philosophical model for the development of teaching practices in postsecondary music programs, then a fundamental change in the structure of American curricular design seems necessary.

The transformation of educational foundations is slow and arduous, and sociocultural tendencies—such as the institutional control of education—do not make the task any easier (Jorgensen, 2003). The difficulty in achieving large-scale curricular change may help to explain why many constructivist educators have ignored the logical contradiction that is illustrated in the previous discussion, choosing to implement aspects of constructivism in courses that address subject matter that is not necessarily motivationally relevant. But what are the particular manifestations of constructivism that exist (or have been proposed) within postsecondary music programs? Examples may be found within the context of the applied studio.

Constructivism in the Applied Studio

The applied studio, as the name might imply, provides an opportunity for the undergraduate student to integrate and apply the various dimensions of music addressed in other courses. This suggests that a constructivist approach might be appropriate. Domenico E. Zarro (2003), chair of the Pedagogical Committee for the New Jersey Chapter of the Percussive Arts Society, provides insight by outlining the traits that may exist in a constructivism-based applied studio. He defines these traits by juxtaposing the approaches of traditional and constructivist applied studios.

Whereas in the traditional studio all curricular choices are made by the instructor, Zarro (2003) states that the constructivist will design the curriculum around the students' interests and abilities, allowing students to decide what they wish to learn, what and how often they will practice, and what performing ensembles they will join. This may be accomplished through the development of a portfolio that consists of both a record of time spent practicing and a daily journal of thoughts addressing a particular piece of music, composer, or time period. The correlation between practice time and understanding displayed through journal writings will help the teacher guide the student's identification of progress and deficiencies (Jorgensen, 2003).

Zarro (2003) suggests that while the traditional applied studio focuses each lesson on the individual student, the constructivist instructor may combine individual lessons with group lessons that require students to focus on a given work, composer, or time period in a cooperative learning environment. "In turn, the constructivist teacher guides their [*sic*] students toward those topics that primarily interest them, coupled with those areas that are deemed necessary to study" (p. 5).

In contrast to the traditional applied studio instructor, a constructivist teacher may encourage creative discovery by inviting students to explore musical interpretations. In addition, to facilitate the students' analysis of their own developmental needs and progress, the constructivist may guide student compositions based on a technical skill, time period, or composer. Zarro (2003) states, "This process engages students while enlightening them to the creative process that is so essential to the arts" (pp. 6–7).

When viewed singularly, the teaching techniques addressed by Zarro (2003) are not necessarily exclusive to constructivist educators; however, they do reflect adherence to the tenets provided by

Wiggins (2004). The concurrent and persistent use of these relatively common strategies would yield an applied studio starkly different from that of a traditional model.

Conclusions

If constructivism is to flourish within the American music education system, teachers trained in constructivist programs must achieve a degree of success equal to—or perhaps greater than—that of educators who have received training in more traditional settings. With this in mind, the existing trend toward the use of behavioral objectives presents a subtle but substantial problem for constructivist educators.

Constructivism dictates that successful instruction depends on the teacher's ability to guide students toward a conceptual understanding that can be demonstrated through, but is not necessarily indicated by, the performance of appropriate behaviors. Constructivist educators, by definition, must focus on building conceptual frameworks. The "why" and "how" of behaviors are more important than the behaviors themselves. The success of constructivist educators could therefore seem less efficient than direct instruction within the current system.

It is my belief that, while the theoretical foundations of its tenets are valid, an all-encompassing shift to constructivism in postsecondary education is unlikely to occur. The implementation of true constructivist principles requires a fundamental change in curricular design, and such a transformation could negate nearly all the current practices in every field of education. However, as has been illustrated, constructivism can be implemented on the smaller scale of individual courses. Thus, it is my opinion that a comprehensive constructivist theory of education, should one be identified, will not be introduced in its entirety; however, further implementations of constructivism may be able to provide practical applications that can be integrated into the existing eclectic American educational design.

References

Abeles, H. F., Hoffer, C. R., & Klotman, R. H. (1994). *Foundations of music education* (2nd ed.). New York: Schirmer.

Adler, M. (1970). Jean Piaget, school organization, and instruction. In I. J. Athey & D. O. Rubadeau (Eds.), *Educational implications of Piaget's theory* (pp. 1–12). Waltham, MA: Xerox College.

Avriham, A. (2000). Beyond constructivism: Autonomy-oriented education. *Studies in Philosophy and Education, 19*, 465–489.

Barros, N. R. A. (1971). Applications of Piaget's theory to education: A critical study (Doctoral dissertation, University of Illinois, 1971). *Dissertation Abstracts International, 32*, 10A.

Broomhead, P. (2005). Shaping expressive performance: A problem solving approach. *Music Educators Journal, 91*(5), 63–67.

Bruner, J. S. (1968). *Toward a theory of instruction*. New York: Norton.

Bruner, J. S. (1979a). The act of discovery. In *On knowing: Essays for the left hand* (Rev. ed.) (pp. 81–96). Cambridge, MA: Bellknap Press of Harvard University Press.

Bruner, J. S. (1979b). After John Dewey, what? In *On knowing: Essays for the left hand* (Rev. ed.) (pp. 113–126). Cambridge, MA: Bellknap Press of Harvard University Press.

Cobb, P. (2005). Where is the mind? A coordination of sociocultural and cognitive constructivist perspectives. In C. T. Fosnot (Ed.), *Constructivism: Theory, perspectives, and practice* (2nd ed.) (pp. 39–57). New York: Columbia University Teachers College.

Dewey, J. (1950). *Experience in education.* New York: Macmillan. (Original work published 1938)

Driver, R. (1995). Constructivist approaches to science teaching. In L. P. Steffe & J. Gale (Eds.), *Constructivism in education* (pp. 385–400). Hillsdale, NJ: Lawrence Erlbaum Associates.

Elliott, D. (1996–1997). Putting matters in perspective: Reflections on a new philosophy. *Quarterly Journal of Music Teaching and Learning, 7*(2–4), 20–35.

Fosnot, C. T. (2005). Preface. In C. T. Fosnot (Ed.), *Constructivism: Theory, perspectives, and practice* (2nd ed.) (pp. ix–xii). New York: Columbia University Teachers College.

Glasersfeld, E. von (1995). A constructivist approach to teaching. In L. P. Steffe & J. Gale (Eds.), *Constructivism in education* (pp. 3–15). Hillsdale, NJ: Lawrence Erlbaum Associates.

Glasersfeld, E. von (2005). Introduction: Aspects of constructivism. In C. T. Fosnot (Ed.), *Constructivism: Theory, perspectives, and practice* (2nd ed.) (pp. 3–7). New York: Columbia University Teachers College.

Jorgensen, E. R. (2003). *Transforming music education.* Bloomington, IN: Indiana University Press.

Lord, C. (1993). Harnessing technology to open the mind: Beyond drill and practice for aural skills. *Journal of Music Theory Pedagogy, 7,* 105–117.

Maclellan, E. (2005). Conceptual learning: The priority for higher education. *British Journal of Educational Studies, 53*(2), 129–147.

Ormrod, J. E. (2003). *Educational psychology: Developing learners* (4th ed.). Upper Saddle River, NJ: Merrill Prentice Hall.

Reimer, B. (1989). *A philosophy of music education* (2nd ed.). Englewood Cliffs, NJ: Prentice Hall.

Rinaldo, V. (2004). Subject matter is the vehicle and not the focus of learning: A constructivist perspective of music education. *Canadian Music Educator, 45,* 31–34.

Stendler-Lavatelli, C. B. (1970). Aspects of Piaget's theory that have implications for teacher education. In I. J. Athey & D. O. Rubadeau (Eds.), *Educational implications of Piaget's theory* (pp. 36–46). Waltham, MA: Xerox College.

Wiggins, J. (2004, Spring). Letting go—Moving forward. *Mountain Lake Reader, 3,* 81–91.

Zarro, D. E. (2003). A comparison of the traditionalist and constructivist applied studio. *National Association of College Wind and Percussion Instructors Journal, 51*(3), 4–11.

Call for Research Poster Presentations

American Orff-Schulwerk Association National Conference
San Jose, CA
November 14–17, 2007

The American Orff-Schulwerk Association (AOSA) will sponsor a research poster session to disseminate the results of innovative and thorough research at its 2007 AOSA National Conference to be held in San Jose, CA, November 14–17, 2007. Research reports on music learning through movement, speech, playing instruments, singing, improvisation, or composition in general music or music therapy settings are particularly appropriate.

Posters of accepted research reports will be displayed. The author(s) of each accepted paper must be present at the conference poster session to discuss the research project with interested participants. The author(s) must also furnish 25 copies of a report summary as well as 10 copies of the completed report.

The following guidelines will inform the paper selection process:

1. Please submit a research summary not exceeding 1,000 words (in English) via e-mail attachment to kathy.robinson@ualberta.ca using Microsoft Word. If e-mail is not possible, please submit five paper copies of the summary to the address listed below. Authors must outline and report: (a) objectives or purposes; (b) perspectives or theoretical framework; (c) methods, techniques, or modes of inquiry; (d) data sources or evidence; (e) results; (f) conclusions/point of view; and (g) implications for and applications to the profession.
2. The author's name, institutional affiliation, and address (including e-mail) should appear only on a separate cover page. The summary should contain no clues to the author's identity.
3. Papers submitted for the conference must comply with the *Code of Ethics* published in the fall issue of the *Journal of Research in Music Education* (and also available on the World Wide Web at http://www.menc.org).
4. Submissions should be sent to: Kathy M. Robinson, Asst. Prof. of Music Education
   Faculty of Education: Elementary Education
   551 Education South - University of Alberta
   Edmonton, AB, Canada T6G 2G5
   E-mail: kathy.robinson@ualberta.ca
5. All submissions must be postmarked or e-mailed by MAY 1, 2007.
6. A panel of qualified reviewers will read all submissions. Authors will be notified by July of the panel's decisions. Summaries will not be returned.

Membership Invitation

MENC: The National Association for Music Education

invites you enjoy the benefits of membership in

the only professional association dedicated to music for all!

Are you a music teacher?

A music education student?

A parent? A caregiver? Retired? Collegiate? Corporate? Or simply a friend of music?

There's a place for *everyone* in music education.

MENC: The Largest Arts Education Association on Earth.

Come see where you belong: www.menc.org

1-800-828-0229 (outside the U.S., call 703-860-4000)

Music. Learn it. Live it. Love it. For Life.*

*©2007 by MENC: The National Association for Music Education

www.ingramcontent.com/pod-product-compliance
Lightning Source LLC
Chambersburg PA
CBHW080551230426
43663CB00015B/2794